C000229144

WILLIAM DEAN

the greatest of them all

Jeremy Clements

NOODLE **N.B.** BOOKS

© Kevin Robertson (Noodle Books) and Jeremy Clements 2012

ISBN 978-1-906419-92-9

Printed in England by Berforts Information Press.

First published in 2012 by Kevin Robertson under the **NOODLE BOOKS** imprint
PO Box 279
Corhampton
SOUTHAMPTON
SO32 3ZX

The Publisher and Author hereby give full notice that all rights to this work are reserved.
Aside from brief passages for the purpose of review, no part of this work may be reproduced, copied by
electronic or other means, or otherwise stored in any information storage or retrieval system without
written permission from the Publisher. This includes the illustrations herein which shall remain the
copyright of the author unless otherwise stated.

www.noodlebooks.co.uk

Front Cover - Dean Goods on foreign soil. The third consignment sent to France in support of the British Expeditionary Force comprised 14 locomotives (WD Nos 109-118 and 181-184). They crossed the English Channel in November 1939, following eight (WD Nos 101-108) that had been shipped the previous month. Because of pressure on Swindon Works at the time, fourteen were prepared at Eastleigh for military service and this photograph was taken prior to despatch of the first four from those works. Nos 181 (ex-GWR No 2402) and 182 (2403) can be identified; presumably the other pair were Nos 183 and 184.

Installation of Westinghouse brakes was intended for French service but supplies were not available for the first 22 locomotives to leave Britain. It is believed that most were fitted with this equipment either in the workshops of the Royal Engineers in France, or later by French operators although two or three may never have so treated.

Rear cover - Reduced to menial duties, Dean Goods No 2462 on permanent-way train duties at Sapperton Tunnel, 27 April 1952. This engine was one of 36 survivors of the class still at work (on paper at least) in that year. Twelve were lost before the end of December, leaving 24 at work. No 2462 would not survive much longer and was withdrawn in 1953.

Frontispiece - Dean Goods No 2537 of Lot No 108 was built in July 1897 with an S4 type round-topped boiler, as shown here. This locomotive carried an earlier Type S2 boiler (with dome on front ring) from 1903 until November 1905, followed by an S4 again until December 1914 when it acquired a Belpaire boiler. It seems likely therefore that this photograph was taken pre-1903 on what is believed to be the Greenford loop.

This posed study is taken from "Safety Movements", a GWR publication prepared to warn employees of the hazards of working on the railway. The engine is in clean condition and its brass dome has yet to be painted over. The cab is fitted with large-diameter spectacle plates; these had to be reduced in size to accommodate the shoulders of the Belpaire firebox when later fitted. The tender is a pre-Dean vehicle and has been modernised with side fenders; there appears to be a sleeper in the coal space – perhaps a prop to be used in another safety related photograph. The oncoming train is in the hands of a Standard or Armstrong Goods 0-6-0, also with a splendid brass dome.

The "message" of this picture is that the man on foot is stepping out of the path of the Standard Goods into the six foot without having first checked whether a train is approaching from behind. Another photograph of the same scene from a slightly different angle reveals that while the signal in the distance governing the movement of the Standard Goods is down, that for the line on which the Dean Goods is running is up. The latter signal is close to the signal box but on the right hand side of the double track. Thus there is an additional warning message that with a signal in the up position, it should not be assumed that there is no train in the vicinity. In this case, the Dean Goods would have been running slowly, intending to stop at the signal.

Finally, the GWR was owner of extensive surplus land, some of which has been put to good use by a local employee to grow a fine crop of vegetables.

CONTENTS

Publisher / Author's note:
Every effort has been made to identify and credit images wherever possible.
Prints obtained with nothing annotated on the rear have been deliberately left unaccredited.
Should an error have occurred this is entirely unintentional.

INTRODUCTION

The intention when work started several years ago was to write about the GWR's Dean Goods 0-6-0s. Such a subject might be considered so mundane as to warrant little more than a few paragraphs, or at the most a chapter, in a broader motive power survey. However, this ordinary class was called upon to perform under extraordinary conditions in some extraordinary places, well away from Great Western territory. That accounts of these wanderings occasionally conflict and are frequently incomplete injects a note of exoticism into the story. There are several references to these adventures in railway literature but up until now, apparently there has been no attempt to concentrate them in a single volume.

Recording facts, such as they are known or can be deduced, was a key element in the writing but in trying to establish the "why" of certain events, lines of investigation led to digression from the main theme which in the author's view contributed directly or indirectly to the account. The first of the class appeared in 1883 and this remoteness in time made verification of information sources that much harder. In this regard, the time-line of events was helpful in understanding the evolutionary chain.

When reviewing this chronology, it was striking that construction of the class should have been sandwiched between two bouts of experimentation where Dean seemed determined to push the boundaries of what might then be possible in locomotive design. Enquiry and innovation were persistent features of his career but it was intriguing that such a simple yet effective type should have been associated with so much design complexity and practical failure.

The GWR was indeed fortunate that the Gooch-Armstrong-Dean-Churchward succession provided a stable continuum. Nonetheless, assessment of the Dean Goods within the company's motive power fleet opened fields of enquiry which induced unfavourable conclusions about aspects of engineering strategy. In particular, although the ascendancy of the 0-6-0T during Dean's tenure was right for the time, later enshrinement of this type in 20th Century policy did not serve the company well economically. After his re-stocking programme, the most significant aspect of Churchward's reign was cessation of construction of this wheel arrangement. Its enthusiastic revival from 1929 onwards became perhaps one of the most misguided of the GWR's key 20th Century investment decisions.

Mindful of Prime Minister Benjamin Disraeli's alleged admonition "there are lies, damned lies, and statistics", certain data indicate over-spending on the 0-6-0T fleet when diversion of resources elsewhere might have proved more fruitful. This in part stemmed from poor management information. In the context of the company's extended love affair with tank engines, it is perhaps remarkable that the Dean Goods appeared at all. It is also noteworthy that despite its continuing importance in certain locations, there was manifest failure to produce a modern replacement.

Exploration of why the class was so widely accepted in foreign parts and by foreign enginemen (be they from Scotland or Italy) was a more positive field of study. Down the years there has been much debate about the superiority of one engine type over another, based on comparative testing, practical experience and prejudice. The Dean Goods passed with flying colours far more rigorous trials – in the hands of operators from diverse backgrounds, and often in circumstances where there was a strong nexus between operational success or failure, and life or death. Trying to assess why the class was so widely trusted led to recognition that it stopped as well as it went – a handy feature when hauling sensitive loads such as high explosives.

Writing a book invites many emotions, not least among which is enjoyment. In this regard, it has been a pleasure and a revelation to discover the importance of William Dean, and just what he meant to the GWR. The process also engendered frustration because so little has been recorded about the man personally. This is a shame in view of the length of his career, of the proportion of it spent holding high office, and of the unusual and demanding challenges that faced the company during the last quarter of the 19th Century. William Dean bore the unique burden of chief executive officer in motive power matters during a particularly difficult phase of the company's history and for a period exceeded in years only by Daniel Gooch. Taking all these factors into account, it is stated without equivocation that he was indeed the greatest of that illustrious sextet that held ultimate command at Swindon.

Devotees of the Great Western mourn the loss of *North Star*, *Lord of the Isles* and 2-2-2 No 14, but are eternally grateful that before creation of the National Collection and before the Barry saga, there were railway officers who, blessed with a sense of heritage, ensured that *City of Truro* and *Lode Star* were saved, and also No 2516, just an ordinary 0-6-0.

Those for whom the Great Western Railway is the focus of their affections are the most blessed of enthusiasts, for the subject of their passion, for the numbers of artefacts extant, and for the abundance of writing that records so much of the company's affairs. Yet another book risks repetition in a crowded field but the two-fold objectives of this volume address areas that have received rather less attention than is their due. The Dean Goods as a significant element in motive power matters spanned many years and a review of its activities at home and overseas helps fill an important gap.

Additionally it became apparent that the story of this extraordinary machine would be incomplete without an appreciation of its designer. In turn, this revealed a corner of the GWR story that has yet to receive the thorough and exhaustive treatment that has been accorded the events of 1900 onwards. Recognition of the traumas and difficulties of the final quarter of the 19th Century, and the manner in which they were overcome by William Dean, does not diminish but rather adds to the splendour of the Edwardian decade. Telling the tale of a locomotive class introduced almost 130 years ago and finally withdrawn 75 years later has

meant reliance on many published information sources. Singling out particular references can be invidious but it would be churlish not to recognise the work of certain authors. Harry Holcroft's reminiscences have special appeal because they seem so relevant and up-to-date making it hard to believe that he knew Churchward personally, along with other giants of the 20th Century's golden age. The survey by William Aves of the Railway Operating Division on the Western Front post dates Holcroft by many years yet masterfully opens up important aspects of operations under extreme conditions that have remained unacknowledged for far too long.

No survey of any part of the GWR locomotive story should be risked without the aid of the volumes produced by the Railway Correspondence & Travel Society. These publications are treasured not only for their abundance of reliable information but also for providing the author in a career spent in 14 countries and usually many miles from Swindon, constant companionship and a cherished reminder of what the Old Company means to him, and to its countless admirers.

Acknowledgements are best if they are brief. Thanks to a publisher whose multi-facetted talents have been thoroughly tested and not found wanting, and to Jeremy English who in the unenviable role of book designer setter showed great patience and provided much wise advice. Also not forgetting a daughter who proved effective in the hunt for images at a photographic fair. Her technique: . Her technique:

Daughter: *Do you have any pictures of Dean Goods?*

Trader: *Do you know what a Dean Goods looks like?*

Daughter: *Yes, it's old-fashioned, has three wheels on the side, and a big bell on top.*

Trader: *But what colour?*

Daughter: *Preferably pink.*

Trader: *Do you know how many people in this room would kill you for saying that?*

This lamentable exchange was sufficient to enlist the help of two kindly, unnamed gentlemen standing close by her – so many thanks to them also.

Jeremy Clements

County Meath, Ireland

October 2012

WILLIAM DEAN

William Dean was a first-rate engineer and his goods locomotive was a cogent statement of functionality. Other aspects of his work showed him to be an artist also, as is apparent in this view of 4-2-2 Class 3031 (or "Achilles Class") No 3074 *Princess Helena*. The evolvement of this group was quite complex and in their final condition, there were several variations between the 80 examples. The version shown here displays the form in which they were best known, and which led to their being widely regarded as the most graceful steam locomotive design ever. Their working lives were sadly shortened by the introduction of heavier trains for which single drivers were ill-suited

Nos 3021 to 3028 were constructed between April and August 1891 as broad gauge 2-2-2s and were converted to narrow gauge after May 1892. In broad gauge form, they exhibited none of the style that later typified the class. No 3023, as yet unnamed, is on shed coupled to a vintage broad gauge tender. The broad gauge locomotive in the background has been identified as a "Sir Watkin" Class 0-6-0ST – either *Sir Watkin* or No 2159 *Saunders*, the only two remaining in service in 1891. The unusual allocation of a running number to a broad gauge engine of GWR origin resulted from Saunders having been sold to the South Devon Railway in 1872. On takeover of that company in 1876, it was allotted a running number along with all engines absorbed at that time.

In the foreground can be seen a good example of Brunel's "baulk road" broad gauge track.   *Rod Blackaller/ The Broad Gauge Society*

Chapter 1

COMETH THE HOUR . . .

During the 113 years' independent history of the Great Western Railway, there were only six individuals who carried the ultimate responsibility for the company's motive power fleet. Of this distinguished group – Gooch, Joseph Armstrong, Dean, Churchward, Collett and Hawksworth – perhaps the least well-known to students of the GWR is William Dean. This is a paradox as his tenure as Locomotive Superintendent coincided with the most intriguing and challenging period of the Old Company's motive power story. His achievements in that demanding role during that difficult period rate him as the greatest of the six men who reigned at Swindon.

The span of Dean's career embraced a period of extraordinary change. It started at a time when the company had only recently acquired some narrow (standard) gauge routes and when the Broad Gauge network was still expanding. It ended with the introduction of classes (Badmintons and Aberdares) that marked the dawn of a new era and a revolution in locomotive design. In between, Dean met the universal challenges of growing traffic levels as railway services matured while facing and overcoming difficulties that were entirely unique to the Great Western.

The events that led to Dean's ascendance had their roots in the northward expansion of the company beyond the geographic limits of the Broad Gauge. The outcome of the Gauge Commission of 1846 had sounded the death knell for any hope of adoption of the 7ft 0¼in gauge on a nationwide scale but it was not until 1854 that the company started standard gauge operations. This occurred through a merger between the Great Western, the Shrewsbury & Chester Railway, and the Shrewsbury & Birmingham Railway to form the Northern Division of the GWR. This organisation was to serve for some years as the focus of the company's standard gauge locomotive activities, and was based at the SBR's works at Stafford Road, Wolverhampton.

Joseph Armstrong, a member of a prominent engineering family from the north east with close connections to the Stephensons, was appointed Locomotive Superintendent of the SBR in 1853. This followed the expiry of an agreement whereby the company's motive power was serviced by outside contractors. He took control of the SBR's and SCR's combined locomotive fleet following the merger and

manufacture of standard gauge locomotives commenced at Wolverhampton in 1859. Up until then GWR narrow gauge locomotives had comprised those supplied by the absorbed companies, plus a few built to Gooch's designs by private manufacturers and at Swindon.

William Dean was born in January 1840, the second son of Henry Dean who was manager of a soap factory at New Cross, East London. From an early age he displayed a vibrant interest in technical matters and after education at Haberdashers' School, he was apprenticed at the age of 15 years to Joseph Armstrong at Wolverhampton. He thus started his eight year apprenticeship shortly after formation of the Northern Division and prior to commencement of locomotive construction. The facilities at Stafford Road were compact for the range of tasks undertaken. This intimate atmosphere aided the assimilation of a variety of skills and techniques, making this an excellent training ground for those with talent and ambition. Dean's practical training was complemented by studies at the Wolverhampton Working Men's College where he excelled in mathematics and engineering, winning many prizes. He was appointed Chief Assistant to Joseph Armstrong on completion of his apprenticeship.

Joseph Armstrong's period in charge at Wolverhampton was a little over 10 years. In April 1864, he moved to Swindon to succeed Daniel Gooch who had been Locomotive Superintendent since the company's early days. Gooch had left to take up the chairmanship of the Great Eastern Steamship Co Ltd, owners of Brunel's famous ship which had been chartered to lay the first transatlantic cable. He had already been contemplating retirement prior to his resignation, partly due to dissatisfaction with the manner in which the GWR's affairs were being conducted. Gooch was the last survivor of a remarkable quartet – the others were Brunel, Russell, and Saunders – who had done so much to build the GWR as an industry leader. The other three died prematurely through overwork and illness, and he was conscious that those now in charge had not been cast in the same mould.

Russell had retired in 1855 after 20 years as Chairman, dying soon afterwards. Six men occupied the chair in the next 10 years and neither they nor the

WILLIAM DEAN

other directors had been able to cope with the consequences of 20 years' headlong growth. Cash resources had drained away, the company had ambitious investment plans that were not viable, and shareholders were unhappy with their treatment. In 1865, the Board recognised the need for drastic action and pleaded with Daniel Gooch to return as Chairman. He agreed to do so once the transatlantic project was completed, but stipulated that he must have a free hand in running the company.

There followed an anxious period as in May 1866 a banking crisis hit all railway companies. In desperation, the GWR sought aid from the Bank of England, which was rejected. James Grierson, recently appointed in the new post of General Manager, knew that the company was within a whisker of bankruptcy and expected the imminent appointment of a Receiver. Gooch finally re-joined the company in September 1866, immediately imposing austerity and severe cuts in expenditure. He remained in office until his death in 1889, and his period as Chairman was marked by continued spending restraint in motive power matters.

Gooch's resignation in 1864 led to significant management changes. Joseph Armstrong's move to

Swindon was more or less concurrent with the retirement of J Gibson who had been in charge of carriage and wagon matters. The roles were combined and Joseph assumed the new title of Locomotive, Carriage & Wagon Superintendent. George Armstrong, who was his younger brother by five years, succeeded as Locomotive Superintendent for the Northern Division. Under him, Dean remained as Chief Assistant but also became Works Manager at Stafford Road. Not long after, the Chief Clerk at Wolverhampton was also transferred to Swindon and as there was no replacement available, Dean took over this position as well. This was an unusual combination of three important roles in the hands of one man and a graphic illustration of his capacities.

On the locomotive front, this was a period of extraordinary pressure. The Broad Gauge empire was at its zenith with a fleet of around 400 locomotives. No new designs appeared after 1866, although rebuilding and renewal of existing machines was to continue until 1888. Motive power needs were otherwise covered through the progressive contraction of the network, which allowed for the re-deployment of otherwise surplus locomotives. The Swindon-Gloucester line, the route to South Wales and the branch to Weymouth were early candidates for gauge conversion while

Recurrent themes during Dean's tenure was how to meet impending demands for larger engines and how to extract more power from existing units, and the Achilles Class was not excluded from these efforts. Invention of steam standing had given the single driver locomotive a brief Indian summer in the 1890s but the inexorable growth of train weights increasingly taxed power and adhesion. After Dean had retired, a solution to this problem was sought without success. Conversion to 4-4-0 with smaller driving wheels was investigated but rejected on grounds of cost. Different types of boiler were applied but the height of the driving wheels restricted the maximum permissible diameter, which ruled out use of the tapered boilers then being successfully introduced. No 3004 *Black Prince*, which received a parallel Standard No 2 boiler in 1906, is seen here at the head of 9 or 10 bogies. The stain on the lower part of the smokebox door seems to have been caused by scorching, suggesting that the locomotive has had to work very hard.

To prove that the Achilles Class was not alone in good looks, No 8 *Gooch* is seen here in workshop grey. The four locomotives of this class were nominally rebuilds of experimental 2-4-0s; all were later reboilered as they were considered under-boilered in original 4-4-0 form. Driving wheels of 7' 1" diameter were used (7" less than the singles). If the proposal to convert the singles had proceeded, the result would have resembled this class.

other important routes became dual gauge. By 1875, broad gauge services had all but disappeared except for three minor branches and for traffic to the West of England that used the dual gauge London-Bristol main line. There was an expansion in broad gauge mileage and the locomotive fleet the next year on takeover of the Bristol & Exeter, South Devon and Cornwall railways thereby magnifying the challenge of the final gauge conversion.

During this period, Stafford Road played an important role in standard gauge construction. Nonetheless, the main burden of locomotive building and maintenance fell upon Swindon as the standard gauge fleet grew to meet traffic growth and to provide for newly converted lines. Concurrently the remaining broad gauge services exerted a different set of needs, pending complete standardisation. To cope with these demands, Joseph Armstrong required first class executive assistance. Accordingly, he brought William Dean to Swindon and appointed him Chief Assistant in 1868. Advancement to such seniority at the age of 28 years might have raised eyebrows but obviously he was trusted as the best man available for an important job. Further, it was a public acknowledgement of his candidacy to succeed Joseph on retirement. By the standards of the time, this would have occurred around the age of 70 years or even later i.e. some 20 years hence.

Joseph Armstrong was a truly remarkable individual, fully committed to the interests of the 13,000 personnel for whom he was responsible. During his 13 years in charge at Swindon he managed the construction of nearly 600 new engines while brother George turned out another 250 at Wolverhampton. The unusual circumstances arising from the protracted metamorphosis from broad to standard gauge would have been demanding enough but there were other aspects to the man that placed major calls upon his time.

He was patriarch to what was to become a pre-eminent Great Western family. In contrast to George who remained a lifelong bachelor, he was a devoted family man who fathered six boys and three girls. The four boys who survived to attain their majorities were all apprenticed at Swindon and two went on to full careers. One of their descendants was the last Armstrong to work for the company, not retiring until 1946. Joseph was also a patriarch in the broader sense of the Great Western "family" and he initiated many schemes to improve the living conditions of the Swindon work force.

As the leading citizen he chaired the Swindon New Town Local Board, presided over the Mechanics' Institute, was a director of Swindon Water Works and held several important positions in local charitable and

WILLIAM DEAN

benevolent organisations. As a man of strong religious principles he was a preacher with the local Methodist church. Almost inevitably, the onerous nature of his professional, administrative and social obligations took its toll, and he experienced heart trouble in early 1877. At first he chose to continue working but was eventually persuaded to take convalescent leave in the summer of that year. Unfortunately this came too late and he died of a heart attack in June, aged just 60 years. Such was the respect he had enjoyed that an estimated 6,000 people attended his funeral at St Mark's on 9th June 1877, including the Board and senior management, senior officers from other companies, colleagues from Wolverhampton, and many of the ordinary Swindon workforce.

With the position of Locomotive, Carriage and Wagon Superintendent falling vacant in this unexpected fashion, the question of succession presented a conundrum. The criteria of age, date of appointment, executive seniority and years of experience favoured George Armstrong. Against these credentials, his experience on the GWR had been limited to the smaller arena of Wolverhampton. (He had started his career at a colliery, followed by a period on the Hull & Selby Railway. He had then worked as a driver on the Nord Railway in France, which culminated in some colourful adventures during the Second French Revolution of 1848). Perhaps most importantly, his absence of experience in broad gauge matters counted against him.

On the other hand, Dean had extensive knowledge of Wolverhampton Works and had then spent the preceding nine years working for Joseph Armstrong at Swindon. He thus had a thorough appreciation of motive power requirements on a strategic plane throughout the system. In this regard, responsibilities at Swindon had been magnified by absorption of the other broad gauge companies, and of narrow gauge railways such as the West Midland, Birkenhead, Vale of Neath etc. Counting against him was his age of 37, making him 18 years younger than George Armstrong.

The board, which effectively meant Sir Daniel Gooch himself by then, seems to have hesitated over Dean's promotion. Sir Daniel had been 21 years old when appointed Locomotive Superintendent in 1837 but the company's circumstances had changed vastly in the interval. He more than any other person would have understood the pressures of the job, and the implications of the constraints placed upon it by virtue of the company's financial condition. There is a comment in his diary that he hoped Dean would do well when the appointment was confirmed in late June 1877.

Any reservations that Gooch might have harboured were to prove misplaced but Dean faced an awkward situation at a point when he had many fresh issues to address. George Armstrong made it patently clear that he would not recognise as his boss a person who was significantly younger and who had previously worked for him. Dean's attitude gives some insight into his character as he apparently chose to react passively and to leave George Armstrong largely to his own devices at Wolverhampton. Harry Holcroft, usually an eloquent commentator on GWR locomotive affairs, only briefly referred to this episode by noting that despite being a martinet, Dean chose not to make an issue of the matter. Holcroft did not elaborate upon or attempt to justify this judgement which is unfortunate as it does not accord with what is known of Dean's character from elsewhere.

The possibility of confrontation was to arise in another way around about 1890. Swindon had been established to cope with the grand design of the Broad Gauge whereas the origins of Wolverhampton were quite different. The northern works had grown to service a variety of locomotives acquired from different sources. In due course, a range of standard designs emerged but the heterogeneous origins of the fleet maintained there in the early days had helped develop a valuable pool of skilled labour. In conjunction with the elimination of the Broad Gauge, consideration was given to concentration of locomotive manufacture and servicing at Wolverhampton. There were strong arguments in favour including close proximity to sources of base materials such as coal, iron and steel, and the plentiful local supply of skilled engineering labour. These factors were thought less important in the manufacture and servicing of carriages and wagons, which activities would have remained at Swindon. However, the plan was dropped when it proved impossible to acquire sufficient land adjacent to the Stafford Road site.

Had this scheme proceeded, George Armstrong's position in the management hierarchy would have re-emerged as an issue. In reality, he remained in post until retirement in 1897 at the age of 75, only 5 years before Dean's own departure. The sturdy independence of Wolverhampton waned thereafter with the last locomotives built there being two batches of small Churchward prairie tanks between 1905 and 1908.

Returning to the point at which he took over the reins at Swindon, William Dean had to cope with funding constraints driven not only by Gooch's austerity programme but also by the civil engineering budget. From the earliest days, the River Severn had presented a major obstacle to efficient services between London and South Wales. The capital commitment to eliminate this impediment in spite of

No 378 *Sir Daniel* was the first narrow gauge passenger engine to be built at Swindon (Works No 69 of the 1st Passenger Lot). It appeared in September 1866, the same month that Sir Daniel Gooch took up the role of Chairman. This class underwent the usual range of boiler changes typical of the later half of the 19th Century, and also received improved cab weather protection. Unusually, the majority of this class of 30 were significantly rebuilt quite late in their careers.

Gooch's financial policies reflected the importance accorded to the project. Construction of the Severn Tunnel commenced four years before Dean took up office and it would be 13 years before it was completed with a length of the 4 miles 624 yards. The project was plagued with problems that were overcome through dogged corporate determination and by the extraordinary bravery of some individuals when disaster threatened. In financial terms, the cost at £1.8 million (contemporary prices) was an enormous burden upon the company's capital resources.

It has been suggested that there was reluctance finally to eliminate the Broad Gauge during Gooch's lifetime, a proposition that is unconvincing. As a hardnosed businessman, he would have known better than most how much this fundamental incompatibility had cost. At one time there had been over 30 breaks-of-gauge where Great Western territory was contiguous with that of other companies. He would have had little sentimentality for a system that had long since become an expensive anachronism. It is far more likely that gauge conversion under his financial stringency had to be delayed until the expense of the Severn Tunnel had been absorbed.

In any event, standardisation of the West of England mainline in May 1892 was not so much the end of the matter as more the beginning of another major civil engineering project. The busy weekend during which the final broad gauge route was despatched with such efficiency has become a romanticised subject. However, in straight engineering terms, the conversion of the South Wales route via Gloucester was a greater task but less well-known, being more remote in time.

The events of May 1892 marked the start of an overdue up-grade of the route to Penzance. As far as Exeter, trains worked over a double-tracked trunk line, laid out for express speeds. Beyond, the character changed entirely as a result of the hilly terrain and the unfounded engineering assumptions born of the misguided atmospheric project. Not much could be feasibly done about the stiff gradients and sharp bends but modernisation to match the line capacity east of Exeter was to prove expensive. Many miles of track had to be doubled and the remaining baulk road replaced. There were tunnels to be widened, a sea wall to be built and numerous timber viaducts to be replaced. Throughout his period in office, Dean had to work under financial constraint imposed by Gooch, in a programme of civil works that had few parallels.

WILLIAM DEAN

While the broad gauge remained, he was required to keep trains moving with an ageing locomotive fleet that required augmentation. A new build programme for service restricted to the broad gauge only was not viable because of impending obsolescence. Dean therefore expanded upon a tactic started by Armstrong – new engines that could be readily converted from narrow to broad gauge and vice versa. The idea was elegantly simple, even if the broad gauge versions were rather less than elegant. Unfortunately, although the benefits of standardisation were increasingly obvious, this unique problem meant continuation of some dated construction methods and more locomotive diversity than would otherwise have been desirable.

Elimination of the broad gauge left a residual, albeit less pressing, split in motive power needs. Express services could be worked as far as Newton Abbot with the GWR's single driver fleet but beyond that point, a more sturdy strain of locomotive with a superior adhesion factor was needed. This led to the creation of a sub-fleet (eg the Duke Class 4-4-0s) able to work efficiently over the gradients of the far west – a specialised need not fully removed until the arrival of larger engines in the Churchward era.

William Dean's abilities as a practical engineer were matched by an appetite for scientific analysis and experimentation. Although some of his designs reflected the orthodoxy of Joseph Armstrong, he was keen to extend the boundaries of knowledge of the steam locomotive. Shortly after moving to Swindon, he brought WH Stanier from Wolverhampton in the role of Chief Clerk. In addition to his clerical responsibilities, Stanier had a keen interest in materials and with Dean's support, he set up facilities to test the mechanical and chemical properties of metals used in locomotive construction. Before space became available at the works, a room in Stanier's home was used as a temporary laboratory. (A possible benefit of Mrs Stanier's tolerance was early stimulation of technical interest by one of her three boys, who was to become Sir William A. Stanier FRS).

With the eventual establishment of a properly equipped laboratory in the works, Dean's continued investigations led in 1893 to presentation of a paper to the Institute of Mechanical Engineers entitled "Tensile Tests and Chemical Analysis of Copper Plates from Fireboxes on the Great Western Railway". That this was the first, and for long the only, published paper on metallurgical analysis of materials used in locomotive construction shows a scientific engineer well in advance of his time.

Dean's backing of Stanier's efforts is reflective of his attitude towards subordinates in encouraging initiative, and in acknowledging and praising their efforts. He was abrupt with those of inadequate commitment but adept in identification and advancement of young engineers with the right potential. This is at odds with Holcroft's terse assessment, but perhaps other factors were involved. Holcroft admitted that despite becoming a premium apprentice to Dean in 1899, he never actually met him but always had to deal directly with Churchward.

The little that has been written of William Dean the man seems to have been drawn mainly from the closing years of his working career. Inevitably this invokes comparisons between the ageing Victorian with failing abilities and the Rising Star of the new century. Thus there is a tendency to look at Dean though the prism of Churchward's presence, achievements, and manner of doing things.

Churchward had a most effective style of leadership and was an accomplished exponent of MBWA. During his frequent visits to the Drawing Office, he might come across a young draughtsman wrestling with a design problem. He would take over the draughtsman's stool and drawing board, and summon those within earshot to an impromptu meeting to evaluate the best possible solution. All would be encouraged to contribute, regardless of their seniority.

Churchward thus blended his practice of "Management By Wandering Around" with a collaborative approach that generated a powerful cohesion. Unlike most modern business "leaders" who fool themselves that they know what is happening by staring at a computer screen, Churchward really did know what was being broadcast on Radio Corridor. Anyone doubting the efficacy of this approach should reflect on how else was it possible to create in his first decade a range of new locomotives of varying capacities that from the start were so competent?

In contrast, shy, self-effacing William Dean could be easily overlooked by history. However, the difficulties he faced during his 27 years as Locomotive Superintendent, and his perseverance is the measure of the man. He had been appointed to an important position when only 23, and for the next 39 years bore a heavy executive burden through the Wolverhampton -Swindon stand-off, the Severn Tunnel saga, and the Broad Gauge abolition and its aftermath. Churchward was never under such pressure; indeed by 1911 it was possible for him to introduce a brand new class more or less out of existing components. It could be claimed that by then his mission was virtually complete.

Dean's leadership ability is also evident in his experimental locomotives, which could not have been possible without the unified support of his subordinates. The number and variety of his innovations was extraordinary and although many were unsuccessful, or proved that some lines of enquiry were dead ends, the knowledge garnered must have proved invaluable, especially for his successor. Although not directly the focus of this work, a summary of these experimental engines appears in **Appendix B**.

Assessments of Dean have often assumed a negative tone, based on adverse interpretation of his abilities during his final years in office and on the nature of his relationship with Churchward. It has been held that by about 1897-8, Dean was no longer mentally capable and that his role had been reduced to one of a figurehead with Churchward as his deputy exercising the real executive power. There is no firm information to support this contention thereby suggesting that it has gained acceptance through repetition. In fact, there is real and circumstantial evidence that points to the contrary.

There are indeed indications that by the close of the 19th Century, Churchward did have a hand in some novel developments. The fitting of pannier tanks (an idea that emanated from Belgium) to 4-4-0PT No 1490 could well have been an early sign of his willingness to embrace foreign engineering ideas, as he was soon to do with respect to French and American practice. Also, the search for a replacement for the Dean Goods led to the Krugers which embraced so many novel features as to suggest that a younger, fresher mind was possibly on the case. These elements notwithstanding, Dean had shown firm commitment to assumption of responsibility throughout his career, and it would not have been in his nature to share ultimate accountability with a subordinate. It is not tenable that a man of his qualities would have entertained a relationship with a deputy to whom blame could be delegated, should something have gone wrong.

Other evidence that he was still in charge concerns the 2-2-2 "Sir Daniel" Class. By 1900, Dean had been

By 1900 train loadings were becoming too heavy for singles of modest proportions and after three had been withdrawn, Dean rebuilt 23 of the 2-2-2 "Sir Daniel" Class as 0-6-0s. This was a relatively simple process resulting in a more practical type that was used on goods duties. The low-cost nature of the exercise reflected the sort of economies that Dean had sought in earlier years under the financial constraints of Sir Daniel Gooch. Churchward had other ideas about motive power for freight work and the programme ceased with the conversion of No 381 in July 1902, when only four remained to be rebuilt. These engines were immediately distinguishable by the hump in the running plate and elevated springs over the centre driving wheels, as with No 384 shown here. It was to be 28 years before the GWR created any more 0-6-0s.

WILLIAM DEAN

thinking about building more of his Class 2301 goods engines but then opted to convert the singles to 0-6-0s. These had been sound engines but their inferior adhesive qualities made them obsolete with trains becoming heavier. Twenty-three were treated but the programme ceased immediately after Dean's retirement as Churchward had not agreed with the concept, his sights being firmly set elsewhere. If he had really exercised control in locomotive matters in 1900, the conversions would never have commenced in the first place.

Then there was the manner of Dean's departure. In February 1902, in his annual address to the Swindon St John Ambulance Association, he made reference to his approaching retirement by stating it to be common knowledge that his connection with Swindon was drawing to a close. A few days after his retirement in June 1902, a large crowd gathered at the Mechanics' Hall for a speech by Churchward following which he was presented with a grandfather clock. This had been purchased out of the almost £400 (a substantial sum in those days) raised through a collection among the engineering staff. Dean had selected this gift, giving the balance of the monies to a local sanatorium. His response was lengthy, detailed and witty, including an extempore joke when his words were interrupted by the chiming of his clock.

These events emphasise that at the conclusion of his career, William Dean was still in command of his faculties, and unambiguously in charge up to the formal hand-over to Churchward. Equally, he would have known that he was no longer able to take new ideas forward but that he could provide a protective umbrella while his successor worked on the concepts that would take GWR locomotives into a new era. These two men, so very different in manner and approach, formed an unusual tandem partnership that facilitated a smooth transition, helping to lay out the ground for the company's brilliant Edwardian phase.

Although a quiet and retiring person, William Dean accepted social obligations beyond his management duties, in the mould of Joseph Armstrong. He founded the Swindon Works branch of the St John Ambulance Association, over which he presided until his retirement. He also presided over the Mechanic's Institute and expended much effort in making that organisation a success. Outside the company, he was an officer in the 2nd Volunteer Battalion of the Duke of Edinburgh's Wiltshire Regiment, and served for many years as a County Magistrate.

The new order, 1884 style. No 2350 displays the early "standard" style of Dean Goods class with dome mounted on the front boiler ring, round-topped boiler and outside boiler feed through clack boxes mounted on the firebox sides. The ornate livery comprised Indian red below the running plate, lined copper green for the superstructure, brass for dome/ safety valve cover/ works plates/ beading, copper rim to the chimney, and burnished handrails/ smokebox hinges/ dart. The tender is an early Dean vehicle with springs mounted below the running plate on the outside frames. Judging by the height to which the coal has been careful stacked and packed in the tender, a long journey is anticipated. Tender modifications, first of coal rails and later side fenders to make the coal more secure have yet to be applied. A high degree of cleanliness was normal in those days as goods engines were expected to match their passenger counterparts in spit and polish.

The old order, 1954 style. No 2411, one of the last dozen Dean Goods in service stands bereft of tender, outside Swindon "A" shop, ready for the final short journey. Changes are prominent in the superheated boiler, ATC equipment, style of buffers and couplings, and in the absence of copper, brass and green. Any colour has long since disappeared under the grime. Despite the vicissitudes of inadequate cleaning, hard work and a long working life, the DNA of glamorous old No 2350 is prominent in No 2411, proud and distinguished to the end.
Arthur Carpenter

Viewed from a modern standpoint, it is difficult to appreciate just how massive was the GWR as an enterprise within the industrial firmament of the 19th Century, and how heavily the leadership of that monolithic organisation bore upon the shoulders of a small group of giants. Gooch was the exception in living a full yet long life; most of the others went before their time, as with Joseph Armstrong. While allegations of mental incapacity can be refuted with authority, it is entirely likely that the years of unremitting pressure seriously damaged Dean's physical health. The opacity surrounding the man prevents grounded conclusions, and this is accentuated by the etiquette of

the time that declared taboo the public admission of some illnesses that today are openly discussed.

The company bought a house at Folkestone for William Dean's retirement but he did not enjoy that reward for long, passing away in 1905. Nothing is known of this period but it must have been lonely for him after the hectic years at Swindon and because of the tragic nature of his family life. He had married in 1865 but his wife died shortly after the birth of their third child. He remarried in 1878 but his second wife predeceased him in 1889. Also his two daughters died young, and only his son was to survive him.

At the time Dean succeeded Joseph Armstrong, the difference in the Wolverhampton and Swindon design schools was strongly evident in tank locomotives. Built in 1877, the year of Dean's promotion, No 1431 of the variegated 0-4-2T Class 517 is seen at Exeter St Davids. There were several alternative styles of rear frames, cabs, and bunkers within this numerically large class which first emerged as saddle tanks from Wolverhampton in 1868. They were better known for the side tank version introduced in 1873. This engine has a Belpaire firebox but retains half cab and inside trailing bearings; the enlarged bunker does nothing for the looks.

Class 517 No 219 is actually a year older than the engine in the previous photograph but is in more modern condition with a Belpaire firebox, outside frames to the trailing wheels, enclosed cab and enlarged bunker.
Real Photographs

Chapter 2
EXPERIMENTATION AND PRACTICE

An important early stage in the evolution of the British steam locomotive was acceptance that four-wheeled power units, as exemplified by the designs of Edward Bury, would be insufficient to cope with heavier loads at faster speeds. Thus the six-wheeled locomotive of basically modest proportions became the norm for motive power during much of the 19th Century (with the honourable exception of the Broad Gauge). An industry-wide consensus emerged that the 2-2-2 type was preferred for the fastest services, that the 2-4-0 (and to lesser degree the 0-4-2) should cover heavier and intermediate duties, and that the 0-6-0 was ideal for goods and general utility work. The longest-lived in significant numbers in tender and tank form was the 0-6-0, which came to be regarded as the archetypal British steam locomotive.

As the Broad Gauge receded, the critical mass of the GWR's locomotive fleet increasingly conformed with those of other companies – almost exclusively six wheeled and conservative in nature. At the end of 1877, the year William Dean took charge at Swindon, the make-up of the GWR's standard gauge fleet was:

Tender locomotives	No.	Tank locomotives	No.
2-4-0	125	2-4-0	83
2-2-2	80	0-4-2	132
0-6-0	538	0-6-0	364
Other	10	Other	19
Total	**753**	**Total**	**598**

The Swindon school preferred 2-4-0Ts with Class 455 introduced in 1869, later known as "Metros". No 986 built in 1874 is shown in basically original condition, cabless and with condensing gear installed for working through the tunnels of the Metropolitan Railway.

As with the Wolverhampton Class 517, the Metros evolved through various styles. No 3597 of 1899 was one of the very last built. This was a "large Metro" – a sort of de luxe version – with fully enclosed cab, larger side tanks, and volute springs in place of the earlier front leaf springs.

By 1880, the composition was 684 tender and 777 tank locomotives and from then, tank engines were consistently in the majority. By December 1892 the division was even more pronounced with 848 tender and 1201 tank engines. The year 1899 was another landmark as the number of 0-6-0Ts in service exceeded 1000 for the first time and the total with this wheel arrangement remained above that level for the next 60 years.

In 1877, there was clear dichotomy between Swindon and Wolverhampton construction practices. Most new building activity at the northern works concerned six-wheeled tank locomotives, those intended for passenger duties being 0-4-2Ts, initially with saddle and later with side tanks. Originally inside-framed throughout, later modifications involved outside frames for the trailing axle. Six-coupled engines were almost exclusively inside framed saddle tanks, most of which later went through the pannier transformation.

At Swindon, passenger tanks used the 2-4-0T wheel arrangement with outside frames only on the leading axle. Six coupled tank engines had double or sandwich frames and saddle tanks, up until 0-6-0T

Class 1813 which was introduced in 1882, shortly in advance of the Dean Goods.

The differing approaches to frame layout had their roots in the company's origins. The southern area embraced most of the Broad Gauge network, which used Brunel's "baulk road". This consisted of bridge rail laid on longitudinal sleepers held apart to the correct gauge at intervals by cross transoms, a method that was used also with dual gauge track. Conversion to narrow gauge was effected by cutting the transoms and bringing the longitudinal sleepers closer together. Installation of conventional cross-sleepers in broad gauge areas had commenced before the final conversion but this programme was not completed for several years. The baulk road was superior in producing a smoother, quieter ride but was less yielding than conventional cross-sleepered track. This placed greater stress on the frames and hence on crank axles, making use of double-framed engines preferable. On the other hand, most of the Northern Division had been narrow gauge from the start, which made the use of cheaper, inside-framed engines more practicable.

Mention of GWR four-coupled tank engines conjures pictures of Class 48xx 0-4-2Ts skipping along with a couple of auto trailers. However, immaculate Metro No 1411 has been called up for excursion duty. The train comprises two bogies vehicles, then eight 4 or 6 wheelers, and finally two or three more bogies – estimated aggregate tare of 200 tons before weight of men, women, children, buckets and spades. The location is not recorded but it could have been a Bristol to Weston-Super-Mare service. *Pamlin Prints*

Why there should have been a distinction between the wheel arrangements of the four-coupled tank engines is less easy to explain. Construction of 2-4-0Ts (the "Metro" Class) at Swindon continued until 1899 whereas production of Wolverhampton's Class 517 0-4-2T ceased some 14 years earlier. This is curious as a better case could be made for the 0-4-2T arrangement in a small, four-coupled engine as it naturally allowed more room at the rear end for cab and bunker. When there was a need for new four coupled tank engines in the 1930s, the

Wolverhampton design school was revived through Class 48xx. Further conformity with Wolverhampton's later practice was the use of outside frames for the trailing wheels of the modern engines.

Dean's early explorations reflected the prevailing bias towards tank locomotives and his first experimental design, appropriately numbered "1", was an attempt to enlarge upon the Metro. This 4-4-0T was notable for its long side tanks when built in 1880 but the real interest lay below the running plate.

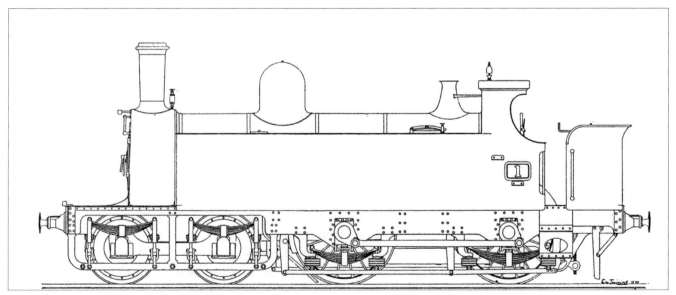

Figure I - Wiliiam Dean's first experimental design - 4-4-0T No 1 of 1880.

WILLIAM DEAN

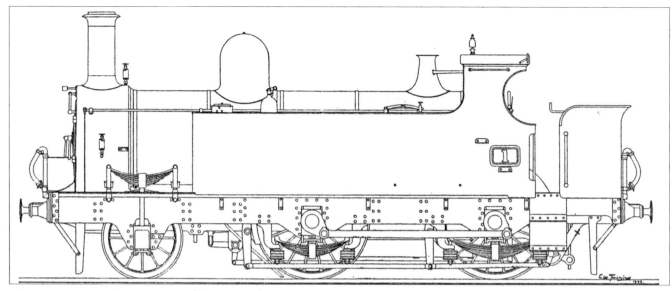

Figure II - No 1 as rebuilt to a 2-4-0T with shortened tanks.

Swindon had built a pair of broad gauge 4-4-0Ts (*Corsair* and *Brigand*) in 1849 using Gooch's ball and socket swivel joint for the bogie. However, when No 1 appeared, modern designs were in their infancy, the Midland Railway having introduced Britain's first bogie coaches as recently as 1874. Dean was therefore investigating the building of a larger and heavier tank locomotive that required an extra carrying axle to achieve an acceptable weight distribution.

With minimal empirical evidence available, he had to start somewhere and the result was most unusual, lacking any centre pin or conventional stretcher between the outside frames. The frame plates were very narrow, carrying the outside axleboxes and thereby maintaining the spacing between the axles. The frame plates were connected to each other by a single transverse plate strip (5" deep and ¾" thick) set midway between the two axles. The only connection between this ultra-lightweight truck and the engine superstructure was indirectly through the spring hangers. These were secured by a link and shackle arrangement to two long U-profiled flat plates (4" deep by ¾" thick) that extended down to a few inches above rail level. These U-plates were attached to (1) the sub-frame supporting the buffer beam (2) the footplate valence equidistant between the bogie axles and (3) the forward part of the outside frame in front of the leading driving axle. The U-plates were cross-supported by three stay rods in front of the leading axle, equidistant between the axles, and behind the rear axle.

Effectively the only "flex" was achieved through limited transverse movement of the axles in the axle boxes. Thus the bogie had no rotational properties in the accepted sense as the wheel flanges, regardless of side play in the axle boxes, remained parallel with the

engine's centre line. The set up was complex yet flimsy, and led to front end instability.

The long side tanks had a reported capacity of 935 gallons (the early Metros had 740 gallons) but which might have been understated, judging by the drawing (**Figure I**). Mansell bogie wheels with teak centres were used as they were thought stronger and less prone to breakage through casting faults than the contemporary spoked variety. This feature later appeared on other Dean bogie engines, and also on some tenders.

The intention was to create an engine with an operating range and haulage capacity greater than would be possible with a 2-4-0T. Not surprisingly, No 1's life as a 4-4-0T was short and it returned to service in 1882 as a 2-4-0T with lengthened outside frames and shortened tanks. In this form, it was a popular and effective singleton that remained at work until 1924 (**Figure II**).

Dean's next experiment was to be a pair of 4-2-4Ts, Nos 9 and 10. This essay has been described in terms akin to "outrageous folly" although the rationale was logical enough. With a shortage of practical knowledge about what might be achieved with bogie engines, Dean seems to have been inspired by a broad gauge design with which he would have been familiar. Since 1853, the Bristol & Exeter Railway had operated 4-2-4WBTs with 9' driving wheels (designed by Pearson) on express passenger duties. They were fast and much liked, and between 1868 and 1873, Nos 39 - 42 were renewed with 8' 10" flangeless driving wheels, becoming GWR Nos 2001 to 2004. In 1876, No 2001 was derailed in a fatal accident and withdrawn; the other three were rebuilt as 4-2-2s with driving wheels reduced to a "mere" eight feet in the year that Dean took up office.

William Dean was familiar with the unusual 4-2-4T wheelbase through Pearson's designs for the Bristol and Exeter Railway. No 44 shown here was one of the first series of 4-2-4WBTs, built by Rothwell in 1854 with 9' driving wheels. Dean's experimental narrow gauge 4-2-4T No 9 was a large locomotive but one that fades into insignificance compared with the grandeur of Pearson's creation.

The final form of the Pearson engines was assumed by 4-2-2s Nos 2002-2004, following the derailment of 4-2-4WBT No 2001. No 2002 (B&E No 40) is seen at Newton Abbot after rebuilding which created a handsome locomotive that looked more modern than contemporary Broad Gauge 4-2-2s of GWR origin.

WILLIAM DEAN

The Pearson engines were larger than contemporary and more conventional tank locomotives by a considerable order of magnitude and they appeared to offer a template for a downsized narrow gauge version. Recorded dimensional details are sketchy but No 9, which appeared in 1881, had 7' 8" flanged driving wheels. The water and coal capacities were 2535 gallons and around 4 tons respectively. These dimensions suggest an express passenger engine with an operating range matching that of a tender locomotive.

New ground was broken with other features. The boiler was the first in this country to be built with two rings, a hallmark of Dean's subsequent designs including his 0-6-0 goods engine. The cylinders at 18" x 28" were the largest yet used on the GWR. The overall wheelbase was long at 30' but frustratingly no definitive information remains about the bogie design although a clue lies in the valve motion.

The transverse bracing rods of No 1's novel bogie combined with the long side tanks had made access to the motion almost impossible. With No 9, this aspect was improved by using outside Stephenson's eccentrics which were connected by rocking shafts to the inside valves, mounted above the cylinders. This unusual layout suggests that an unconventional form of front bogie frame had been used but no details have survived. EW Twining's drawing (**Figure III**) is based on interpretation of known dimensions and sundry data obtained from Swindon sources. A modified version of No 1's bogie might have been installed at the rear of No 9.

No 1 had undertaken little testing because of instability; distances covered by No 9 were even less as in this respect its shortcomings were even more extreme. If the engine had ever worked at any speed, more instability might well have occurred from water surge in the long side tanks, although the enclosed sandboxes might have acted as baffles. Little information survives about No 9 as it seemed to be later policy to deny its existence. Only when confronted with third party evidence did Churchward concede that it had actually been built. Perhaps the reason for secrecy was that Dean was only recently appointed and with a reputation to establish and protect, he needed to play down his second experimental failure, particularly one as spectacular as No 9.

Strangely, history was repeated in 1924 with a newly appointed Locomotive Superintendent, by then CME, and a prototype tank engine. The first movement of No 5600 in steam was only a few yards before failure. This resulted from a design fault whereby inadequate support of the valve spindles and connecting extension rods led to severe bending of the spindles. The problem was swiftly solved, and the relevant drawings were dated August 1924 although they were actually prepared in December, following the incident. Collett completed the cover-up by warning all involved that *any* further discussion of the matter would invoke instant dismissal. It took some years for the story to emerge, and emphasises the point that official information should not necessarily be assumed as 100% accurate.

The unfortunate adventures with No 9 meant that construction of No 10 was halted in its early stages. The second locomotive was to have been fitted with Joy valve gear for comparison purposes. As this equipment had already been acquired, it was used in a further experiment – involving yet another tank locomotive.

Dean took a seminal decision regarding six-coupled tank engines in the forty members of Class 1813 introduced in September 1882. With these loco-

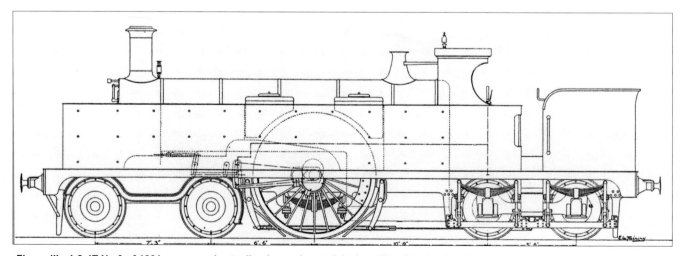

Figure III - 4-2-4T No 9 of 1881, an even shorter-lived experimental design. This drawing is an interpretation based on the comparatively small amount of information recorded about this locomotive.

EW Twining

GWR 0-6-0T side tanks were a rarity but Wolverhampton produced 12 of Class 633 in 1869. Some were condenser-fitted for working over the Metropolitan Railway as with No 633 shown here at Old Oak Common. *RK Blencowe Negative Archive*

motives, he switched to the Wolverhampton school by adopting inside frames; all subsequent 0-6-0Ts used this format except for Class 1661, which employed double frames for their possible use as broad gauge convertibles. Class 1813, which was also distinctive for having side tanks and domeless boilers (the latter à la Nos 2301-2320), was built in two batches of 20. Inserted in this number series was No 1833, also a side tank but fitted with the Joy valve gear set surplus from the abandoned No 10.

0-6-0Ts from Swindon were also uncommon. The first batch of outside-framed Class 1076, the "Buffalos", (Nos 1076 to 1081 of Lot 22) appeared as side tanks. The remainder of this 266-strong class were built as saddle tanks; most examples later acquired pannier tanks. *F Moore's Railway Photographs*

Opposite, upper - Swindon continued construction of Buffalo 0-6-0STs of Class 1076 from 1870 until 1881. These engines worked mainly in the south and for many years hauled long distance mineral and goods trains e.g. Aberdare to Swindon via Gloucester, and later to Salisbury via the Severn Tunnel – journeys of 108 and 103 miles respectively. They were later favoured for auto-train services. No 1287 was fitted with pannier tanks in 1925, withdrawn from normal service in 1946, used as a stationery boiler at Leamington until 1953, and is seen awaiting cutting up at Swindon. There were failed attempts at preservation in view of its historic importance as the last surviving 0-6-0 with double frames.

Opposite, lower - The last "large" Wolverhampton 0-6-0STs were of Class 655, built from 1892 until 1897. No 1773 of 1893-vintage acquired pannier tanks in 1925 and survived until 1950.

Above - Wolverhampton maintained its commitment to inside-framed tanks well into the 20th Century by continuing to build small Class 2021 0-6-0STs, as first introduced in 1897. No 2148 of 1904 is seen here at Swindon in May 1953 carrying pannier tanks fitted 30 years earlier.

No 1833's role in this series of experiments was pivotal. It is reasonable to speculate that if the formula had proved successful, later examples of Class 1813, or the following Class 1854, might have been changed to conform. Unlike the complexity of Nos 1, 9 and the proposed 10, this engine's only novel features were the valve gear and the 17" x 28" cylinders (originally intended for No 10). There was thus little risk of confusion about causes in the event of failure to perform satisfactorily. Recorded dimensional details are incomplete but the boiler barrel and wheelbase were longer than that of Class 1813, and the engine was significantly heavier. It was found that variation of water levels in the side tanks disturbed the valve gear settings and for this reason, withdrawal took place in August 1884 after covering just over 11,000 miles.

The final stage in this round of innovations was to rebuild No 1833 in October 1884 as an 0-6-0. The valve gear, cylinders with their long stroke, and domeless two-ringed boiler were retained. The wheelbase was unchanged at 7' 7" + 8' 3" but the frames were shortened, and a tender from a Beyer 0-6-0 added. Apart from slight upward curves in the running plates to allow for clearance of the coupling rod bosses, the rebuilt engine externally resembled a Dean Goods of the 2301-2320 series. These had appeared in the interval between the introduction of No 1833 as a tank engine and its rebuilding. In its latter form, No 1833 maintained its similarity with the Dean Goods by receiving a back dome Belpaire boiler (Type B4) in 1902. Withdrawal took place in 1906, having covered over 315,000 miles.

Summarising these tank locomotive experiments, it is apparent that only No 1 as a conventional 2-4-0T could be judged satisfactory in a normal operating sense. However, in terms of size and haulage capacity, it fell short of the step change that Dean had been seeking. Benefits were nonetheless derived such as proving the applicability of the two-ring boiler. Also, there were elements of the curious bogie on 4-4-0T No 1 that were to prove more useful in the famous centre-less carriage bogie. Nonetheless, the over-riding conclusion must have been that under prevailing conditions, a large tank locomotive was not feasible.

Dean was not alone in encountering difficulties in this regard. It was a challenging concept to combine a large boiler with adequate coal and water capacity on a single carrying frame, and to contain the result within loading gauge and weight restrictions. Many years later, the efforts of JR Bazin in designing his 2-6-2T Class P1 No 850 of 1928 for the Great Southern Railways were closely monitored by his erstwhile colleague, Nigel Gresley, who was then designing his Class V1 2-6-2T for the LNER. No 850, the GSR's only truly modern tank engine, was never completely satisfactory. A similar judgement might also be passed on Thompson's 2-6-4T Class L1 for the LNER, which went through many design iterations before construction started. Experiences like these make the instant success of Churchward's pioneering large and small prairies all the more laudable.

Above - The narrow gauge 0-6-0 tender locomotive tradition at Swindon commenced in 1855 with Class 57 – No 59 shown here carried Swindon Works No 3. Renewal of several took place at Wolverhampton in 1873-5 and No 59 was so treated during that period, although how much of the original remained is questionable. More modifications followed but that most relevant to this discourse was the fitting of a round-topped boiler with rear dome (RCTS Code S4) in January 1901 which it carried until withdrawal in 1912. This is the form depicted – few photographs are available of this type of boiler on the Dean Goods although most of the class carried them at some stage during their careers.

Opposite, upper - To illustrate the diversity possible even within a numerically small class during this period, this view shows Class 57 No 68 with an R3 type boiler (RCTS Code). This was a three-ring boiler with dome on the front ring and round-topped raised firebox.

Opposite, lower - Class 79 was an enlargement of Class 57, introduced in two batches in 1857/8 and two more in 1861/2. No 122 was the only member of the two later batches to remain a tender engine; the others were converted to 0-6-0ST. It is seen carrying an S2 boiler acquired in 1892. An S4 Type followed in 1906 and then a B4 type in 1909; withdrawal came in December 1918.

Above - Class 77/167 comprised six locomotives built by Beyer Peacock (two in 1857 and four in 1861). Their inside frames made them unusual among contemporary GWR 0-6-0s; they spent their lives almost entirely in the Northern Division. The class was re-boilered twice, the first time with a Wolverhampton version of the Swindon three ring boiler with dome on centre ring – as shown here with No 169 which stayed in service until 1904. With the second re-boilering programme, much more variety was injected into the class which emphasises the hazards of locomotive identification in the late 19th Century.

Below - Class 131 was a Swindon design and more in keeping with current GWR standards. The story of this class is complex but not that of No 317 which was built in 1865 and withdrawn in 1883, a remarkably short working life. Other examples were renewed and survived into the 1920s.

Daniel Gooch was so impressed with Beyer Peacock's product quality that when he placed an order for 0-6-0s, he left the design work entirely in the hands of the manufacturers. The result was Class 322, colloquially known as "Beyers" with 20 built in 1864, and ten more ordered by Joseph Armstrong in 1866. They were handsome machines, proving popular for their efficiency, and enjoyed long lives. No 354 was the last to be withdrawn in August 1934; it is seen at Leamington, very likely in post-Grouping days, carrying a B4 boiler.

This and the two images overleaf are included because they provide good views of B4 boilers fitted with top feed, as also applied to some Dean Goods. No 328 carried this type of boiler from 1914 until withdrawal in 1929.

The right hand side of Beyer No 355 . . .

. . . and the left hand side. Note that the engine now carries the more modern form of smokebox door.   *Photomatic*

Above - Inclusion of yet another Beyer photograph – this time of No 337 – is justified on grounds that this engine is living up to the class's reputation regarding looks. After delivery of the Beyers, it would be many years before the GWR ordered new engines from outside manufacturers. On this evidence this was a pity as Beyer Peacock could have continued to supply some very attractive locomotives to the company. *F Moore's Railway Photographs*

Below - The old bias in favour of tank locomotives re-surfaced with the Beyers when six were converted to 0-6-0STs between 1878 and 1885. Five were later converted to pannier tanks but they lost none of their attractive looks through those processes. 0-6-0PT No 326 was converted to that form in 1919 and is seen in company with a saddle tank.

The 12 members of Class 360 were built at Swindon in 1866. They were very similar to the Standard or Armstrong Goods that appeared shortly afterwards, the main differences being in length and frame detail. No 363 seen here was the last in service, being withdrawn in 1933.

Rail Archive Stephenson

The need to rely on outside manufacturers was unnecessary from 1866 onwards as Swindon had developed the capacity to build in large numbers. Between that year and 1876, 290 examples were built of Class 388 (the Standard Goods – also referred to as the Armstrong Goods to differentiate from Dean's 0-6-0s). No 426 seen here was built in 1868 and fitted with an S2 boiler in 1892. (A further 20 engines of Class 927 were built in 1874. Known as "Coal Engines", they varied only in having 4' 6" driving wheels).

Above - This view of No 601 is undated which is unfortunate as it is carrying either an S4c boiler fitted in 1910 or an S4 boiler fitted in 1919. (The S4c type had small dimensional variations from the standard type – refer to Appendix A.2 for further information).

Below - Armstrong Goods No 44 with a B4 boiler carried from 1912 to 1921.   *M Whitworth*

The final evolution of the pre-Grouping GWR 0-6-0 was the Dean Goods. No 2462 was at Carmarthen in August 1950.

With no evidence that tank locomotive practice then offered any avenue of sustainable advance, Dean reined back on his predilections and opted to construct tender engines for longer distance work. Thus the tank to tender transformation of No 1833 in parallel with the domeless boiler and inside frames of 0-6-0T Class 1813 formed the precedents for significant aspects of the first batch of Dean Goods, the key design features of which will be considered in the next chapter.

Sixteen years after No 2301 appeared and with Dean Goods construction drawing to a close, there was another spate of experiments. These were to explore what form a larger goods engine might assume and centred around four locomotives, in the chronological order of their introduction Nos 36, 2601, 33, and 2602. They were traditional in retaining the double frames that Swindon still adhered to with its larger tender locomotives and their role was as test beds for new ideas, mainly in boiler design.

The first of the quartet was constructed to meet the specific need of freight haulage through the Severn Tunnel. Mineral traffic over this route was heavy and with significant gradients on the approaches and within the tunnel, the consequences arising from a train stalling could be far reaching. No 36, the GWR's first 4-6-0 (and soon nicknamed "The Crocodile") was pure Dean in design with the largest boiler constructed under his aegis, a wide firebox and an unusual grate

profile. The engine demonstrated a substantial reserve of power in taking through the tunnel loads that were greater than a pair of 0-6-0s could manage, and at a higher overall speed. During its working life from 1896 to 1905, it achieved a reasonable mileage.

Next came another 4-6-0, No 2601 with a high pitched boiler that included other fresh ideas, most noticeably a 3' 6" long combustion chamber, a grate which at 32.2 sq ft was the largest then in use in Britain, and a boiler pressure of 200 lbs/ sq in. This engine appeared in December 1899 and had none of No 36's rakish elegance. It was fitted with a large saddle sand box that accentuated the awkward appearance; it soon earned the nickname "Kruger" after the country's public enemy No 1 in the contemporary Boer War. Eighteen months later in June 1901 the second of the type, No 2602, appeared as an equally ungainly 2-6-0 – the company's second mogul. Neither engine was successful, the boilers giving trouble that was not alleviated by reductions in working pressure, first to 180, and then to 165 lbs/ sq in.

There was an enigmatic quality to the Krugers. The design seems to have been a classic Dean-Churchward fusion of ideas with most of the latter's input apparent above the running plate, where the shortcomings were most evident. However, there is little information about what was the precise nature of the boiler problems. Another curiosity is that despite

Around the end of the 19th Century, several companies broached the question of larger locomotives for goods work with varying degrees of success. The 4-6-0 type was explored and some were found wanting – as exemplified by the London & North Western "Bill Baileys" and the Great Southern & Western Class 362. None however had quite the distinctive appearance of experimental No 36, an engine whose typical Dean styling hid innovations in boiler design. It was a powerful performer but clearly of a passing era.

Further innovation was found in 4-6-0 No 2601., which had none of No 36's handsome looks.

the prototypical pair failing to perform as hoped, a further eight of the mogul version with only minor changes from No 2602 were constructed between January and June 1903.

The working lives of these eight engines were very short, officially around three years but actually less in most cases. Their very existence was contrary to the normal practice of building a single prototype and only adding more after it had proven satisfactory, or after its deficiencies had been identified for subsequent modification. With this class the number of innovations would have complicated identification of the cause of problems, and it made little sense to multiply a design already known to be sub-standard.

An official photograph of the experimental goods 2-6-0 No 33, as built in August 1900. Features typical of the Dean-Churchward transition period are displayed:- the boiler is an early parallel Standard No 2 of the D0 type; the tender has yet to receive side fenders; the livery is as ornate as that used on passenger locomotives. This engine differed from the production series in the heavy compensating beam mounted between the pony truck and the leading driving wheels, and in the vertical spring hangers for the latter. No 33 otherwise conformed with the later style of the Aberdares by receiving a Standard No 4 boiler in early 1903; it was renumbered 2600 in late 1912 by which time it had also been superheated.

One of the enigmas, 2-6-0 "Kruger" No 2610 was built in June 1903 and officially withdrawn in August 1906, although thought to have been taken out of service earlier. Series production of the successful (and much better looking) Aberdares had started in March 1901 and materials from the withdrawn Krugers are believed to have been used in later examples of that class. Several Kruger boilers served on for a many year in a stationary capacity at Swindon Works.

The building of Nos 2603-2610 was more strange considering that the remaining prototype – No 33 – which appeared in 1900 had proved to be essentially sound, and that 60 of the production series had actually been built before No 2603 appeared. A further puzzle is that the Krugers had piston valves mounted above the cylinders, a typical Churchward feature, but the cylinders themselves were inclined at 1 in 7. Inclined cylinders were anathema to him and it might be speculated that either the failure of the Krugers was the source of that hostility, or that this feature was installed against his better judgement on the instructions of Dean.

The Kruger episode suggests the possibility of confusion in the year of the Dean-Churchward transition. Certainly, the affair was uncharacteristic of the normal approach to innovation and Churchward might have been reluctant to let too much become common knowledge. Regardless of who accounted for which features, production of Nos 2603-2610 was clearly on his responsibility and he might have been sensitive about association with a high profile and profligate failure so soon after his appointment. This experience could have been similar to that which William Dean had faced over 4-2-4T No 9, and to that which Collett later met with 0-6-2T No 5600.

The GWR's first mogul was No 33 which appeared in 1900 and became the prototype for the successful Aberdare Class of which 80 more were built. Several styles of Standard Nos 2 and 4 boilers were tried before settling on the tapered No 4 type. They took over the working of mineral traffic emanating from Aberdare that previously had been handled by Dean Goods. As the freight version of the fleet of double-framed 4-4-0s, they were good strong engines but with the Achilles heel of steam reversing gear. No 2680, built December 1902, is seen at Banbury in 1939. By then withdrawals were well under way but this engine was given a stay of execution by the war and was one of the last in service, remaining until June 1948   *Photomatic*

The Dean/Churchward partnership was also evident in the remaining member of the experimental quartet. No 33 was a simpler machine than the others and its main experimental role was in the evolution of boiler designs that followed Churchward's principles. Different versions of the Standard Nos 2 and 4 boilers were tried on No 33 and the earlier members of the production series. Eventually, the normal tapered Standard No 4 was fitted throughout the class, and in this guise, the type could be regarded as the goods version of the "Cities".

Officially designated Class 26xx, these engines initially took over the principal mineral workings from South Wales, for which they earned the nickname "Aberdares". Sound, strong engines they retained one feature from the spell of innovation that had surrounded No 36, 2601 etc – steam powered reversing gear. This troublesome gadget was contrary to the Dean Goods tradition of simplicity and was to remain a feature of the Aberdares, despite its early removal from contemporary 4-4-0s. The operating mechanism required the maintenance of oil under pressure but wear would lead to leakage. With a consequent fall in oil pressure, an engine that had

been notched up would drift back into full forward gear, irritating the driver, adding to the fireman's labours, and increasing coal consumption. However, the greater inconvenience was experienced off duty as in light steam at 120 lbs/ sq in or less (as would be customary while on shed), the reverser could not be worked at all. Equally, the valves could not be adjusted without jacking up the engine.

It is ironic that introduction of the Dean Goods should have been accompanied by so many attempts at innovation. Dean's classic was the simplest of designs, born partly of proof that larger tank engines could not then meet emerging traffic demands, constrained by financial stringency, and enriched by importation of Wolverhampton design practice. There was also irony in the search for a successor. The Aberdares were the only product of complex and quite expensive experiments capable of taking over from the Dean Goods in any acceptable operating sense, and then only partially. Sightings of Aberdares on passenger work were rare and they never developed comparable operational universality. The first Aberdare appeared 17 years after No 2301; the last went eight years before the final Dean Goods was withdrawn.

WILLIAM DEAN

A broader and more complex issue concerns comparison of the rival merits and disadvantages of tank and tender locomotives. Other than the 120 members of Class 2251 that appeared between 1930 and 1948, after 1899 the only additions to the 0-6-0 tender fleet were the 23 "Sir Daniel" rebuilds and the engines absorbed at the Grouping. Construction of the vastly larger 0-6-0T fleet continued until 1905 and after a 24 year hiatus was resumed with a vengeance until 1956. Although the Dean Goods might be considered an archetypical GWR design, by the late 1930s it was becoming a scarce type in comparison with the sustained number of tank engines.

The GWR's attitude was borne of tradition, but this did not always show motive power policies in the best light. By definition, a tank engine was expected to work shorter services, and to spend more time in shunting and pilot duties than its tender counterpart, but it was still subject to the same mileage-defined maintenance regime. Locomotive mileage when working defined journeys could be measured with acceptable accuracy but this was less of a science where duties included frequent stops and starts, reverses of direction, and lengthy periods stationary. Recourse was thus taken to a standard figure for notional miles covered per hour in steam.

This approach could lead to substantial distortions in recorded mileages as exemplified by the case of 0-6-0ST Class 1361 No 1365. In a career lasting from 1910 until 1962, its official mileage was 936,000, an average of 18,500 per annum. Assuming a 270 day working year (allowing time out for Sundays, light repairs, wash-outs etc), a locomotive with 3' 8" driving wheels and confined to dock shunting and shed pilot duties was supposedly covering around 65 miles per day, ie roughly the equivalent of a Plymouth – Newton Abbot return trip.

Another example of mileage distortion concerned the case of 0-6-0PT No 1508 at Cardiff Canton in 1959-61. Railway author Peter Rowledge commented on this locomotive's daily duties: *"...apart from moving the odd dead engine around the yard (it) made a daily run to nearby sidings with empties to return with loco coal, about one and a half miles, but every day it was credited with 40 miles. In truth with a realistic mileage figure it would have hardly needed scheduled maintenance other than the boiler on an hours in steam count. A lot of money spent on un-needed exams...".* Of course by the 1960s, dieselisation was making steam power surplus to requirements but this example of chronic under-use of a modern locomotive designed as a round-the-clock shunter identifies

In October 1949, BR at Swindon started to deliver the first of 70 0-6-0PT Class 16xx. This was a pure GWR design intended to replace the useful small panniers of Classes 850/ 2021, the youngest of which dated from 1895. Selection of a traditional number series for six coupled tank engines was a nice gesture to the past but the arrival of lightweight diesel shunters was imminent. Withdrawals

38

The provision of so many of Class 16xx late in the story of steam might have seemed lavish but pales into insignificance compared with Class 94xx. The GWR produced ten and another 200 were constructed by contractors between 1949 and 1956; withdrawals in significant numbers commenced in 1959. The class offered little, if anything, beyond what a Class 57xx could deliver – in fact rather less given its Red route availability and the higher cost tapered boiler. On introduction of No 9400, a GWR director reputedly expressed satisfaction that the company at last had a modern-looking shunting engine. So much for the board's views on aesthetics. They might have more usefully enquired into the financial justification for a class that was the final expression of the company's long -standing extravagant attitude towards supply of six-coupled tank locomotives. No 8439 was built by Bagnall in June 1953 and withdrawn in October 1962.

money wasted in an under-utilised capital asset and in unnecessary overhauls. (Wildly exaggerated mileage figures for shunting locomotives were not the sole preserve of the GWR. Great Southern & Western Railway 0-6-0T *Jumbo* allegedly clocked up 1,610,000 miles in a 61 year career almost entirely confined to the goods yard at Waterford, Ireland!).

Routine maintenance practices could also lead to waste, as shown where GWR services intermingled with those of other companies making direct comparison possible – eg Tredegar where LNWR and GWR locomotives worked side by side. In this area, the local water is very soft but nevertheless the GWR engines were subjected to the system-wide policy of boiler washouts every 10 days or so. If done properly, this would put an engine out of commission for about two days and was essential to maintain a boiler in sound condition if confined to hard water locations. Thus in some areas engines stood out of use on boiler

washouts for no real benefit. The combination of over-stated mileages and unnecessary routine maintenance resulted in more engines than would otherwise have been required – hardly in the best interests of the shareholders, and later the taxpayers.

Whether this contention is fair can be tested by considering the situation elsewhere. In this regard, the LMS provides an objective basis for comparison being the only other member of the Big Four to pursue extensive fleet modernisation. (The profile of the impecunious LNER with its numerous classes and sub -classes was quite different, while the Southern's situation was peripheral to that company's extensive electrification programme). Both the GWR and the LMS in the inter-war years extensively replaced older equipment but the latter was operating with substantially fewer locomotives per miles of route by 1947:

	Tender engines	Tank engines	Total	Route miles	Engines per 100 route miles
GWR	1420	2436	3856	3595	93
LMS	5570	2235	7805	6260	80

WILLIAM DEAN

When considering what had been achieved through their massive re-stocking programmes, it is obvious that the LMS did better than the GWR:

	Fleet total 31-Dec-23	Fleet total 31-Dec-47	% Change
GWR	3944	3856	-2.2
LMS	10313	7805	-24.3

For all the effort at replacement of older types, it is remarkable that the GWR's fleet total should have remained so little changed. A further element was that the addition of 40 diesel passenger units should have replaced at least a matching number of steam locomotives. Part of the LMS's success derived from a corporate re-organisation that emphasised improved operating methodologies and a better-tuned approach to fixed asset utilisation. There were undoubtedly surpluses in the LMS fleet following the Grouping and

unquestionably the 1920s were dominated by wasteful factional strife, but the 24% reduction in fleet total was a notable achievement.

The conclusion may be drawn that the GWR's new build programmes had replaced old engines on a like-for-like basis without consideration of how a better return per individual power unit could be achieved. Design stagnation at Swindon during the 1930s has been much commented upon but there is a suggestion that the malaise ran deeper in lavishing money on new locomotives without improving the overall financial return. Putting it in brutal modern management terminology, the LMS was far better at "sweating" its locomotive assets.

In addition to its design attractions, the Dean Goods was a class to be valued for its comparative rarity among the armada of pannier tanks, and for the superior return on investment that it delivered for its owners over 70 years and more of working life!

The initial conception of the Dean Goods: No 2319 of Lot 61, built in 1883. Only the first 20 class members were built with domeless boilers and although rotation of boiler types was later common throughout, the domeless variety was confined to this batch. A feature was the fitting of clack boxes to firebox sides. A pre-Dean vintage tender is attached, partly modernised with coal rails.

Locomotive Publishing Co

Chapter 3

THE GOODS PEDIGREE

William Dean's initial policy was to perpetuate the design principles established by his predecessor, and this was evident in the first locomotives attributed to him. These were ten 2-2-2's (numbered 157 to 166) that had been supplied by Sharp Stewart to the Northern Division in 1861. They were so comprehensively rebuilt as to be considered new engines despite retaining sandwich frames, a feature that by then had been largely discarded. In 1881 the 2-4-0 Class 2201 appeared which closely followed Armstrong's Class 806 of 1873. Over the years there were numerous detailed changes in the older 2-4-0 fleet in a constant process of modernisation and renewal. Broadly speaking, Dean persisted with the standards set earlier for this locomotive category.

The 0-6-0ST Class 1076 construction programme continued until 1881, thereby maintaining the sense of continuity as this numerically large class was effectively the tank version of the Standard Goods.

Adherence to Armstrong's policies with tank locomotives was even more pronounced with the sustained construction of Metro 2-4-0Ts up until 1899. Progressive modifications yielded such a bewildering variety of bunkers and cabs as to undermine the concept of "class" implying uniformity (Wolverhampton's tank engines were similarly variegated). This individuality contrasted strongly with the standardised Swindon approach of the next century.

Concurrent with these developments, the need for more motive power on the Broad Gauge demanded special attention. Younger locomotives were created through the reincarnation of Gooch's stately "Iron Duke" 4-2-2's. The last appeared as late as 1888; just how much was new and how much re-cycled material in their creation is a matter of debate but there was no doubt about their purpose. They were to keep expresses running until the final gauge conversion.

No 2312, also of Lot 61, is shown here in the second condition assumed by the class. In October 1894, this engine received a boiler with dome on the front ring (RCTS Code Type S2) which it carried until April 1900. A Roscoe-type lubricator was fitted behind the chimney - a practice that ceased with new boilers built after 1892. This was followed by a boiler with dome on rear ring (Type S4) between then and August 1907, when it reverted to an S2 type until February 1911. This view very likely dates from the 1894-1900 period. Pre-Dean tender attached. *Locomotive Publishing Co*

The second batch, of which No 2325 was a member, was built with domes on the front boiler ring (Type S2). This locomotive received a boiler with dome on the rear ring in February 1900. The tender is pre-Dean and has yet to have its coal capacity increased by means of rails or side fenders. The location appears to be Worcester.

Locomotive Publishing Co

No 2351 is also carrying a front-domed boiler but in this case, clack boxes are mounted on the firebox sides with a hydraulic jack standing alongside. The tender is of Dean design, with coal rails rather than the later side fenders. In the background there are two Broad Gauge locomotives of the 2-4-0 Hawthorn Class. To the left is *Fenton* (built Slaughter Gruning & Co, July 1865) and to the right is *Blenkensop* (by the same makers, by then renamed Avonside Engine Co, December 1865). Both were withdrawn in May 1892.

Locomotive Publishing Co

This is an intriguing photograph as it shows No 2397 apparently fitted with Automatic Train Control. The first ATC installation for normal operating took place between Paddington and Reading in 1908 and this engine might have been early recipient as the class was still regularly working front line freight duties at that time. Also the fitment might be connected with modifications to the front running plate, most of which has been removed. A further query relates to the boiler which is an S2 type whereas records show this to have been replaced with a Belpaire boiler in 1902, which it carried for the remainder of its career   *Locomotive Publishing Co*

In parallel with this renewal programme, Dean expanded a locomotive fleet designed for easy conversion from narrow to broad gauge and vice versa. The first examples built with this purpose in mind had actually preceded his appointment. The last used on the Broad Gauge under this programme appeared as late as 1891, implying a dearth of serviceable engines in the surviving fleet that could cope with expanding traffic. The history of the convertible engines pre-1892 is too complex to discuss in detail but is summarised in **Appendix C**.

Thus in 1883 on the eve of his famous goods locomotive, there were diverse issues facing William Dean. He had been unexpectedly elevated to his position six years earlier, and had reached a working accommodation with the independently minded George Armstrong in his northern redoubt. He had initiated a programme of experiments that explored the limits of what might be possible under contemporary design and construction practices. He had maintained the status quo by continuing with designs introduced by his predecessor, and by expanding upon Armstrong's initiative with convertible locomotives. These differing endeavours were set against the stringencies imposed by Gooch in preserving the company's overall financial condition, and against the enduring nightmare and uncertainties of the Severn Tunnel project.

Dean's cause was obliquely aided by personalities and circumstances. Gooch's financial restraint was timely in view of the difficult economic conditions that afflicted the country for 20 years or so from 1873. This policy was reflected in the attitude of GN Tyrell, Superintendent of the Line from 1864 until 1888. The innately conservative Tyrell was reluctant to see speeds exceed 40 mph and through his seniority, he successfully resisted most proposals for acceleration of services. As the GWR enjoyed a monopoly in much of its territory, it was able to get away with laggardly speeds and standards of passenger comfort that compared adversely with other companies. A poor reputation with the travelling public resulted but Dean was relieved of the need to create designs suitable for faster speeds.

With economy the watchword, this sentiment was apparent in the conception of the Dean Goods. The preference for a tender design over enlarged tank locomotives had been proven through the experiments involving Nos 1, 9, 10, and 1833, as discussed in the previous chapter. The new design foreshadowed changes to come and in certain key respects differed from preceding 0-6-0 goods locomotives.

Earlier, consolidation and expansion of the standard gauge network had stimulated growth in goods traffic. The concomitant need for more motive power was met

WILLIAM DEAN

in 1866 by Armstrong's 0-6-0 Class 388, designated the Standard Goods. This marked a key change heralding construction of large numbers of tender locomotives of standardised dimensions, as opposed to the preceding small classes. Construction was continuous between 1866 and 1876, penetrating every part of the narrow gauge system. The type's versatility was underlined by conversion of the final batch of 20 in the 1880s to augment the remaining broad gauge fleet.

After a hiatus of seven years during which the need for more goods engines was met by tank locomotive construction, the first of Class 2301 – the Dean Goods – entered traffic in May 1883. There was similarity with the Standard (Armstrong) Goods in leading dimensions:

NB There were many variations in boiler dimensions with the Standard Goods; those quoted are indicative.

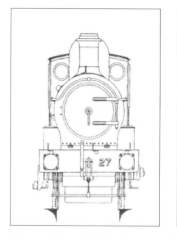
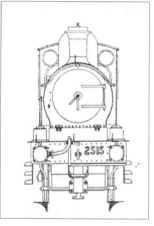

Class	Standard Goods (Nos 1186-1195)	Dean Goods (Nos 2301-2320)
Cylinders	17" x 24"	17.5" x 24"
Boiler		
- barrel	11' 0"	10' 3"
- diameter	4' 2"	4' 3"
Firebox length	c. 4' 9"	5' 4"
Heating surfaces		
- tubes	1187.8 sq ft	1079 sq ft
- firebox	98 sq ft	113.6 sq ft
Grate	16.3 to 17 sq ft	16.4 sq ft
Boiler pressure	140 lbs/ sq in	140 lbs/ sq in
Wheels	5' 0"	5' 0"
Wheel base	7' 4" + 8' 4"	7' 3" + 8' 3"
Weight	c. 30 tons	33 tons
Maximum axle loading	c. 11t 8c	11t 12c

Figures IV and V (left above and below): Class 388 Standard Goods 0-6-0, with type S4 boiler, later known as the "Armstrong Goods" to distinguish it from the Class 2301 "Dean Goods", figures VI and VII (right above and bottom), with type B4 boiler.
JN Maskelyne

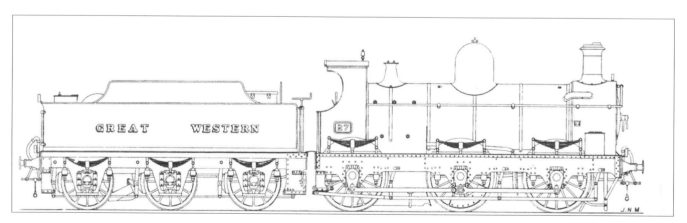

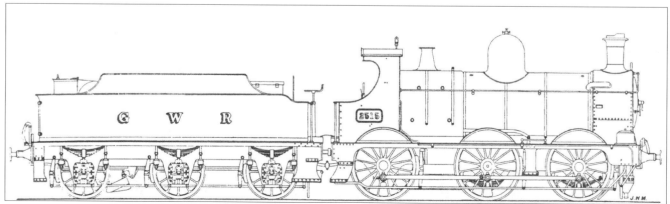

An unidentified engine with front dome boiler on goods duties; the pre-Dean tender has received coal rails.   *LGRP*

The key difference was the use of inside frames with the new design. Although Swindon had slight experience of building narrow gauge engines with inside frames throughout (e.g. 2-4-0 Class 439 in original form), this layout had been more typical of the Wolverhampton design school. With his experience at the northern works and mindful of the need to minimise costs, Dean was well placed to exploit this economic simplicity.

However, this configuration prevented conv-ersion to Broad Gauge should the need arise. This could only be accomplished by modifying more of the Standard Goods or by introducing a suitable variant on the Dean Goods theme, as later took place with Nos 2361-2380. In the event, no further gauge conversions of 0-6-0s proved necessary.

The boiler design was also a change from earlier practice. 4-2-4T No 9 had inaugurated the two ring boiler and, it is believed, the domeless style. Dean's designs from 1877 forwards (excluding examples of Joseph Armstrong's designs built by him) followed this configuration. In the case of the Dean Goods, the domeless type was comparatively short-lived being confined to the first 20 members of the class but two rings formed the basis for all other types of boiler used.

In other respects the locomotive employed traditional features. The driving wheel diameter was nominally 5 feet but in reality closer to 5' 1"; this dimension later

increased to 5' 2" with use of thicker tyres. The motion was similar to that of Armstrong's *Queen* Class with slide bars of the two bar type but modified with rectangular guides bolted to the motion plate. The overall impression was one of maximum simplicity to minimise construction cost. Success was proven in the total of 280 examples built between 1884 and 1898:

Lot No.	Nos	Works Nos	Built
61	2301-2320	946-963	1883
62	2321-2340	966-985	1884
63	2341-2360	986-1005	1884
67	2361-2380	1032-1051	1885-6
82	2381-2400	1181-1200	1890
87	2401-2430	1271-1300	1891-2
92	2431-2450	1361-1380	1893
99	2451-2470	1453-1472	1895-6
100	2471-2490	1472-1492	1896
104	2491-2510	1511-1530	1896
108	2531-2550	1572-1591	1897
108	2531-2550	1572-1591	1897
111	2551-2580	1632-1661	1897-9

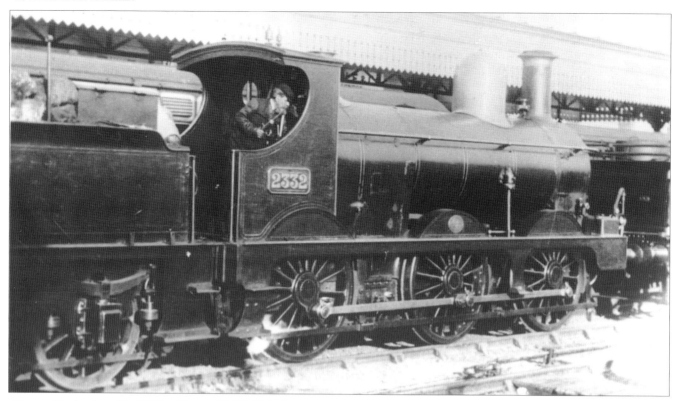

Above - Plenty of pre-World War 1 finery with No 2332; the boiler has clack boxes mounted on the front ring and the Dean era tender has yet to have its coal capacity increased.
RK Blencowe Collection

Below - An unidentified engine with front dome boiler leading a double-framed saddle tank on a down goods at South Brent; the Kingsbridge branch trails in on the right.

Nos 2361-2380 as "convertibles" were not normally regarded as part of the Dean Goods class proper because of their double frames, under-slung driving wheel springs, longer wheelbase and (in the early years) differing boiler dimensions. For these reasons they are covered separately in **Chapter 7**.

When introduced, the first 60 Dean Goods were coupled to the traditional Armstrong-vintage GWR tender with springs mounted above the frame on the running plate. However, concurrent with the rebuilding of 4-2-4T No 9 as a 2-2-2 tender locomotive in early 1884, a new form of tender (No 852 of 3000 gallons and 5 tons capacity) was provided. From 1889, this type was built in significant numbers until 1906.

Above - Construction of Lot 99 (locomotives Nos 2451 to 2470) commenced in October 1895 and introduced the third and final style of boiler to be fitted to the class when built. This form was a combination of round-topped firebox with the dome mounted on the rear ring (RCTS Code S4). All locomotives from No 2451 through to No 2580 appeared with this boiler type, and most of the earlier engines carried it for a period before graduating to the Belpaire fireboxes. Curiously however, while photographs of locomotives with front dome boilers and round-topped fireboxes (Type S2) are reasonably plentiful, views depicting the later and numerically far larger S4 version seem scarce. In this view, No 2340 is seen with an S4 boiler which it carried from June 1904 until October 1913. This locomotive is in interim condition, retaining copper rim chimney, brass safety valve cover, and works plate, and a coal rail tender. On the other hand the dome has been painted as a step towards the more muted livery of later years.

Below - Comparison of this photograph of No 2399 (S2 boiler) with that of No 2340 above highlights the difference in length of smoke

WILLIAM DEAN

Above - Another view of a Dean Goods west of Exeter. No 2305 has just passed the Sea Lawn Gap at Dawlish with an up goods on 17th June 1906. The engine is in as built condition except for the front dome boiler carried from June 1892 until November 1906.

Below - Following the decision to adopt Belpaire fireboxes as the new standard, some existing round-topped boilers were rebuilt. This resulted in the hybrid B2 type, which combined a new Belpaire firebox with the dome on the front ring. These boilers were around 8-10 years old when rebuilt and only about 25 were so treated before it was judged more economic to build brand new boilers of the well-known B4 type.

Good photographs of Dean Goods with B2 boilers are rare so this view of Class 131 No 142 has been substituted. No 142 was built by Slaughter Gruning in 1862 to the orders of Daniel Gooch and "renewed" at Wolverhampton in 1886: reputedly no material from the original machine was used. This engine carried the B2 boiler from April 1912 until January 1918 when it reverted to a much older three ringed domeless boiler with raised round-topped firebox, and was withdrawn in August 1919.

Brian Stephenson

The boiler arrangement by which the class is best known was rear domed with Belpaire firebox, fitting of which commenced in the autumn of 1901. No 2322 was so fitted in November of that year. *Locomotive Publishing Co*

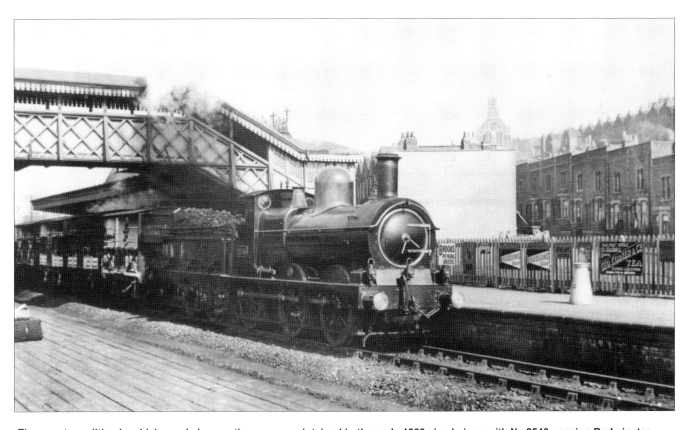

The smart condition in which goods locomotives were maintained in the early 1900s is obvious with No 2543 passing Bedminster, Bristol on a down train. This engine carried a Belpaire boiler from November 1903; its condition is splendid with the usual brass and copper, but augmented by burnished handrails, smokebox door band, hinges and handles plus buffer heads. *LGRP*

49

Above - Another early Belpaire era view. In this case, neither location nor locomotive identity has been recorded but a fairly substantial passenger train is being hauled. The engine is not as ornately finished as in the previous view but overall it is very clean. The pre-Dean tender has been modernised with side fender.

Below - From 1913, about 40 Belpaire (B4) and a small number of S4 boilers were built or fitted with top feed, and at least one of the former survived into the 1950s. Not long after being so equipped, No 2309 is at Birmingham Snow Hill in January 1914. Despite the modern top feed, the old-fashioned dished smokebox door is still in place. *CM & JM Bentley*

A year after tender No 852 appeared, a smaller version was introduced with a 6' 6" + 6' 6" wheelbase (two feet shorter) and with capacities of 2500 gallons and 4 tons 10 cwt. Both tender sizes came to be habitually associated with the class. With early examples, the sides terminated at the top of the outwards flare necessitating careful stacking and packing of coal to prevent loss overboard. Coal rails were soon fitted and later these gave way to the familiar side fenders.

Dean's re-location of the springs below the running plate and immediately above the axle boxes allowed for a wider tank and thus greater carrying capacity. While the Armstrong tender type continued to appear with the Dean Goods, the introduction of the class is associated with the arrival of a tender layout that stayed with GWR engines to the end of steam. Thereafter, the only significant visual changes were higher sides to accommodate greater fuel and water capacities, and variations in the profiles of the side fenders. However, the essentials remained unchanged until the wide-bodied all-welded tenders introduced in 1945 for the 4-6-0 Counties.

Simplicity of design, excellence in construction, and superb steaming qualities helped make the Dean Goods popular within and well beyond the boundaries of the GWR. Often, footplatemen would learn to live with the foibles of "home" designs and tolerate driving conditions that "foreign" crews found unacceptable. However, the Dean Goods was well received by all shades of footplate crews wherever the class was used. In view of the number of other 0-6-0 types of broadly similar size that were called up for military service in World War 1, there had to be something more that set the design apart.

It is contended that this difference derived from the nature of freight train working in the 19th Century. On the narrow gauge, the company's strong orientation towards tank locomotives meant that 0-6-0ST's were used not only for shunting and short distance work but also for main line freight services over quite long distances. This is best reflected in the employment of Buffalo 0-6-0STs on trains between Bristol and London. To modern eyes, such workings might seem extraordinary but schedules were pedestrian with frequent pauses for refreshment thereby allowing for the passage of faster traffic. Under these conditions, elimination of a tender was attractive as this reduced the non-revenue earning weight. On the other hand, a tender significantly added to braking power.

No 2356 also received a top feed boiler. In this undated view there appears to be another top feed-fitted member of the class behind.
RK Blencowe Collection

WILLIAM DEAN

Much has been written about haulage capacity and speed in motive power development but rather less about making trains stop. For example, it is only recently that thorough analysis has advanced a convincing explanation for the cause of the Grantham accident of 1906. In this case, an Ivatt Atlantic in the hands of an experienced driver and a premium apprentice over-ran adverse signals during a night of good visibility, in a location where there was little chance of the crew mistaking their position. The analysis convincingly argued that operating omissions led to the continuous brakes not being connected at Peterborough (the previous stop) where the engine had been changed. On the approach to the Grantham stop at express speed it became apparent that the only the engine and tender brakes could be engaged; the terrible consequences underlined the hazards of working a train with inadequate brake power.

These were exceptional circumstances with tragic results but evidence from elsewhere suggests that the braking of unfitted goods trains could be an uncertain "science". In his work *LNWR Eight-Coupled Goods Engines*, Edward Talbot quotes ES Cox as stating that how the London & North Western Railway worked unfitted freight trains at all was "something of a mystery". This notion was heightened by brake tests conducted soon after the Grouping with unfitted trains of equal loads descending a 1 in 100 gradient at 20 mph. A vacuum-braked Lancashire & Yorkshire 0-8-0 brought its train to a halt in 1,520 yards. In contrast, a vacuum-braked LNWR G2 0-8-0 had increased its speed to 22.5 mph after 3,860 yards of full brake application; restraint was then imposed by another engine that had been inserted in the train as a precaution. A LNWR G1 0-8-0 performed even worse in the same tests. The conclusion drawn was that skilled application of the reverser was more important than the brakes in persuading locomotive and train to stop at the right place.

A factor in the use of saddle tanks on long distance freight workings was the effectiveness of the powerful steam brake fitted to all GWR locomotives. Tank engines were fitted with a single vertical cylinder that activated brakes on all driving wheels concurrently. The arrangement was simple in operation and apparently adequate for the task on the main line. In the case of tender locomotives though, the same linkage system was actuated by *two* cylinders of similar dimensions located horizontally beneath the cab and backed up by a single vertical cylinder (tank engine style) mounted below the tender running plate to work the tender brakes.

No 2410 in process of being re-railed. The Spartan nature of the footplate is very evident.

Above - No 2475 has adopted much of the style by which the class is best remembered, except for what seems to be retention of the dished smokebox door. The more austere livery of later years is now apparent in the painted dome and safety valve cover, and in the plain chimney.

Below - No 2488 on shed displays a clean condition but the previously unpainted and polished metalwork is now painted over. ATC has been fitted and although it is difficult to be certain from the camera angle, the tender appears to be of the 2000-gallon variety originally introduced for use with the Duke Class 4-4-0s in Cornwall. *Real Photos*

WILLIAM DEAN

A post-1934 view of No 2576, also shorn of the original brass and copper bright work. This was one of the few thought never to have received ATC. It was a Welsh engine during the 1930s and was sold to the government in 1940, becoming WD No 196. It served on the home front during the war and ended its service on the Shropshire and Montgomeryshire Railway.   *Real Photos*

Other railways economised by relying on mechanical linkage between engine and tender which was actuated by one or two brake cylinders on the engine. The problem was that when slowing a train, the effect of wagons bunching up slackened the coupling with the locomotive thereby reducing tension in the linkage and so diminishing the effectiveness of the tender brakes.

By the early 1870s, increasing speeds and heavier loads made installation of competent continuous braking systems in passenger trains a matter of urgency. Companies experimented with alternative methods, and in some instances more than one was in use by the same organisation. Apart from the importance of establishing which was the most effective form of brake, the chaotic nature of the situation created problems for standardisation and for operation of trains over other company's routes. Under the influence of the Board of Trade, alternative braking methods were evaluated through comparative trials at Newark on the Midland Railway in 1875 and a number of companies participated. The key choice was between the Westinghouse air and the automatic vacuum braking systems; in due course most companies favoured the latter.

The GWR stayed aloof from these proceedings but took a close interest in the results. The following year the company conducted its own trials with the Sanders brake, and then with the more advanced Sanders-Bolitho system. Dean believed that there remained room for improvement and that the GWR should develop its own brake. In 1880, he gave this task to Joseph (known to all as "Young Joe"), the brilliant but sadly short-lived fourth son of his predecessor. In due course, he designed a neat fitting mounted on the back of the firebox that combined the working of the steam and vacuum brake application valves, and the ejector. A young engineer recently transferred to Swindon from Newton Abbot – GJ Churchward – assisted in the project. Because he did not bother to patent his invention, Young Joe never received due recognition when his design, which served the GWR with minimal modification until the end of steam, was copied by other companies.

An important outcome of this work was to bless the Dean Goods with brake power to match its performance. This feature was particularly welcome when handling sensitive loads – such as ammunition and high explosives. Compared, for example, with the lottery of the LNWR braking system, it is under-

Above - No 2301 in an undated view but most likely taken in the late 1920s as this engine was fitted with ATC in the 1930/ 31 programme.   *Real Photos*

Below - A grimy No 2513 on shed at Chester.   *Ian Allan Library*

Above - No 2554 on shed at Chester

Ian Allan Library

Below - No 2486 in May 1919 with Old Oak Common East Signal box as an impressive backdrop.

standable why this feature should have helped make the Great Western engine so readily acceptable to foreign crews.

Details of duties undertaken during the 19th Century are scarce but as the company's main long distance goods type, it can be deduced that allocations were concentrated at principle sheds handling freight traffic including Paddington, Swindon, Bristol, Cardiff, Aberdare, and Wolverhampton. Official records from 1902 onwards are available and although faint in places with some slight ambiguities, but it is possible

to draw a picture of pre-World War 1 deployments.

Records have been extracted for 1902, 1909 and 1913. During the first of these years, the Aberdare 2-6-0s were entering service, being the first type to displace the class from the heaviest duties. In 1909, the Aberdares had in turn been replaced by Churchward's 2-8-0s while in 1913, numbers of Class 43xx 2-6-0s were increasing and also encroaching on the class's traditional work. Allocations by shed at the start of each year:

	1902	1909	1913		1902	1909	1913
Aberdare	1	5	1	Newport	4	1	3
Aberystwyth	-	-	3	Newton Abbot	2	2	1
Banbury	5	4	5	Oxford	8	4	4
Barnstaple	-	1	-	Paddington	23	21	19
Bristol	33	29	37	Plymouth (Millbay)	4	3	1
Cardiff	5	12	13	Pontypool Road	7	2	4
Carmarthen	-	16	14	Reading	14	13	12
Cheltenham	-	-	1	Salisbury	1	-	-
Chester	-	-	1	Slough	3	4	3
Chippenham	2	-	-	Southall	6	4	4
Chipping Norton	1	-	-	Swindon	13	18	15
Crewe	1	-	-	Swindon Works	30	16	15
Didcot	6	7	8	Taunton	1	9	5
Exeter	8	6	7	Tondu	-	-	1
Fishguard	-	-	1	Trowbridge	6	6	-
Gloucester	21	5	7	Tyesley	-	4	6
Hereford	4	-	-	Weston-Super-Mare	-	2	1
Honeybourne	-	1	1	Weymouth	2	6	3
Kingham	-	-	1	Whitland	-	-	1
Laira	6	3	1	Winchester	1	-	1
Landore	1	-	1	Wolverhampton	15	12	13
Ledbury	1	-	-	Worcester	24	23	20
Llantrisant	-	-	1	Yeovil	1	-	-
Neath	-	2	4				

WILLIAM DEAN

There was notable stability in the pattern of distribution. Some remained in the same general area (eg. rotating between locations such as Didcot, Reading and Swindon) whereas others stayed at one shed for long periods. In particular, Wolverhampton and Worcester seemed to be possessive regarding certain engines with Nos 2307/2379/2380/2390/2403/ 2521/2538/2569 long term residents of the former and Nos 2321/2324/2326/2328/2331/2332/2334/2336/ 2344/2347/2350 at the latter.

It is generally thought that the class was always little used in Devon and Cornwall which makes the allocation of 20 at Exeter and further west in 1902 rather surprising, although this number had halved by 1913. Wider dispersal was evolving immediately prior to World War 1 but the majority remained at traditional locations. Withdrawals of the Standard Goods had commenced in the early 1900s, together with earlier

0-6-0 classes, and it would appear that many Dean Goods were retained at larger sheds to take over duties previously handled by the older generation.

Finally, an indication of the pre-1902 deployment may be deduced from the 1902/1909 allocations of the Aberdares as the first class to displace the Dean Goods from front-line work:

	1902	1909		1902	1909
Aberdare	8	7	Swindon Works	8	12
Pontypool Road	–	9	Tyseley	–	8
Severn Tunnel Jct	–	5	Wolverhampton	–	11
Swindon	12	5	Other sheds	7	24

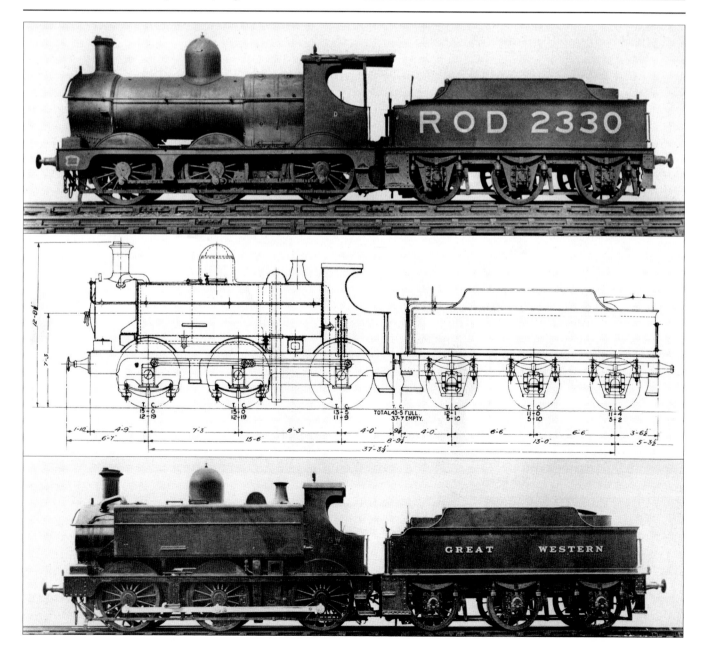

Chapter 4

YOUR COUNTRY NEEDS YOU!

The 1914-1918 War was different from any conflict before or since in the vast numbers of men deployed and the enormous volumes of food, materials and munitions consumed by opposing forces that remained essentially static. From the outset, logistics were crucial to both sides in holding their positions on the Western Front, which extended through France from the English Channel to the Swiss border. Over the course of the war, the British Army through the Railway Operating Division of the Corps of Royal Engineers developed an extensive standard gauge railway network using existing domestic routes and by adding many more miles laid for military purposes. These services were co-coordinated with a complex network of temporary narrow gauge railways that carried men and materials close to the front line positions.

Initially, indigenous motive power, either lent by the French companies or hired from the Belgian state, coped with most needs. However, by late 1916 the unremitting demands placed on the ROD forced the creation of its own motive power fleet. By the Armistice, approximately 1600 standard gauge locomotives were working overseas, requisitioned from the British railway companies and manufacturers, or built to order by British, American and Canadian commercial manufacturers.

Above - The German military authorities in drawing up the Schlieffen plan for the invasion of Belgium failed to anticipate that nation's efficiency in evacuating a major portion of their locomotive fleet to safety. This led to a locomotive surplus available for hire by the British Expeditionary Force and it was not until late 1916 that recourse to motive power from the UK became necessary. Depicted here is an Etat-Belge Class 25 0-6-0 near Boesinghe on a typical duty – hauling troops in open trucks to the front line in August 1917.

At the outbreak of war, a total of 472 of this class were in service and 272 escaped the German advance. They were sturdily built with good haulage capacity but rather poor brakes. With outside frames and Belpaire firebox this could be a continental version of GWR Class 2361, although the chimney is unlikely to have come from Swindon or Wolverhampton! *IWM Reference Q2747*

Opposite, upper - No 2330 was one of the older examples requisitioned and is seen here in ROD livery and with extended cab roof in place. The date of this view is unknown but the general condition of the locomotive suggests that this might have been an official photograph taken after the locomotive had returned from service in France.

Opposite, middle (Figure VI) and lower - No 2578 as uniquely equipped during World War I with pannier tanks and condensing equipment. The capacity of the pannier tanks was 800 gallons and the modifications added approximately 2 tons to the maximum axle loading which negated one of the advantages of the class i.e. its ability to operate over lightly laid lines.

British companies provided almost 500 locomotives of the 0-6-0 type from their existing fleets, many of which were unsuited to work in continental Europe being old, small and under-powered. As the war progressed, eight-coupled locomotives played an increasingly important role and the 2-8-0 type came to be regarded as the ideal for war service, a viewed perpetuated in 1939-1945. A brief survey of the role of railways in the war, and of the ROD locomotive fleet appears in **Appendix D**.

The contribution made by the GWR consisted of 22 Class 388 0-6-0s (the Armstrong Goods) which went

to the Mediterranean, 11 Class 43xx 2-6-0s which served in France only, and 62 Dean Goods, all of which were first deployed in France with 16 later moving to Greece and Turkey. In addition, the GWR provided eight purpose-designed ambulance trains which mainly used the then modern "toplight" carriage stock.

More importantly, 25,460 GWR employees or 32.6% of the total 1914 workforce joined up. Most of the early volunteers served in the infantry; later recruits by and large joined the ROD where better use could be made of their professional skills and knowledge.

Opposite, upper - The ROD was responsible for increasing the capacity of the railway network by doubling single track routes and by laying extra sidings at key locations. Also, a considerable mileage of completely new standard and narrow gauge routes were laid from scratch as in this case where grading is complete and delivery of track material is awaited.

Opposite, lower, and this page - Track-laying in progress.

Overleaf, upper - The 0-6-0 seen here propelling a train of track materials appears to be one of the Etat-Belge locomotives based on Caledonian Railway Class 812, designed by JF McIntosh. An estimated 345 were evacuated in advance of the invasion of Belgium and they comprised three separate classes (30/ 32/ 32S). Being essentially British with Westinghouse brakes and certain continental fittings, they were popular with ROD crews but by 1916 were in poor condition as a result of overwork. The single bolster wagons loaded with rails appear to be of British origin.

Overleaf, lower - Another view of an Etat-Belge 0-6-0 of McIntosh design hauling a load of materials and propelling a flat wagon on which a detachment of troops have hitched a lift.

All: Royal Engineers Library & Archive

Armstrong Goods (Class 388) 0-6-0

The war-time service of these locomotives was chequered. Six were sold to the government in late 1915 only to be re-sold to the GWR in March of the following year. The rationale behind these transactions has not been established. Three of these locomotives returned to normal GWR service thereafter; the other three were part of the first batch of six sold to the ROD (as opposed to the government) in August 1916. Four of these were supposedly despatched to Serbia but this information, despite being reported by a number of sources, is considered inaccurate. By the time of their despatch overseas, Serbia had been invaded and under German control for a number of months. It seems more probable that they were sent direct to Greece.

The second batch comprised eight locomotives which were shipped in May 1917 and destined for Salonika in Greece; all were lost at sea. The final shipment in September 1917 also consisted of eight locomotives, which ran the gauntlet and arrived safely in Salonika. Thus only 14 of the 25 locomotives that passed through governmental/ ROD hands actually served overseas.

These locomotives (all with saturated boilers) seem to have been selected on the grounds of their being older than the Dean Goods and thus more suitable for sale (rather than loan) for use in remote locations from where repatriation was less likely. No record has been traced of their actual duties in Serbia (if any), Greece and later Turkey.

GWR No.	Built	Sold to Govt	Repurchased by GWR	Sold to ROD	ROD number	Disposal
24	Feb-72			May-17	n/a	Sent to Salonika but sunk in English Channel
27	Jan-76	Nov-15	Mar-16		n/a	Withdrawn by GWR Jun-20
39	Feb-76			Sep-17	39	Sent to Salonika; returned to GWR Apr-21; withdrawn Dec-21
427	Oct-68			Sep-17	32	Sent to Salonika; sold to Ottoman (Aidan) Railway Oct-19 – their No 100
434	Mar-68	Nov-15	Mar-16		n/a	Withdrawn by GWR Jul-19
438	Apr-68			May-17	n/a	Sent to Salonika but sunk in English Channel
447	Jul-68			Aug-16	§	Sent to Serbia (?)
451	Aug-68			Sep-17	§	Sent to Salonika; returned to GWR Apr-21; withdrawn Dec-21
495	Mar-70			Sep-17	34	Sent to Salonika; sold to Ottoman (Aidan) Railway Oct-19 – their No 101
508	Aug-70	Nov-15	Mar-16	Aug-16	40	Sent to Serbia (?); sold to Ottoman (Aidan) Railway Oct-19 – their No 103
674	Jan-72			Sep-17	§	Sent to Salonika; returned to GWR Apr-21
716	Nov-72			May-17	n/a	Sent to Salonika but sunk in English Channel
781	Jul-73			May-17	n/a	Sent to Salonika but sunk in English Channel
784	Aug-73			May-17	n/a	Sent to Salonika but sunk in English Channel
794	Nov-73	Nov-15	Mar-16	Aug-16	§¶	Sent to Salonika; returned to GWR Apr-21; withdrawn Dec-21
796	Nov-73			Sep-17	§	Sent to Salonika
878	Jan-74			Sep-17	36	Sent to Salonika; returned to GWR Apr-21; withdrawn Dec-21
1084	Jul-70			Sep-17	37	Sent to Salonika; sold to Ottoman (Aidan) Railway Oct-19 – their No 102
1091	Nov-70			Aug-16	§¶	Sent to Salonika; returned to GWR Apr-21; withdrawn Dec-21
1100	Nov-70	Nov-15	Mar-16	Aug-16	§	Sent to Serbia (?)
1107	Apr-71			May-17	n/a	Sent to Salonika but sunk in English Channel
1186	Mar-76	Nov-15	Mar-16		n/a	Withdrawn by GWR May-23
1189	Mar-76			May-17	n/a	Sent to Salonika but sunk in English Channel
1191	Mar-76			May-17	n/a	Sent to Salonika but sunk in English Channel
1198	May-76			Aug-16	§	Sent to Serbia (?)

§ Renumbered in the ROD 30-43 series but actual number not known
¶ Some records indicate initial despatch to Serbia but for reasons stated above, this move is unlikely to have occurred

WILLIAM DEAN

Churchward Class 43XX 2-6-0

In 1917, the ROD formally asked the GWR to provide a batch of eight-coupled locomotives but Frank Potter, General Manager, responded that the 43s were practically-speaking the equal of other companies' 0-8-0s. Such was the faith in this archetypal Churchward creation, and it was not to prove misplaced. Immediately after construction, 11 of the class were sent to northern France, having been painted in military khaki with the initials "ROD" and their GWR number in large white digits on their tenders. Unfortunately, they were not fitted with Westinghouse brakes, which restricted their potential usefulness. The 43s on war service were distinctive for two reasons. They were the only brand new locomotives requisitioned from the British railway companies and apart from the American 4-6-0s built by Baldwin (the "spiders"), the only officially designated mixed traffic tender locomotives in the ROD fleet.

Based at Calais and Andruicq, their main duty was to haul the nightly divisional supply trains from Rivière Neuve, the marshalling yards at Les Fontinettes (Calais), to the railheads at Hazebrouck and St Omer. These trains were not air-braked but had French screw-link couplings. They usually consisted of around 40 wagons aggregating 800 tons although loads up to 1000 tons were not uncommon. Other duties for which they were favoured were troop and ambulance trains made up of British vacuum-braked vehicles.

All except No 5319 (completed August 1917) were built in September 1917 and lent that month to the ROD; they returned to the GWR in either April or May 1919. The locomotives concerned were:

GWR No.	Withdrawn	GWR No.	Withdrawn	GWR No.	Withdrawn
5319	Nov-59	5323	Jun-58	5328	Jul-58
5320	Sep-48	5324	Sep-60	5329	Mar-39
5321	Sep-59	5325	Aug-57	5330	Jun-64
5322	Apr-64	5326	Mar-62		

On return to the GWR, they took up normal duties. No 5322 is preserved and in 2010, it returned to steam in ROD livery and largely original condition, except that it retained the outside steam pipes fitted in October 1949.

An example of different military transport routes where a standard gauge line made a flat crossing of a road and an adjacent roadside 60 cm gauge tramway.
Royal Engineers Library & Archive

Above and below - Troop trains on the narrow gauge.   *Royal Engineers Library & Archive*

Troops moving up to the Front near Ypres by narrow gauge in February 1917, hauled by Hunslet 4-6-0T No 309. Given their circumstances, these men seem in remarkably buoyant mood.   *IWM Reference Q1695*

The Dean Goods on the Western Front

Sixty-two members of the class were lent to the ROD. The loan was recorded as a single transaction, commencing in April 1917 and completed the following month. Ports of embarkation are not known but are likely to have been Portsmouth and Southampton, both of which had suitable harbour cranes. Certainly 10 LNWR 0-8-0s were transported from Portsmouth to Le Havre in May 1917.

Before leaving the GWR, their brass number plates were removed and painted white shaded figures substituted. Continental style side chains were mounted on the buffer beams and several acquired cab extensions in France, supported by vertical pillars at the rear of the footplates with the intention of reducing firebox glare. Prior to the war, the Dean Goods carried the standard GWR livery of lined green but by 1915, plain green was being applied to locomotives passing through Swindon Works. In 1916, a number of engines acquired a browner form of the military khaki although a reversion to standard unlined GWR green occurred in January 1917. With 62 locomotives being prepared for overseas service in a short space of time, it seems likely that not all received

khaki livery before despatch and that some would have arrived overseas in either lined or unlined GWR green but with painted running number and "ROD" on their tenders and GWR running numbers.

Uniquely, No 2578 was fitted with pannier tanks and condensing equipment to reduce emission of steam that could betray the locomotive's position. The tanks increased the water capacity by 800 gallons and combined with the condensing equipment, the weight was increased by over 6 tons. This obviated a basic advantage – the modest axle loading – and the modification was not repeated.

While some companies had made only their older goods locomotives available for military service, the GWR was more generous. Every Lot was represented except for No 104 of 1896, withdrawal of which had been completed in 1910. All carried Belpaire boilers of the final type (B4) to be fitted to the class and 20 had been superheated, making them almost as modern as the class was ever to get. Nos 2313, 2430, and 2461 had been fitted with superheaters only four months before shipment to France, which implies a recent return from a works visit and thus good condition.

In March 1917, German forces strategically withdrew from the Western Front between Arras and Soissons to pre-prepared positions that formed part of the Hindenburg Line. In so doing, they laid waste to the ground yielded up and destroyed the rail network. The early locomotive shipments to France mainly comprised small 0-6-0s, which were ideal for use in the reconstruction of devastated railway lines. With their low axle loadings, Dean Goods, LNWR Coal Engines and GER class Y14 proved invaluable, and the network was restored with remarkable speed. With minimal infrastructure surviving, these engines were maintained where they worked.

At first, it seems that imported locomotives were deployed in ad hoc fashion but as numbers increased and the ROD's physical facilities developed, classes were concentrated at particular locations. Specific

details are sparse but it is possible to form a view of how the Dean Goods came to be most commonly employed.

ROD maintenance depots varied widely, some having fully fledged service and repair facilities while others were very basic. In August 1917, 20 locomotives were based at Gombremetz on a single line military route built specifically to link Warlincourt with Acq, thereby improving access to Arras. This "shed" comprised a number of sidings in a wood with equipment stored in covered vans. Three of the allocation were Dean Goods (Nos 2316/ 2452/ 2517). At this time, 28 locomotives of nine different types were based at Bergues near Dunkirk, an important railhead that supported the Ypres salient; four of this allocation were Dean Goods (Nos 2306/ 2457/ 2566/ 2578), all sub-shedded at Dosinghem.

Images of the Dean Goods at work in France are not common. In this case, work is underway apparently to lay new track alongside an existing route. In the far distance to the left, a member of the class is engaged in this helping with this endeavour.
Royal Engineers Library & Archive

WILLIAM DEAN

Above - The canal system of northern France was adapted by using tow paths for laying standard and narrow gauge track. Grading and curvature would have made these paths ideal for temporary track, and presumably the main risk was subsidence of canal banks under the weight of trains. Here a contingent from the British Third Army is constructing a ramp from the towpath to the floor of the Nord Canal in November 1917 with a works train hauled by a Dean Goods in attendance. *IWM Reference Q47167*

Below - An unidentified Dean Goods hauling a track laying train on the Achiet-Marcoing Line. *IWM Reference Q47112*

None of the Dean Goods appear to have been fitted with Westinghouse brakes, which restricted their range of operations. The introduction of armoured tanks in 1917 presented unique operating challenges. Tanks weighed up to 30 tons and were limited to a maximum speed of about 4 mph. Rail transport was therefore essential for their delivery to combat zones in significant numbers quickly and for tactical reasons, at night. Set trains were operated which weighed around 600 tons fully laden. Transport over the standard gauge network, using temporary track closer to the trenches, was the only practical means of efficient delivery. Further difficulties were encountered with no cranes for unloading, so they had to be driven off the ends of their special flat wagons, originally based on the Macaw B and later developed as RECTANKS.

Reliable locomotives with low axle loadings were needed for these duties. It is believed that the ROD depot at the village of Buire on the Amiens to Arras mainline provided the motive power from its allocation of 25 locomotives. The preferred arrangement was an Etat-Belge 0-6-0 Class 30 or 32 as train engine, with a Dean Goods as pilot. Use of the Belgian engine "inside" was very likely to operate Westinghouse brakes if continental flat wagons formed part of the train.

Above - Etat-Belge Class 30 No 2823 hauling a British rail-mounted 14" naval gun. This particular artillery piece was taken out of store at the start of World War II and stationed on the Elham Valley line in Kent, where it was attended by Dean Goods. *WM Reference Q35197*

Left - Artillery played an important role in both defensive and offensive actions, and the largest guns deployed in the field were rail-mounted. This gun was manned by British troops who are in the act of pulling camouflage covers over the barrel.
Royal Engineers Library & Archive

A batch of ROD 2-8-0s newly built by North British Locomotive Co Ltd, awaiting despatch to France.
Royal Engineers Library & Archive

With vast numbers of locomotives required in France in the later stages of the war, rail ferries were important for moving machinery across the English Channel as in this view of brand new ROD 2-8-0s loaded on board.
The Railway Gazette

The main British ammunition depot was at Zeneghem (south-west of Dunkirk), where there was an allocation of 29 ROD locomotives. Pairs of Dean Goods from this shed hauled ammunition trains from Boulogne during 1917. Artillery was intensively used in support of troops in the trenches so these services were vitally important – by the war's end over 187 million shells had been manufactured in Britain and sent to France. Working such trains would have demanded skilful driving and reliable motive power. Dean Goods were used in pairs, one hauling and one banking. Presumably, this method was adopted to eliminate the risk of a train parting while on the move, and to facilitate reversal at places where there were no run-round facilities. When available in sufficient numbers, ROD 2-8-0s replaced the Dean Goods on this work.

A new train ferry service from Richborough in Kent to Dunkirk started operating in February 1918, which up-graded the importance of the French port. The 4th Australian Broad Gauge Operating Company, previously at Péronne, took over the working of the docks. The ROD locomotive allocation totalled 74 locomotives of American, Belgian and British origin, the most numerous type being 26 Dean Goods. Other reports suggest that up to 30 were allocated to Dunkirk for dock shunting work.

On 21st March 1918, the Germans launched the "Kaiser's Offensive" against the British Expeditionary Force in the St Quentin area and ROD personnel were engaged in a hasty and largely successful evacuation of rolling stock and materials. During clearance of sidings at Tincourt, the fireman of No 2357 was killed by enemy fire.

In early 1918 a further new ferry service connected Southampton with Dieppe and some Dean Goods were allocated to nearby Rouxmesnil for shunting work at the docks. Apart from the previously described duties, the class seems to have been favoured by the Royal Engineers for numerous ballast workings and in assisting in the construction of new workshops and other facilities.

By 1918, the influx of large numbers of ROD 2-8-0s and locomotives from the USA, and the shortening of supply lines as a result of enemy advances in northern France early that year, rendered a surplus of motive power. A few newly arrived Baldwin 4-6-0s were even placed in temporary store while 16 Dean Goods rendered surplus to requirements were transferred to the Eastern Mediterranean. Plenty of work could be found for the remaining 46 on shunting and permanent way work.

The most distinguished duty fell to No 2531. This engine in company with a Caledonian Railway Class 294 0-6-0 "Jumbo", worked the first ROD train to cross the River Rhine into Cologne after the Armistice. No 2531 and its crew remained in Germany for some weeks and the engine aroused much interest among local railwaymen who seemed fascinated with the amount of polished brass and copper on show. This is unlikely to have reflected the engine's typical condition while in France; presumably it had been "bulled up" for the occasion. This was the first, although by no means the last, occasion on which a member of the class worked in Germany.

The railway systems of France and Belgium were restored to normal in 1918/9 much faster than the military planners had anticipated so that by October 1919 the only British loading gauge engines remaining were some Caledonian Jumbos and a few ROD 2-8-0s. The remaining French contingent of Dean Goods had been kept busy until mid-1919 when they were returned to the UK. It was policy to service locomotives returning from France at Swindon, facilities being freed up by letting out the servicing of other locomotives to contractors. All those brought home returned to normal duties although some worked for a period bereft of cabside number plates due to a shortage of brass.

By the closing stages of the war, men and materials from the United States were arriving in vast quantities. With the English Channel ports working at full capacity in support of the British Army, the Americans had to use the Atlantic coast ports and then cross France to reach the Front. Narrow gauge locomotives built by Baldwin are seen here at St Nazaire on 1st November 1918, awaiting transhipment eastwards. Standard gauge Pershing type 2-8-0s are standing in the background. *IWM Reference Q69533*

Although the ROD fleet is typically associated with Great Central-based 2-8-0s of Class 8K and locomotives requisitioned from the British companies, engines were also acquired from Canada and the USA. This Canadian-built 2-8-0 is at the workshops at St Etienne.
The Railway Gazette

As the war progressed, bombing became more accurate and in late May 1918 the bridge over the River Canche at Etaples on the Boulogne-Abbeville line was damaged. North Eastern Railway Class T1 0-8-0 No 1177 is crossing a section that has been temporarily repaired by a bridging unit of the Royal Engineers.
IWM Reference Q47359

The hazardous nature of railway working conditions is apparent with this view of derailed and overturned 2-8-0 ROD No 1859 (North British Works No 21836 – 1918). ROD No 1328 was a 2-8-0 built by Canadian Locomotive Works in mid-1917.

IWM Reference Q10005

War service on the home front. Greatly increased demands were placed on the UK railway network leading to substantially heavier traffic being handled by secondary cross-country routes and railway companies. Dean Goods No 2409 was lent to the Midland & South Western Junction Railway to help out and is seen here at Chiseldon. People in the way can be a problem with old locomotive photographs but rarely to this extent. A major proportion of the MSWJR's workforce seems to have got in on the act. The photograph has another significance in depicting an engine with the photographically elusive type S4 boiler

The Dean Goods in the Eastern Mediterranean

The history of the class in this region is intermingled with that of the Armstrong Goods, and is incompletely documented. In addition to the normal hazards of determining the identity of individual locomotives at specific dates and locations, there is uncertainty about deployment of engines between Serbia, Greece and Turkey. The information supplied below is based on the few records that appear to have survived, plus an element of speculation.

As mentioned earlier, the chronology of the war in the East makes it doubtful that the Standard Goods destined for Serbia actually reached that country. It would seem more likely that they were re-directed and that all 14 engines that survived the sea passage were initially landed in Northern Greece to support British forces on the Salonika Front. With the growing British presence and with the northward advance of allied forces extending supply lines, there was a need for more motive power by 1918. Concurrently, the flow of larger, eight-coupled locomotives into France had rendered surplus some smaller locomotives in the ROD fleet. On basis of proven performance, the Dean

Goods was deemed the best choice for re-deployment although apparently the less advanced servicing facilities in Greece made it preferable to send only saturated engines.

Sixteen Dean Goods were despatched from France in 1918, and presumably received prior attention in the ROD workshops, which by then had been extensively developed. Shipment was a protracted affair as the first two (believed to be Nos 2308 and 2488) arrived at Salonika in June, whereas that same month Nos 2329/2336/2453/2557 and probably 2563 were still working at Dunkirk. The Greek contingent was allocated a new ROD number series (71 to 84), which suggests that the final pair arrived after conclusion of hostilities. The final two *might* have been diverted en route to Turkey without receiving new numbers as of the five still at Dunkirk in June, only Nos 2453 and 2563 never returned home.

The ROD operated both standard and narrow gauge railway services in Greece but most routes laid under their auspices were 60 cm gauge. Thus it is deduced that unlike France where the ROD laid an extensive temporary standard gauge network, the Dean Goods

The Dean Goods worked in three continents and the first occasion for inter-continental transfer was after the Armistice of 1918 when a contingent was sent from northern Greece to Asian Turkey. An unidentified class member is being shipped on barges across the Bosporus at Constantinopoulos

(and also the Armstrong Goods) were more used for mainline services. Details of the nature of their duties seem almost non-existent although there was a magazine report of a Dean Goods bringing an ambulance train down the valley of the River Vardar on the line from Skopje in Macedonia to Salonika.

Unlike the situation in France, it was impossible to bring British locomotives home from the Eastern Mediterranean during 1919. Following the war, the deployment of GWR locomotives was apparently split. Firstly, the line from Salonika through northern Greece to the border with European Turkey and on to Constantinopoulos was in poor condition and short of motive power. Thus 15 of the ROD fleet remained to help keep services operating in that region. The Armstrong and Dean Goods concerned were apparently renumbered 25 to 39 for post war Greek

service but the corresponding GWR numbers are not recorded. By 1921, these engines could be released from Greece and returned to the UK.

Secondly, under an article of the Armistice of Mudros signed on 30th October 1918, control of the Turkish railway system was ceded to Britain and its allies, in conjunction with their occupation of Anatolia. It is believed that 15 GWR locomotives were shipped across the Bosporus for service in Asia Minor but information on where they were used is confusing and incomplete. Some records state they were acquired by Chemin de Fer Ottomans d'Anatolie (CFOA), the principal Turkish railway company which operated between Asian Constantinopoulos and Ankara. Other sources record the Ottoman (Aidan) Railway as the acquirer.

WILLIAM DEAN

During the next four years, the political situation in Turkey was unstable with confused fighting in the country's War of Independence. It is believed that GWR locomotives were used on the railway line through Anatolia to Ankara, and separately in the Izmir area. The latter was an enclave occupied by the Greek army from which an abortive attempt was made to expand control of the Turkish mainland. Fighting in these conflicts was intense and a number of locomotives are known to have been intentionally destroyed. Hostilities around Izmir ended with defeat of the Greek army in 1922. The following year saw the evacuation of remaining allied forces, the departure of the last Ottoman Sultan and the declaration of the Turkish Republic. CFAO came under complete Turkish control in September 1923 and by this time, only a small element of the ex-GWR fleet remained in service.

Of the 30 locomotives that actually reached the Eastern Mediterranean theatre (14 Armstrong and 16 Dean Goods), it might be deduced where actual locomotives were employed after World War 1. Fifteen engines were returned to the GWR in 1921, the Dean Goods to resume normal duties and the older engines to be scrapped:

Class 388		Class 2301	
GWR No.	ROD No.	GWR No.	ROD No.
39	39	2318	not known
451	not known	2322	"
674	"	2327	"
794	"	2329	"
878	36	2336	"
1091	not known	2454	"
		2488	"
		2533	"
		2557	"

It would seem that these were retained in Greece to work Salonika-Constantinopoulos services until they could be replaced.

Details about disposal of the other 15 locomotives believed to have reached Turkey are uncertain. The eight Armstrong Goods (originally purchased from the GWR in 1916/ 1917) were sold in 1919 whereas the seven Dean Goods, still being GWR property, were lent and not formally sold until 1921. The precise identities of the purchasers/ acquirers under these transactions are unclear but it would seem that those used on the line from Constantinopoulos to Ankara were purchased by CFOA. Only two ex-GWR engines remained in service by 1922, the rest reputedly having been destroyed. This pair were numbered 38A and 83A, one being an Armstrong Goods and the other a Dean but there are no other details.

The group used further south appear to have faired better with six surviving for acquisition by the Ottoman (Aidan) Railway (which was taken over by CFAO in 1935). Aidan is a region of Turkey near Izmir and these engines seem to have been used there during the fighting between Turkish nationalist forces and the Greek occupying army. Those numbered in the Ottoman Railway series were:

Armstrong Goods			Dean Goods		
GWR No.	ROD No.	Ottoman (Aidan) Rly No.	GWR No.	ROD No.	Ottoman (Aidan) Rly No.
427	32	100	2308	73	110
495	34	101	2542	84	111
508	40	103			
1084	37	102			

No 2308 apparently survived in service until the 1950s and was noted derelict in 1955 while the younger engine was withdrawn in 1929. There were several sightings of GWR tenders being used as water carriers in Turkey in the 1930s and later.

This leaves the following locomotives unaccounted for:

Armstrong Goods: Nos 447/796/1100/1198
Dean Goods: Nos 2334/2387/2420/2453/2563.

The GWR's books were straightened out in 1921 through a transaction whereby all seven Dean Goods (i.e. Nos 2308 and 2542 plus the missing five) were formally sold to the government. Settlement took the form of the return of the six Armstrong Goods brought home from Greece, which had been in government ownership, plus a cash payment for No 2563. As the older engines were deemed fit only for scrapping when they arrived at Swindon, it is hoped that the cash payment made up for any shortfall.

The delayed repatriation of the surviving members of the Greek contingent (Nos 2318/ 2322/ 2327/ 2329/ 2336/ 2454/ 2488/ 2533/ 2557) meant that they did not resume their normal working lives until 1921. The immediate post-war years were a particularly busy period for all railway companies in tackling the backlog of locomotive repairs, and outside contractors were engaged to assist. The Great Central Railway sent 12 of its Sacré 0-6-0s to the Vickers Works at Erith in Kent and reportedly, they were repaired alongside some Dean Goods. The identity of the latter is not recorded but they may have been part of the Greek contingent although the engines brought home two years earlier had received attention at Swindon.

Above - A tragic irony of World War I was that the opposing armies were sustained in an essentially inefficient conflict by efficient railway networks. The ROD was equally effective in helping to ease human suffering through the manner in which ambulance trains were operated. The GWR contributed to this effort by assembling 238 passenger vehicles, marshalled mainly into 16-coac ambulance trains. Twelve trains were deployed in France while three remained in England. Modern coaches were mostly used including 181 of the 57' toplight type. Principally they were all thirds and brake thirds either recently built or constructed specially for ambulance train work, and sold to the government. This view is of a hospital train formed of GWR toplight coaches standing at Grevillers Hospital sidings on the Achiet-Marcoing route.
IWM Reference Q47147

Below, left - Nurses arriving at a hospital train at Dernancourt in September 1916. The coach is a GWR toplight; the car is a sleeve-valve 20 hp Daimler open tourer.
IWM Reference Q1297

Below, right - This is the treatment room of a "Pharmacy Car" built 1915; these vehicles were recorded as being created out of Toplight passenger brake vans although in this case it might be an ex-brake third. Most of the ambulance train vehicles were repurchased after the war; three of the pharmacy cars became nondescript saloons.

GWR No.	ROD No.	Superheated pre May-17	Date to Greece	Sold to Govt.	Returned to GWR	Final disposal
						Summary of Dean Goods on military service
2303					Jul-19	Withdrawn by GWR Feb-35
2306					May-19	Withdrawn by GWR Apr-29
2308	73		1918	Apr-21		Transferred to CFOA, Turkey Oct-19 as their No 110; formally sold to UK Govt 1921; survived until 1950s
2309					May-19	Withdrawn by GWR Apr-31
2311		Jan-16			Jul-19	Withdrawn by GWR Nov-34
2313		Jan-17			May-19	Withdrawn by GWR Dec-38
2316					Aug-19	Withdrawn by GWR Nov-34
2317					Jun-19	Withdrawn by GWR Nov-34
2318	§		1918		Apr-21	Withdrawn by GWR Aug-29
2322	§		1918		May-21	Withdrawn by British Railways Jun-51
2327	§		1918		May-21	Withdrawn by British Railways Apr-53
2329	§		1918		May-21	Withdrawn by GWR Sep-38
2330					Apr-19	Withdrawn by GWR Jul-31
2332					Jul-19	Withdrawn by GWR Jul-38
2334	§		1918	Apr-21		No information
2336	§		1918		May-21	Withdrawn by GWR Nov-34
2338					Apr-19	Withdrawn by GWR Apr-31
2339		May-14			Jun-19	Withdrawn by British Railways Mar-52
2348					Jul-19	Withdrawn by GWR Jul-45
2349					Aug-19	Withdrawn by British Railways Mar-52
2355		Apr-16			May-19	Withdrawn by GWR Mar-30
2357		Apr-15			Jun-19	Withdrawn by GWR Jul-35
2383		Apr-15			Jun-19	Withdrawn by GWR Aug-46
2387	§		1918	Apr-21		No information
2403					Jul-19	Returned to military service; sold to Govt Oct-40
2415					May-19	Returned to military service; sold to Govt Dec-40
2420	§		1918	Apr-21		No information
2430		Jan-17			Aug-19	Returned to military service; sold to Govt Oct-40
2446					May-19	Returned to military service; sold to Govt Oct-40
2452					Jul-19	Withdrawn by British Railways Oct-52
2453	§		1918	Aug-21		No information

GWR No.	ROD No.	Superheated pre May-17	Date to Greece	Sold to Govt.	Returned to GWR	Final disposal
2454	§		1918		May-21	Returned to military service; sold to Govt Oct-40
2457		Aug-16			Jun-19	Returned to military service; sold to Govt Oct-40
2458		Jan-16			May-19	Withdrawn by British Railways May-54
2461		Jan-17			Aug-19	Returned to military service; sold to Govt Oct-40
2463					Jun-19	Returned to military service; sold to Govt Oct-40
2469					Jun-19	Returned to military service; sold to Govt Oct-40
2470		Oct-16			Jun-19	Returned to military service; sold to Govt Dec-40
2473		Jun-11			Jun-19	Returned to military service; sold to Govt Oct-40
2476		May-16			Jun-19	Returned to military service; sold to Govt Oct-40
2480					Jun-19	Returned to military service; sold to Govt Oct-40
2484					Jun-19	Withdrawn by British Railways May-54
2488	§		1918		May-21	Returned to military service; sold to Govt Oct-40
2489		Nov-11			Aug-19	Returned to military service; sold to Govt Oct-40
2514		Sep-16			Aug-19	Returned to military service; sold to Govt Oct-40
2517		Nov-15			Aug-19	Returned to military service; sold to Govt Oct-40
2518					Jul-19	Returned to military service; sold to Govt Oct-40
2519					Jul-19	Returned to military service; sold to Govt Oct-40
2520		Feb-17			Jun-19	Returned to military service; sold to Govt Oct-40
2522		Nov-16			May-19	Returned to military service; sold to Govt Oct-40
2528					Aug-19	Returned to military service; sold to Govt Dec-40
2531					Jun-19	Returned to military service; sold to Govt Oct-40
2533	§		1918		Apr-21	Returned to military service; sold to Govt Oct-40
2535					Jul-19	Withdrawn by GWR Jun-46
2542	84		1918	Apr-21		Transferred to CFOA, Turkey Oct-19 as their No 111; formally sold to UK govt 1921; withdrawn Sep-29
2549		Aug-16			May-19	Returned to military service; sold to Govt Oct-40
2557	§		1918		May-21	Returned to military service; sold to Govt Oct-40
2563	§		1918	Apr-21		No information
2566					Jul-19	Returned to military service; sold to Govt Oct-40
2577		Oct-16			Jun-19	Returned to military service; sold to Govt Oct-40
2578					Jul-19	Withdrawn by British Railways Sep-53
2580					Jul-19	Returned to military service; sold to Govt Oct-40

§ The ROD allocated the numbers 71-84 in the "Salonika series" to 14 of the locomotives in Greece but no other details have been traced.

WILLIAM DEAN

The first design attributed to William Dean was the 2-2-2 Class 157 of 1879. It was not always clear what was the difference between "renewal" and "rebuild"; a third process involving a change of boiler type occurred quite frequently but was not considered to constitute a rebuild. The process applied to the 157s was so extensive that they were officially classified as new locomotives. These engines were fitted with outside sandwich frames and initially with domeless boilers of the S0 variety, as shown with No 158 depicted here. The type of frame used and the open splasher sides were reminiscent of an earlier generation but the result was a classically proportioned, attractive design. This engine was seen carrying the name *Worcester* in 1895 which was soon removed as this appeared on 4-2-2 Achilles Class No 3027 in December of that year.

Looks apart, these engines were effective performers on express trains; on one occasion No 162 averaged almost 59 mph between London and Birmingham via Oxford.

An official photograph supposedly dated 1902 of River Class No 69 *Avon.* This engine had been converted from a 2-2-2 in January 1896 when it was fitted with an S4 boiler; in July 1902 an S2 boiler is recorded as having been fitted. However, the boiler depicted is an S4 and as it seems unlikely that an official photograph would have been taken immediately *before* a boiler change, either the photograph date or the date of boiler change is incorrect.

Chapter 5

LEGACIES

William Dean is best remembered for two classes of fundamentally different character, which in their respective ways won recognition well beyond the community of railway officers and enthusiasts. The style and elegance of his express passenger Achilles 4-2-2s captured the attention of a public that normally would not have given a locomotive a second glance while his cheap, simple, robust goods engine won respect and admiration from operators and soldiers both at home and internationally. There is however much more to the Dean story than these two celebrity designs.

Most of the tank locomotives of the 0-6-0, 0-4-2 and 2-4-0 varieties produced under his aegis were continuations of design standards and construction methods that had evolved under Joseph and George Armstrong. Bar some exceptions discussed below, they had no distinctive features that were specially Dean's. There was however one further group of locomotives – collectively his other passenger tender engines – that bore his hallmark.

This group is especially interesting for several reasons. They were diverse in character, delivered in comparatively small batches, and divided into several classes – in marked contrast to the "standard" types that grew numerically large eg the Dean Goods, and the Buffalo 0-6-0STs. The earlier examples of this group reflected the constraints imposed on the GWR's operations during the period from the resignation of Daniel Gooch as Locomotive Superintendent until the mid-1890s. The company's strained financial resources, senior management's repressive policy concerning speeds over 40 mph, a policy of cost containment that encouraged parsimonious use of fuel, and even the notorious, obligatory 10 minute refreshment stop at Swindon were all factors that conspired to keep engines small and of moderate power. Nonetheless, Dean created and sustained a cadre of locomotives noted for their mechanical simplicity, ornate finish and handsome looks.

The sustained trend towards heavier trains dictated a need for fleet modernisation. It was not always entirely clear whether an engine had been renewed or rebuilt, what precisely was the difference between the two processes, and how much of the original machine might be retained with each. Additionally, boiler changes were a frequent feature and some engines carried distinctly different types between an officially

designated rebuild/renewal date and final withdrawal. For a company considered later to have taken standardisation to extremes, these locomotives were bewildering in their variety. To summarise the histories of these varied classes during Dean's tenure, they are separately reviewed by wheel arrangement.

The 2-2-2 tender locomotives

Trends in traffic growth progressively taxed the capacities of the 2-2-2 express passenger engines and Dean's response was reflective of the financial constraints imposed upon him. Of the four principal classes in service in 1877, he extended the working lives of three by quite radical rebuilding.

A little more than a year after taking office, he started renewing the 10 members of Class 157, nicknamed "Sharpies", in such comprehensive fashion as to see them recorded as new engines. They were therefore considered the first class attributed to William Dean, even though their form closely followed the Joseph Armstrong originals. Despite their modest proportions, they were successful engines and similar to the better-known Queen class although differing in the use of sandwich frames. Like the Queens, these engines lasted in service until 1914 by which time they were relegated to the lightest of passenger workings.

The rebuilding of two other types of 2-2-2 involved changes of wheel arrangement. The eight-strong Class 69-76 which had been built in 1855/6 by Beyer Peacock were progressively modernised through two formal re-boilering programmes but by the 1890s their usefulness was diminishing. Between 1895 and 1897, they were converted to 2-4-0s with new frames (but retaining the archaic sandwich method of assembly) – a process that extended their working lives by between 11 and 23 years. During this conversion, they were named after rivers and thereafter employed on light passenger work, and pilot duties. In January 1907, No 70 *Dart* was in a violent accident with Dean Goods No 2448 at Thingley Junction; damage sustained was sufficiently severe for both to become the first withdrawals from their respective classes. (The conversion of 23 of the Sir Daniel Class 2-2-2s into 0-6-0s is described separately in Chapter 1).

The most successful of the 2-2-2s were the famous 7' Queen Class which comprised 21 locomotives constructed 1873-5. These engines remained singles throughout their careers, which commenced hauling

The Queen Class of 1873 were the best known of the 2-2-2s. Introduced only four years before Dean took office, they lasted until 1914 without rebuilding, beyond changes of boiler. Built new with a domeless (S0) boiler, No 1132 (above) acquired a front dome S2 type boiler in 1884 and survived in this condition until withdrawal in 1905 whilst No 1122 *Beaconsfield* is depicted (below) during the last three years of its working life, carrying the BR0 type boiler (raised Belpaire, domeless) that it received in April 1904

expresses to Swindon, Gloucester and Wolver-hampton. No longer capable of front line work and relegated to secondary duties, withdrawals commenced in 1904 but the last survived until 1914, while the last Achilles 4-2-2 went the following year.

In 1881, there emerged from Swindon a particularly interesting 2-2-2 bearing No 9. This was a rebuild of Dean's unsuccessful experimental 7' 8" 4-2-4T No 9,

retaining the outside Stephenson's motion. Five years later, it was joined by No 10 as a more conventional double-framed 2-2-2 with inside motion. This was a new engine that used none of the material ordered for the aborted project for a second 4-2-4T intended to be No 10. In addition to the usual round of boiler changes, both engines lost their 7' 8" driving wheels in favour of the 7' variety in 1900. They were mainly

Above - An almost universal feature of Dean's designs was the use of inside valve motion, which makes the outside Stephenson's link on 2-2-2 No 9 all the more interesting. This engine was a reincarnation of his unsuccessful experimental 4-2-4T of the same number that formed part of the experimental programme that preceded the introduction of the Dean Goods. During conversion from a tank engine in September 1884, the domeless boiler was replaced with an S2 type as shown here.

Above - In July 1890, No 9 was again rebuilt with removal of the outside Stephenson's link, installation of new outside frames, and substitution of the 7' driving wheels. Concurrently it was named *Victoria*. A further change followed in April 1902 with the fitting of a domeless raised firebox Belpaire boiler which remained until withdrawal in early 1905. Mileage exceeded 500,000 over 20 years' service as a 2-2-2 – an entirely respectable performance for a unique machine created from the remains of a disastrous experiment.

No 10 had been planned originally as a 4-2-4T similar to No 9 but with inside Joy valve gear. Following abandonment of that project, an entirely new No 10 appeared in 1886 as a companion to No 9. This engine was more conventional though with double frames and inside motion as shown here but it also was rebuilt with 7' driving wheels in January 1890 when it was named *Royal Albert*. In their final form Nos 9 and 10 strongly resembled the Queen 2-2-2s.

engaged on passenger services to Swindon and Wolverhampton before withdrawal in 1906, having achieved respectable mileages. The history of No 9 demonstrated Dean's capacity to turn a design failure into an effective locomotive.

Dean's ultimate essay with 2-2-2s was the 30-strong 7' 8" 3001 Class of 1891. In terms of size, these engines were a considerable advance over the "Queens" but they were front-end heavy and unstable. Eight had briefly served as convertibles to meet a motive power shortage immediately prior to cessation of the Broad Gauge but all were rebuilt with front bogies and assimilated into the Achilles Class proper by the end of 1894.

Opposite, below - The final batch of 2-2-2's built for the GWR were the 30-strong 3001 Class which appeared in 1891 (Nos 3021-3028 working temporarily on the Broad Gauge). By this time single drivers would have been considered obsolete but for the invention of steam sanding which improved their adhesive qualities. This class had 7' 8" driving wheels and at 44 tons 4 cwt (engine only) they were substantially larger than the Queens (33 tons 10 cwt). They were intended as top link passenger locomotives for the West of England main line but proved unsatisfactory being front end heavy and unstable, leading to rebuilding as 4-2-2s forming part of the famous Achilles Class. No 3024 *Storm King* is shown during the interlude between conversion from broad gauge and rebuilding as a 4-2-2 in December 1894.

This page, below - The derailment of Dean 2-2-2 No 3021 *Wigmore Castle* in Box Tunnel was the incident that led to the conversion of the 3001 series to 4-2-2s. This locomotive is depicted after conversion.

Bottom - 4-2-2 No 3029 *White Horse* at Paddington in 1897.

WILLIAM DEAN

The Wolverhampton 2-4-0s

The northern works were primarily associated with tank locomotive construction during the Dean years. However, it is apparent that most of the 2-4-0s usually allocated to sheds in the north were renewed and maintained under the auspices of George Armstrong with minimal input from Dean. With so much on his plate, the latter was doubtless content with this arrangement although a side effect was to inject even more variety into the numerically larger 2-4-0 fleet.

The oldest were the eight members of the Chancellor class numbered 149 to156, built in 1862. They were the first 2-4-0s built for the narrow gauge and, unusually for the time, intended for express passenger work. Built by outside contractors, they were designed by Gooch but with Stephenson's link motion. They were renewed at Wolverhampton in 1878-1883 retaining little of the original machines, and worked out their lives on secondary duties in the Northern Division, surviving as late as 1920. Apart from the Rivers, No 149 *Chancellor* was the only narrow gauge 2-4-0 to be named by the GWR.

Chronologically, the second 2-4-0 type was Joseph Armstrong's Class 111 of which 18 were built at Wolverhampton in 1863-7. Two more were added in 1886/7, created out of two old Wolverhampton 2-2-2s showing continued adherence to the economically-orientated "make do and mend" philosophy. The 111s proved to be useful secondary locomotives almost exclusively associated with the Northern Division. They did not require rebuilding or renewal beyond the usual boiler changes; the last was retired in 1914 after 51 years.

The first narrow gauge 2-4-0s built at Swindon were Class 439 in 1868. They were nicknamed "Bicycles" because they had inside frames and fully exposed wheels in the contemporary fashion of broad gauge locomotives. Predominantly Northern Division engines, six were renewed at Wolverhampton in 1885/6 and the seventh in 1895. The renewal process was effectively the construction of new locomotives with only small amounts of material retained from the originals. The class survived until the end of 1918 but was another with which Dean had minimal involvement.

By 1889, Wolverhampton's new construction work was focussed on tank locomotives, plus the odd tender locomotive renewal. In that year though, the northern works unexpectedly introduced the 5-strong Class 3226 which apart from minor details was an extension of Class 111. These were the last new tender locomotives built there and their introduction was quite out of character with the established new construction programme. Like the 111s they were useful secondary locomotives, initially concentrated in the Northern Division but later more broadly distributed, the last being withdrawn in 1922.

Chancellor Class No 152 was a classically attractive engine when photographed on shed with a vintage tender.

No 726 of Class 56/717 is recorded as carrying an S2a boiler from 1903 until 1912. This type had been introduced with the 0-6-0 Class 2361 and had minor dimensional differences from the standard S2 type.

The Swindon 2-4-0s

The remainder of the 2-4-0 fleet were, in the main, Southern Division machines and therefore directly under Dean's supervision.

The second type of narrow gauge 2-4-0 built at Swindon was Class 481 in 1869, plus an additional engine in 1887. They were similar in size to the Bicycles but with a different frame layout. Most were renewed at Swindon in 1887-1890 in which process they retained their frames and motion, but received S2 type boilers. Some kept these boilers until withdrawal while others later acquired S4/B4 types – a similar pattern to that applied to the Dean Goods. The 481s were quite small engines and were soon relegated to secondary duties such as Didcot-Southampton services and pilot work. Even so, they proved quite long-lived, the last staying in service until 1919.

Later 2-4-0s were markedly larger and more powerful locomotives that were spared the obscure processes of rebuild and renewal, although they were subject like other Dean locomotives during this period to a multiplicity of boiler changes. Class 56/717 built 1871/2 was fitted with inside frames for the 6' 0"

driving wheels but double frames at the front end. Broadly similar types followed with 20 of Class "806" in 1873 and a similar number of Class 2201 in 1881/2 – although both these classes had 6' 7" driving wheels. The latter two classes demonstrated the sense of continuity at Swindon as the 806's were built by Joseph Armstrong and the 2201's by Dean. All these locomotives were initially engaged on provincial passenger services but followed the usual pattern later in their careers of taking on secondary and branch work. Except for No 810, which managed to linger on until 1926, they were all withdrawn between 1904 and 1922.

After an interval of 10 years, there was a reversion to more of the same genre with the 20 locomotives of Class 3232, which also had 6' 7" driving wheels. These were the last new 2-4-0s to be built at Swindon, and they largely substituted for Class 2201 while also taking over provincial and cross-country services, such as the North-to-West route. They had shorter working lives than the preceding 2201s and the later examples of small wheeled 2-4-0s, anticipating the reduced demand for large wheeled four-coupled locomotives in the 1920s, as was also to affect the 4-4-0s. No 3251 was the last to go in 1930.

No 2220 of Class 2201 was the last in service, working until 1921. These engines presented a relatively modern appearance compared with certain other 2-4-0 classes but by the 1920s there was diminishing demand for four-coupled locomotive with large driving wheels.

No 3251 of Class 3232 had the distinction of being the last new 2-4-0 built at Swindon, and the last of its class to remain in service. The date is not recorded but the pre-Dean era tender is considerably older than the locomotive.

Between classes 2201 and 3232, which were visually speaking modern engines with inside frames for the driving wheels, there was an apparent backward step with double-framed Nos 3201-3205 of the Stella Class. These formed part of an unusual standardisation programme in 1884-7 that embraced four types - 2-4-0 Class 3201; 2-4-0T Class 3501; 0-6-0 Class 2361; and 0-6-0ST Class 1661. They shared the same dimensions for driving wheels, cylinders and motion, and the boilers were similar but with minor variations. The double frames were of an unusual design with under-slung springs.

Stella 2-4-0 Class 3201 No 3201 at Wolverhampton on 11ᵗʰ October 1833, after withdrawal. This class was introduced under Lot 65 in 1884/5 in a programme to produce a cadre of engines that could be readily converted to Broad Gauge use if circumstances so required. The other three classes in this exercise were 0-6-0 Class 2361, 0-6-0ST Class 1661 (Lots 69 & 71 of 1886/7), and 2-4-0ST Class 3501 (Lot 64 of 1885); all four shared many standard dimensions. No 3201 had an unusual history as it was built six months before any more of the type and promptly sold in new condition to the Pembroke & Tenby Railway where it was numbered 8 and named *Stella*. It returned to GWR stock in 1896, took up its originally llocated number and carried its name until 1902.

Coltas Collection

The Class 3501 2-4-0T was one of four classes of standardised convertibles created to cope with possible shortages in the closing years of the Broad Gauge. The first ten were built in 1885 as broad gauge engines; No 3505 was converted to a 2-4-0 BG tender engine in 1890 and rebuilt as part of NG 2-4-0 Class 3201 in 1892. Despite appearances, No 3505 as shown here is a broad gauge engine – it had double frames and an *additional* set of outside frames for the leading wheels.

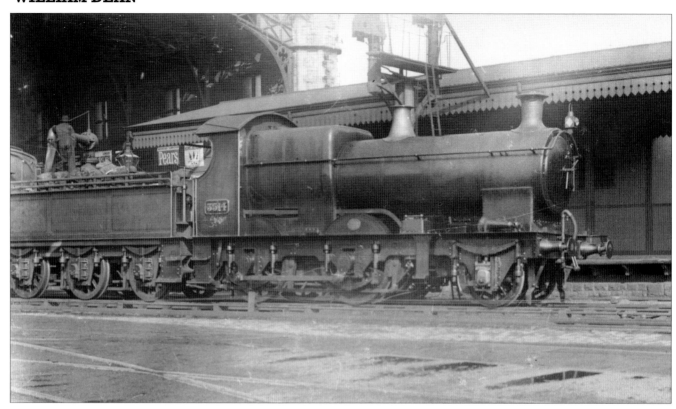

Class 3201 No 3514 at Bristol Temple Meads in about 1905. This locomotive started life as a convertible 2-4-0T but was always a narrow gauge machine. It was rebuilt as a 2-4-0 in 1895, becoming a member of Class 3201. A further change in appearance occurred when it carried a D0 type boiler between 1901 and 1910, thereafter reverting to a conventional domed boiler. The D0 style was unique – effectively an early form of Churchward Standard No 3 boiler – and made the engine quite different in appearance to its classmates.

2-2-2 Queen Class No 1124. This view is presented out of sequence to demonstrate the hazards in trying to identify boiler types during the later Dean period. The BR0 type shown was carried between 1901 and 1905 and at first glance looks similar to the D0 on No 3514 in the previous image. The dimensions of BR0 type were significantly smaller and the lower pitch is emphasised by retention of the round cab spectacle plates. In addition to the poor factor of adhesion, development of the singles was constrained by the driving wheel diameter which prevented installation of tapered boilers.

As explained elsewhere in connection with Class 2361, the purpose was to provide a group of engines that could be easily converted for use on the broad gauge. In the event, only ten of 2-4-0T Class 3501 were so used between 1890 and 1892 and five during that period were converted to broad gauge 2-4-0s. This mixed group of broad gauge tender and tank engines all became narrow gauge 2-4-0s as part of Class 3201 in 1892; they were joined by the remaining ten narrow gauge 2-4-0Ts which were similarly rebuilt In 1894/5. Following standardisation in the West Country, these engines went to Devon and Cornwall to operate passenger services until displaced by Duke Class 4-4-0s. Thereafter, they were distributed throughout the system and remained in service on secondary duties. Withdrawals commenced in 1919; No 3201 was the last, being withdrawn in 1933.

Class 3206 introduced in 1889 was the best known of the GWR's 2-4-0s, allegedly nicknamed "Barnums" after their work as favourites for hauling the heavy trains of Barnum & Baileys Circus. They were subject to a number of modifications in springs, valves and cylinders but their most significant feature was the use of sandwich frames, a long out-moded construction technique. Sandwich frames comprised twin iron plates with oak slabs fitted between. Assembly was time-consuming, as care was needed in alignment of the different components and treatment of the timber to prevent acidic contamination of the metal. Very strong frames resulted with considerable lateral flexibility that yielded smooth running by absorbing much of the stresses exerted by the crank axle. The Barnums were possibly the last locomotives worldwide to be built with this frame type although why Dean used this method is not clear. They were considered mixed traffic locomotives and their popularity saw them well distributed throughout the system. Withdrawals of these 20 locomotives commenced in 1926 with the last going in 1937.

For sake of completeness, mention should be made of four other 2-4-0s built between 1886 and 1888, which formed part of Dean's exploration of design possibilities through experimentation. Stimulated by the success of marine compound steam engines, several engineers researched compound systems and Dean investigated the four-cylinder tandem method. This used low-pressure cylinders with valves above in front of high-pressure cylinders with valves below, the valve spindles being connected through conventional motion. No 7 was built as a narrow gauge engine and No 8 as a broad gauge machine. Both proved unsuccessful and were soon set aside, together with two more experimental 2-4-0s (Nos 14 and 16) built for the broad gauge and fitted with large cylinders and boilers. They were rebuilt in 1894 as the GWR's first narrow gauge 4-4-0s with a close resemblance to the 4-2-2s, becoming known as the Armstrong Class.

An unidentified Barnum Class late in its career with B4 boiler.

WILLIAM DEAN

The 4-4-0s

Experiences with the 2-2-2 Class 3001 and the slightly later 4-2-2 variant created an important watershed in locomotive design policy. Stability problems with the 2-2-2s, culminating in the derailment of No 3021 *Wigmore Castle* in Box Tunnel (see page 85), graphically demonstrated the practical limits of what could be achieved with that wheel arrangement. Dean had been wary of leading bogies which was a reason for his experimental designs on tank engines Nos 1 and 9, but was apparently now reconciled to their inevitability with larger engines. As 4-2-2s, *Achilles* and her sisters proved to be fleet of foot, smooth running, and stable at speed but another challenge soon arose as a result of the inexorable increase in train weights which before long started to tax their adhesive powers.

A further complicating factor was the need to improve services beyond Exeter, following the gauge conversion. Single drivers could handle trains as far as Newton Abbot but beyond that point, something stronger was required. Thus in 1895 appeared what was to be the start of Dean's last major initiative with express passenger engines. The 4-4-0 Duke Class, fitted with 5' 8" driving wheels, was ideal for service over hilly, circuitous routes. They were attractive,

double-framed engines that continued the typical Dean styling including graceful upward curves in the running plate to allow clearance for the coupling rod bosses. Their modest axle loading afforded them a wide sphere of use; until about 1900 they dominated Exeter -Penzance services and thereafter were distributed throughout the system on secondary work, with emphasis on Central Wales later in their careers. When built, they were equipped with small 2000 gallon tenders so that they could use the short turntables still in use in the far west – one of the civil engineering tasks yet to be completed in the infrastructural improvements in the area.

With the proving of the Dukes, consideration was given to 4-4-0s with larger diameter driving wheels for use elsewhere. The Armstrongs were in this category but had not proven entirely satisfactory in practice, the cylinders being too large for the boiler. The Badminton Class of 1897 was better proportioned in this regard and the twenty members of this type marked the start of a series of express 4-4-0s with classic double framing that featured in the later Atbaras, Flowers and the larger-boilered Cities. This type was rather short-lived (the beautifully named Flowers in particular), being replaced by Hall 4-6-0s from the later 1920s onwards.

4-4-0 Duke Class No 3322 *Mersy* in early condition.

Armstrong 4-4-0 Class No 16 *Brunel* at Reading in the 1890s.   *RS Carpenter* **Photos**

Badminton Class 4-4-0 No 3292 *Badminton* as built in December 1897 – the first 4-4-0 with 6' 8" driving wheels.

Flower Class 4-4-0 No 4120 *Stephanotis* as built in July 1908 – the last 4-4-0 with 6' 8" driving wheels. Over ten years' evolution is evident in the tapered saturated boiler (yet to receive top feed), straight running plate over the driving wheels and deep outside frames.

The smaller wheeled variety proved longer lasting as they were suited to a wider range of duties. In due course, the Dukes evolved into the Bulldogs which carried heavier boilers. All these 4-4-0 types were subject to boiler changes, which with the expansion of Churchward's influence meant the proliferation of various tapered types. The Dukes however continued to run with smaller parallel boilers.

Around this time the distinction between Dean and Churchward influences become blurred but perhaps the line can be drawn with the 4-4-0s over the change from flowing curved frames to more austere straight-topped running plates and frames. The Bulldogs embraced both styles with the first of the straight-framed version appearing in Lot No 124 of May 1900.

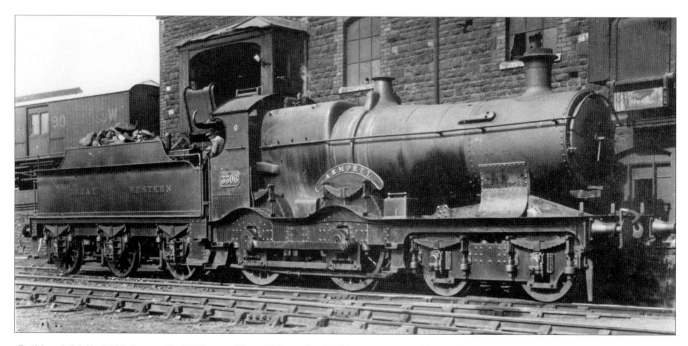

Bulldog 4-4-0 No 3306 *Armorel* in 1920s condition. This engine had been converted from a Duke of the same name in 1902 and underwent boiler changes as typically applied to the 4-4-0s.

94

Dukedog 4-4-0 No 3204 *Earl of Dartmouth* created August 1936 with the frames from Bulldog No 3439 and officially replacing Duke No 3271. The Earls became commoners in June/July 1937.

The 1930s brought an amusing postscript to the Dean 4-4-0s. By then the Bulldogs were becoming surplus while conversely, there was continued need for the older Dukes which were approaching the end of their useful lives. Charles Collett neatly solved the problem by placing Duke boilers on "Bulldog" chassis, creating the Dukedog hybrid which was the last GWR 4-4-0 type in service, surviving until 1960. Collett started to name these new/old engines after Earls and quickly earned the disapprobation of some of their namesakes. The GWR knew its place in society, having often tugged the corporate forehead to the nobility and gentry; placing one's private address on a modern, thoroughbred 4-6-0 was acceptable but placing one's *title* on a mechanical antique of mixed parentage was really going too far, don't you know. The Earls swiftly became anonymous, leaving a suspicion that here was another possible display of subtle sense of humour by the normally inscrutable Collett.

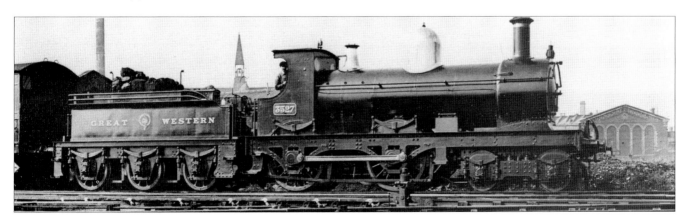

4-4-0 Class 3521 No 3527 as rebuilt from 0-4-4T, fitted with a Dean goods type S4 boiler.

One of the "curiosities", 4-4-0ST No 13 on a Brixham branch train at Churston in 1906. This engine had started life as a unique 2-4-2T built in 1886 and was converted to this state in 1897.   *Photomatic*

0-4-2T Class 3521 No 3525 as built in 1887. The long wheelbase contributed to stability problems which were not solved by conversion to 0-4-4T with shorter tanks in 1892.

Remaining tank locomotives

Setting aside a small group of engines which were curiosities that really played no significant part in the GWR locomotive story, there were some designs that deserve specific mention.

The need for a fleet of convertible locomotives for the closing years of the Broad Gauge extended to a group with a particularly chequered history. In 1887/8, 20 examples of 0-4-2T Class 3521 were built for the narrow gauge, and in 1888/9 a further 20 (Nos 3541-3560) were constructed for use on the broad gauge in Devon and Cornwall. The initial 20 were unstable, as were the later engines, so nineteen of the second batch appeared with full-length saddle tanks. These also quickly proved unstable so the twentieth (No 3560) was built new as an 0-4-4T with short side tanks. In 1891/2 all the first batch were rebuilt as 0-4-4Ts while the nineteen broad gauge 0-4-2STs were converted to conform with No 3560 in 1890/1, before conversion to standard gauge. Envisaged as main line tank engines, serious stability problems persisted and between 1899 and 1902, the entire class was subjected to further and very drastic rebuilding. They re-appeared as 5' 2" 4-4-0s but maintained their reputation for variety. Twenty-six had Dean Goods type boilers (as had been carried while tank locomotives) while the remainder were fitted with parallel, and later tapered, Standard No 3 boilers. Dean's passenger engines were noted for their variety but with this class, this characteristic even out-lived his retirement. Confined to branch and secondary duties, the Standard No 3 type lasted until 1929, and the parallel boiler version until 1930.

Around the turn of the Century, there was increasing recognition of the need for faster schedules to serve a growing suburban population. It was perceived that "double-ender" tank locomotives which could work safely at speed in either direction would be preferred for such duties, which implied the adoption of symmetrical wheelbases. Other companies pursued the concept leading to several types of 2-4-2T, the rare 4-4-4T, and ultimately the 4-6-4T. Dean's entry into the double-ender field was by 2-4-2T No 11, introduced in 1900 and early in 1902, production commenced of 30 to the same design. It might be argued that Churchward's prairie tanks were also double enders but this was not the primary intent of creating a sizeable fleet of 2-6-2Ts; they were simply the best wheelbase for the GWR's specific needs.

"Double ender" 2-4-2T Class 36xx No 3629 at Birkenhead. The 31 engines of this class were nicknamed "Birdcages" on the basis of the high, large cab in relation to the rest of the superstructure.

0-6-4PT crane engine No 18 *Steropes*. (Steropes was a rather obscure figure in Greek mythology being one of the Cyclopes – one-eyed giants. Presumably the connotation was physical strength implied by the crane; No 17 was named *Cyclops*).

Finally in this category, a tank locomotive appeared in the closing years of Dean's superin-tendency that had a feature that was to become an indelible element of the GWR locomotive scene. In 1898, a 4-4-0T with the number 1490 was introduced, the last of his experimental tank engines. This was a possible replacement for Metro 2-4-0Ts on London suburban services but was unsuccessful as it was too heavy; it was sold in 1907. Nonetheless, this engine was the first to be fitted with pannier tanks, an idea imported from Belgium that was eminently practical, as was proven over following years.

The advantages of pannier tanks were exploited in 1901 with a pair of 0-6-4PT crane engines built for works service at Swindon and Wolverhampton. The engine part was a Class 850 0-6-0PT with round-topped, domeless boiler and the crane was mounted behind the cab on a footplate extension supported by the bogie. The jib rested on the domeless boiler for travelling purposes. Two, Nos 17 and 18 appeared in 1901 and were joined by No 16 1921.

4-6-0 No 100

Four months before his retirement, there emerged from Swindon the precursor of the next stage in the evolution of the GWR's large engine policy.

Locomotive No 100 was quite different from anything that had gone before. At a weight (engine only) of 67 tons 10 cwt, it was larger and significantly heavier than the company's preceding two 4-6-0s (No 36 – 59 tons 10 cwt) and (Kruger No 2601 – 60 tons 8 cwt). It signalled the arrival of the modern era with outside cylinders, and with an appearance that alarmed purists who had been used to elegance in Swindon's products. Public dislike for the austere impression imparted by No 100 did not go unheeded and the appearance of later 4-6-0s was improved by some softening of their lines. Although the GWR's 20th Century machines were generally good-looking, there was to be no return to the flowing elegance of Dean's single drivers, or to the colourful exoticism of his livery.

No 100 signalled what was about to happen through the company's large engine policy. While the design was fundamentally attributable to GJ Churchward, the engine's initiation marked a fitting closure to a career that had started shortly after establishment of the first standard gauge operations. No 100 was cogent evidence of how much had changed during the previous 25 years, especially as William Dean's very first passenger class, the 2-2-2s Nos 157-166 were still at work. The difference between the two types stood testimony to progress under his guiding hand through difficult times.

Pioneer outside cylinder 4-6-0 No 100 first entered service unnamed but became *Dean* in June 1902; in November 1902 it was renamed *William Dean* and later renumbered 2900. This engine appeared first with a parallel Standard No 1 boiler but in June 1903, this was replaced with a short cone version as shown here. This engine was later treated as part of the Saint class although it varied from the rest in frames, cylinders and valve gear. This famous engine was withdrawn in 1932 after its non-standard cylinders had reached their re-boring limit.

Post-Grouping

By the time the "greater" Great Western was created through the Grouping, the ranks of Dean's passenger locomotives had been sadly depleted, largely by virtue of the new generation of which No 100, by now No 2900, had been in the van. The single drivers had all gone and the variegated 2-4-0s were heavily reduced in numbers. The larger wheeled 4-4-0s were condemned to enjoy comparatively short lives, victims of the mass influx of the mixed traffic 4-6-0s although the 5' 8" classes hung on longer. Their working lives were extended by World War II but, except for the hybrid Dukedogs, all had gone by 1951.

In keeping with the general trend of 0-6-0s being the longest-lived of British six-wheeled locomotives, at a time when the presence of Dean's passenger tenders engines was in decline, his goods design was still at work in substantial numbers. War service from 1917 to 1921 had marked out the class as something special and the activities for which they were best remembered and respected had yet to unfold. It follows that from the Grouping forward, the story of William Dean and his designs is very largely the story of the Dean Goods.

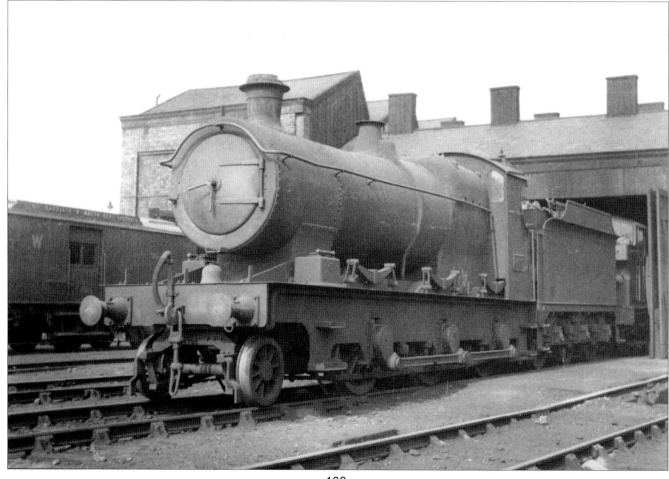

Chapter 6

ON THE MODERN GWR

The Dean Goods was the GWR's principal freight type from inception in 1883 until the turn of the century. By then there was a trend towards larger locomotives for front line duties. The North Eastern, Great Central and London & North Western railways extended the 0-6-0 concept by adding an extra driving axle to create 0-8-0s with either inside or outside cylinders. In eschewing eight coupled designs, William Dean tried out novel ideas with 2-6-0s and 4-6-0s as described earlier; the only effective successor to emerge from that programme was the 81-strong Aberdare Class 2-6-0.

Like the later double-framed 4-4-0s, the Aberdare was essentially a transitional design but what followed was undeniably of the modern era. Churchward's interest in contemporary American locomotive practice led to the introduction in 1903 of No 97, prototype of the Class 28xx 2-8-0. Batch production started in 1905 and by 1919, a total of 84 were in service. Class 28xx presaged the widespread adoption of the Consolidation wheel arrangement, and was arguably the best heavy freight design until the Standard Class 9F 2-10-0 of 1954.

The demand for modern freight power was complemented by the provision of a further ground-breaking design with American connections in 1911. The mogul had become a popular maid-of-all-work in that country, and the Class 43xx 2-6-0 was to prove an early exemplar of a wheel arrangement widely adopted for mixed traffic work. The 43xx was hardly a fresh design but more a fusion of existing components, so embedded had Churchward's standardisation policy by then become.

Opposite, upper - An early post-Grouping view of Dean Goods Nos 2301 (left) and 2466. Both engines have lost their brass domes and safety valve covers but retain their original dished smokebox doors. *Lens of Sutton*

Opposite, lower - The direct successors as the GWR's prime freight type were the 81-strong 2-6-0 Aberdare Class built between 1900 and 1907. Better looking and substantially more successful than the preceding ten locomotives of the 4-6-0/ 2-6-0 "Kruger" series, they never developed the mixed traffic role that the Dean Goods assumed in later years. No 2680 with a tender purloined from an ROD 2-8-0 is on shed at Banbury in 1939. *Photomatic*

Below - Another type that contributed to the removal of the Dean Goods from frontline freight work was the 2-6-0 Class 43xx introduced in 1911. A total of 342 was built between then and 1932. Although Class 28xx very occasionally appeared on passenger workings, the 43xx was a genuine mixed traffic machine whose range of duties was broadly similar to that of the Dean Goods, albeit without the same wide route availability. No.5327 (the only member of the 5319-5330 batch not to join the ROD in France) is seen at work on an express freight. *HMRS*

Two other 2-8-0 classes also had an impact on freight services. Churchward's last design was the nine-strong Class 47xx of 1919, a specialised type intended for overnight fitted goods trains. At the other end of the scale, in March/April 1919 the GWR had purchased 20 examples of war surplus ROD 2-8-0s of the type that had worked alongside the Dean Goods in France. They were bought at attractive prices and their unused condition made them welcome as Swindon was busy attending to maintenance arrears from the war years. The RODs were freight-only machines, equipped just with steam brakes and thus restricted to non-fitted working.

Thus, immediately prior to the Grouping, the company was well provided with tender locomotives intended either for goods duties or with clearly identified mixed traffic objectives:

Class		Introduced	In service
0-6-0 Types:			
57/131/360		1866-1873	6
328 (Beyer)		1864	16
Armstrong Goods		1866	53
927 (Coal engines)		1874	4
Dean Goods		1883	232
Class 2361		1885	20
Sub-total			**331**
Post-Dean Goods:			
Aberdare goods	2-6-0	1900	81
28xx	2-8-0	1903	84
43xx	2-6-0	1911	292
47xx	2-8-0	1919	9
30xx ROD	2-8-0	1919	20
Total			**817**

Opposite, upper - Class 47xx No 4701 at Swindon in British Railways' days. No 4700, the class prototype, was built with a Standard No 1 boiler that proved inadequate for such a large engine. It was rebuilt with a larger Standard No 7 boiler which was used from new with the other eight members of the class. Apart from an extension to the cab roof, the appearance of these engines was virtually unchanged throughout careers spent mainly on fast night goods workings. Nos 4701 to 4704 differed from the others by having their snifting valves mounted outside on the steam chests.

Opposite, lower - The Aberdare 2-6-0s were displaced by Churchward's 2-8-0s of class 28xx, series production of which commenced in 1905. These were Britain's first 2-8-0s and 84 were in service by 1919. Construction recommenced in 1938 with small improvements including side window cabs on the 83 built between then and 1942. No 3825 was one of the later type. Britain never saw a finer 2-8-0 than this archetypical Churchward design.

Below - More Class 28xx 2-8-0s would have appeared in the 1920s, had it not been for the purchase of war surplus ROD 2-8-0s from the UK government. The background to the genesis of these locomotives is discussed in Appendix D. Initially, 20 unused examples were bought, followed by the short term hire of 84 to help cover motive power shortages while Swindon caught up with its repair back-log. Then another 80 were purchased in 1925 at attractive prices. These were a mixed bag and they were progressively whittled down to the best 30. The remainder were withdrawn as soon as heavy repairs fell due although their tenders were kept for further use. No 3016, seen here at Swindon on 9th January 1954, was one of the original 20 that were purchased new.

Above - Another Churchward design overtly for mineral haulage was the Class 42xx introduced in 1910 with the rare 2-8-0T wheel arrangement. One of these impressive performers, No 4271, was built in February 1920

Below - The rebuilding of 54 members of Class 42xx as 2-8-2T Class 72xx was effectively a reversion to the 19th Century practice of using tank engines on long distance freight work. No 7220, first of the class's second series (which retained the old-style straight running plate) is seen starting away from the loop at Aller Junction on the westward assault of Dainton Bank. This being the BR era, the banker is likely to be a Class 5101 2-6-2T

The arrival of the larger types resulted in a cascade of the Dean Goods to lesser duties, and in withdrawal of older 0-6-0 locomotives. Continued emphasis post-Grouping on large freight locomotives forced further displacement. The Class 30XX ROD fleet had been temporarily expanded between 1919 and 1922 by the hire of 84 war-surplus locomotives to help alleviate motive power shortages. Then 80 second-hand RODs were purchased at knockdown prices in 1925. Like the locomotives hired earlier, their condition varied widely and by 1932 they had been whittled down to the best 30. The remainder were discarded as heavy repairs fell due but their tenders were retained for use with the Aberdares. When that class was withdrawn, some moved on to Class 2251 and others found use as sludge tenders – the GWR certainly extracted maximum value for money.

A reversion to old habits concerned the use of tank locomotives on heavy goods duties. Between 1910 and 1940, a total of 205 examples of Class 42xx with the unusual 2-8-0T wheelbase were built mainly for short distance mineral traffic in South Wales. Adverse economic conditions rendered some surplus and in 1932, 20 were placed in store. Between 1934 and 1939, these and 34 others had their operating range increased by frame extensions and the addition of a trailing truck to support a larger bunker. The resultant 2-8-2T was an impressive performer but with its smaller (Standard No 4) boiler and 2500 gallons water capacity, it could not match the abilities of Class 28xx. In later years, the longest journeys habitually handled were mineral trains from South Wales to Salisbury – the type of duty that in the 19th Century had been covered by Dean Goods and earlier still by Buffalo 0-6-0STs.

At the Grouping, the 0-6-0 fleet was increased by 86 engines absorbed from the Cambrian, Midland & South Western Junction, and Taff Vale railways. The new owners could not resist "Great Westernising" them and they came in for varying degrees of attention. This had minimal effect on the smallest Cambrian engines and on the Taff Vale fleet but most of the remainder were modified. They basically continued with their pre-Grouping duties, often alongside reallocated members of the Dean Goods. More information about these engines appears in **Chapter 8**.

As at 31st December 1922, the Dean Goods was distributed throughout the system at 50 locations. The largest individual concentrations were Bristol – 28, Carmarthen – 11, Reading – 14, Wolverhampton – 13 and Worcester - 13. Full details are set out in **Appendix E**.

The Grouping had a major impact upon deployment and the class's importance within the motive power fleet at a time when in other circumstances, a structured withdrawal programme on grounds of age could have been anticipated. In fact, age-related withdrawals did not commence until 1929 and curiously in advance of the last survivors of older 0-6-0 classes. When No 2304 was withdrawn in January of that year, a solitary example of Class 360 was to work for another six months while six Beyer Goods and 18 Standard Goods were still operating – both classes did not become extinct until 1934.

Between 1929 and 1938, 51 Dean Goods were despatched on grounds of condition and age:

No.	Withdrawn	No.	Withdrawn	No.	Withdrawn	No.	Withdrawn
2301	Jan-34	2316	Nov-34	2335	Sep-33	2359	Dec-35
2302	Mar-31	2317	Nov-34	2336	Nov-34	2384	Dec-38
2303	Feb-35	2318	Aug-29	2337	Nov-35	2388	Jun-38
2304	Jan-29	2319	Feb-31	2338	Apr-31	2390	Aug-37
2305	Jun-35	2321	Oct-38	2341	Nov-34	2391	Dec-33
2306	Apr-29	2324	Feb-31	2342	Aug-38	2394	May-38
2307	Apr-32	2326	May-32	2346	Sep-36	2396	Jun-34
2309	Apr-31	2328	Sep-38	2347	Apr-38	2397	Apr-35
2310	Nov-34	2329	Dec-33	2352	May-35	2398	Dec-38
2311	Nov-34	2330	Jul-31	2353	Dec-36	2417	Feb-39
2312	Feb-31	2331	Mar-31	2355	Mar-30	2421	May-38
2313	Dec-38	2332	Jul-38	2357	Jul-35	2450	May-38
2314	May-32	2333	Nov-31	2358	Nov-34		

By year, the number of withdrawals was: 1929 – 3; 1930 – 1; 1931 – 10; 1932 – 3; 1933 – 3; 1934 – 9; 1935 – 7; 1936 – 2; 1937 – 1; 1938 - 12

WILLIAM DEAN

Withdrawals continued unabated during 1939 and by August, ten more had been removed from the active list. However, in view of the international situation, a number of older locomotives of several classes withdrawn that year were held in reserve and by July, a total of 41 were in store at Swindon. The following nine Dean Goods in due course returned to work (No 2417 withdrawn Feb-39 was not re-instated):

No.	Withdrawn	Reinstated
2315	Jul-39	Oct-39
2340	Jun-39	Feb-40
2354	May-39	Nov-39
2419§	May-39	Oct-39
2439§	Apr-39	Oct-39
2447§	May-39	Nov-39
2455§	Aug-39	Nov-39
2480§	May-39	Nov-39
2524§	Aug-39	Oct-39

§ Lent to the Government for military service in 1940 and later sold.

For a company that accorded standardisation such importance, the Grouping presented an organisational challenge in the variety of locomotives that were assimilated. The wide route availability of the Dean Goods made it a popular choice for newly acquired lines with axle loading limitations – principally in what became the Central Wales Division. Thus the class discovered new theatres of operations, working alongside indigenous 0-6-0s.

Steady attrition from 1929 onwards was largely due to the introduction of Class 2251, of which 50 were in service by the end of 1938. The new engines were allocated in the main to English sheds where they replaced Dean Goods that then migrated to Wales. A further 30 Class 2251 were built in 1939/40 to help fill the gap created by the departure of 108 Dean Goods on military service. There were many foreign locomotives lent to the GWR during the World War 2 but the only transfers directly attributable to these wartime losses were 43 ex-Midland Railway 2Fs and 3Fs, and 40 LNER J25s (ex-North Eastern Railway) – all 0-6-0s. At least eight MR Class 2Fs were allocated to the Oswestry-Moat Lane-Brecon area but reputedly there was a reluctance to let them down Talerddig bank, apparently on the unfounded assumption that they lacked the strength to get back up! No record has been traced of their having reached Machynlleth.

Although the Dean Goods had been intended for freight work, by 1922 it was evolving as a mixed traffic type. In 1934, distribution was even more widespread than it had been at the Grouping, being found at 56 locations. Bristol by then was home to 18 while Carmarthen had 10 and Worcester 13. The growing Welsh presence was evident at Aberystwyth (6), Machynlleth (9) and Oswestry (8).

The Dean Goods started its long association with the Central Wales Division soon after the Grouping. No 2457 is seen here adjacent to the coal stage at Oswestry depot on 28th August 1926.
HC Casserley

Above - No 2558 is seen in this undated photograph but likely to be the 1920s as the engine retains its original dished smokebox door.

Below - Post-Grouping, there was less incursion into Devon beyond Exeter, so records of the class west of the River Exe have particular interest. This view is believed to have been taken during the 1920s, and the location is Dawlish Warren. Why a down goods should be standing on the up station loop is not clear. Perhaps single line working (not uncommon between this station and Teignmouth) was in force and this train was waiting for a faster service to pass.

Above - A good study of the exposed nature of the footplate of a Dean Goods; No 2479 is standing at Reading West in January 1929.
HC Casserley

Below - Another undated photograph, this time of No 2450 and the location would appear to be in Wales.

In the inter-war years, apart from different sizes of tenders, variation was usually only evident in the details. No 2541 has a slightly tapered chimney instead of the more usual parallel version. The engine has yet to receive ATC equipment which was fitted in 1930/31.

Retention of small numbers at sheds such as Old Oak Common, Southall and Reading was surprising in view of the growing rural deployment. Didcot always had a penchant for veterans, the complement there being used on Winchester/ Southampton services. The Taunton group worked mainly on the branches to Barnstaple and Minehead. The widespread distribution stood testimony to the Class's general usefulness throughout most of the GWR system, except understandably Cardiff Valleys Division and traditionally by then, west of Exeter.

The extent to which they were still appearing on main line duties was underlined by the number equipped with Automatic Train Control. There had been some very early fitments before World War 1 and one more was so treated in 1927, followed by a major installation programme in 1930/ 31. A further seven were fitted between 1936 and 1938 so that by the end of the decade the remaining non-ATC fitted locomotives formed a negligible minority. This programme ran concurrently with the provision of ATC ramps, the last of 2,114 being installed at Penzance on 9th November 1939 thus completing the main line routes from Paddington to Fishguard, Chester and the West Country.

No 2392 taking water at Leamington Spa in 1931.

Coltas Trust

WILLIAM DEAN

ATC normally conjures visions of 4-6-0s hauling express trains in thick fog at close to normal speeds. It was affirmation of the GWR's commitment to safety that No 2301 itself should have been ATC fitted 47 years after it had been built. Twenty years were to elapse before British Railways started to make similarly safe the routes of the other members of the Big Four. Details of the shed allocations as at 31st December 1933, and of locomotives that were ATC fitted between 1927 and 1938 appear in **Appendix F**.

The company's positive attitude towards the class was evident in yet another way. Superheating started in 1911 and the fitting programme continued steadily into the 1930s. Excluding the 28 locomotives taken off the books prior to the Grouping, none of which had been superheated, all the remainder were so fitted except for Nos 2310 (withdrawn Nov-34), 2312/ 2324 (Feb-31), 2333 (Nov-31), 2341 (Nov-34), 2352 (May-35), 2359 (Dec-35).

The almost universal modernisation of the class in the 1930s was put to good effect. Generally speaking, photographs from that period of passenger train workings depict a Dean Goods on three or four coaches on a rural stopping service but the class was still called upon for heavier work. For example the Cambrian lines could host quite significant trains as in the summer of 1931 when No 2321 piloted 4-4-0 "Duke" Class No 3264 *Trevithick* on 12 coaches from Talerdigg to Aberystwyth.

A type B4 boiler replaced the last round-topped firebox boiler in 1927 (No 2321) and from the 1920s the class

maintained an essentially homogeneous appearance that was unusual for secondary locomotives of advanced years. More variety was evident with the tenders, which predominantly were of 3000-gallon capacity, although the smaller 2500-gallon version was also used. In 1934, tender allocation was:

Diagram Nos	Built	Gallons	Wheelbase	Number
A24	1895	2000	5' 6" + 5' 6"	1
A40	1900-1901	2400	5' 6" + 5' 6"	2
A6/7/9/22/23/26/29/30/33/ 35/37/38/41-44/58	1884-1903	2500	6' 6" + 6' 6"	57
A28	1896	2600	6' 6" + 6' 6"	1
A5/10/11/12/14/15/17/18/ 20/21/31/ 32/36/45/ 47-50/52/54/57/61-64/71	1884-1906	3000	7' 6" + 7' 6"	151

The 2000 gallon tender was No 1122 coupled to locomotive No 2434; this type had been introduced in 1895 to work with Duke Class 4-4-0s in the West Country where short turntables were then still in use. The 2400-gallon tenders were Nos 1357 and 1362 coupled to locomotives Nos 2450 and 2576 respectively. The 2600-gallon tender No 1178 was a unique vehicle built in 1896 for use with Dean's 4-6-0 No 36; by 1934 it was coupled to locomotive No 2579. The oldest 3000 gallon tender in service was No 852, the prototype vehicle built for the Dean's 2-2-2 No 9 following its rebuild from 4-2-4T; by 1934 it was coupled to locomotive No 2423.

No 2404 at Reading in the mid-1930s.

RK Blencowe Collection

As larger locomotives increasingly infiltrated main line freight work, the Dean Goods became well established during the inter-war years in the Central Wales Division. No 2541 is on shed at Oswestry on 31st May 1932. *HC Casserley*

To conclude this account of the class on the modern GWR, it is appropriate to review reported activities from 1938, when significant numbers were still in service, through to the end of 1947. Apart from being broadly representative of their duties during the 1930s, 1938 was the Old Company's last complete year of normal operations before fundamental changes were wrought by the war.

At the beginning of that year, 181 examples were still in service. Following the convention of the GWR's accounting cycle, between the periods ended 8th January 1938 and 7th January 1939, no fewer than 129 re-allocations took place. The number of transfers to each shed was:

Aberdare	1	Exeter	2	Newport	1	Southall	4
Aberystwyth	1	Fishguard	2	Neyland	2	St Philips Marsh	5
Banbury	2	Gloucester	6	Old Oak Common	4	Stafford Road	8
Bath Road	1	Landore	2	Oswestry	17	Stourbridge	1
Cardiff, Canton	3	Leamington	1	Oxford	1	Taunton	2
Carmarthen	4	Llanelly	1	Oxley	7	Tyseley	3
Chester	1	Machynlleth	16	Pontypool Road	2	Westbury	2
Croes Newydd	4	Merthyr	2	Shrewsbury	2	Whitland	4
Danygraig	1	Neath	2	Slough	1	Worcester	7
Didcot	4						

Several involved locomotives that were re-allocated back and forth between two depots. An example concerned No 2465 which was transferred to Oswestry in the period ended 2/4/1938, to Machynlleth 28/5/1938, to Oswestry 10/12/1938 and back to Machynlleth 7/1/939. The pattern reflects a class much in demand within the perpetually changing composition of the motive power fleet.

It might have been expected of locomotives aged between 41 and 55 years that they should see out their years on minor and parochial duties close to their home sheds. However on 1st January 1938, No 2353 (Oswestry) was noted at Oxford on a local goods working while No 2472 (Taunton) was observed at the same location working a south-bound goods. A few days later, No 2313 (Oxford), by then the oldest still in service, was not far from home at Didcot shed. Later that month No 2541, and then in early February No 2349, worked the afternoon Cheltenham-Southampton passenger train, a service more usually entrusted to 2-6-0 Class 43xx. A month later, Nos 2395, 2423 and 2566 were seen on Didcot-Southampton services.

During March 1938, No 2418 was lent by Taunton to Exeter, a noteworthy move as this was the first allocation of an 0-6-0 that far west since the mid-1920s. In the early spring, virtually all services Aberystwyth-Portmadoc-Pwllheli were handled by Dean and ex-Cambrian 0-6-0s with only occasional appearances by "Dukes" and "Dukedogs". Further south, the Moat Lane-Brecon passenger services were exclusively worked by Dean Goods. New Class 2251

Above - As the final survivor in ordinary service, No 2538 was to be photographed many times in the 1950s so here is a view of this engine some 20 years earlier.

Below - No 2447 at Welshpool in August 1936.

This undated photograph is most likely from the 1930s; the locomotive which cannot be identified is of interest because it carries one of the few top feed type B4 boilers. *HMRS*

Below - No 2392 at Tyseley in 1933. Seven years later this engine was to gain distinction as being the oldest of the class sold to the War Department. As WD No 187, it was sent to France in March 1940 and later became SNCF No 0303WO16. After the war it was despatched to China. *CM & JM Bentley*

Above - The class was well represented at Worcester, as with No 2551 in 1932. *Coltas Trust*

Below - No 2481 also at Worcester in July 1932 standing between two vintage tank locomotives. 0-4-2T Class 3571 No 3573 at the rear and what appears to be an 0-4-2T Class 517 with modified bunker in front. *Coltas Trust*

No 2534 on standby for snowplough duty in Swindon Stock Shed.

0-6-0s were on most Aberystwyth-Carmarthen services while Cambrian 0-6-0s made occasional appearances on goods trains.

There was a major re-organisation of motive power on the Barnstaple and Minehead branches that summer, following installation of Automatic Staff Exchange apparatus. It had been the practice to lend locomotive**s** to Taunton to cope with seasonal traffic (in 1936, Nos 2439, 2441 and 2442 had been on loan). However during 1938, the permanent Taunton allocation was augmented by a number of locomotives fitted with the apparatus. These comprised Nos 2410, 2418, 2472, 2527, 2537 and 2578 plus three Class 2251 0-6-0s, three Bulldog 4-4-0s, nine Class 43xx 2-6-0s, eleven Class 4575 2-6-2Ts, and two Class 51xx 2-6-2Ts.

Duties for the Taunton engines were varied – No 2418 complete with shunter's "gig" substituted for a failed 0-6-0PT Class 57xx on goods shunting on 16th January 1939 while No 2537 was working Chard branch trains (tender first in one direction) on 11th February. On 28th May, No 2527 working tender first piloted 2-6-2T No 5501 on a 17 coach train from Minehead to Taunton. By mid-summer, Nos 2472 and 2527 were regularly sharing Taunton-Minehead duties

with a Bulldog. Heavier trains on summer Saturdays called for a Class 4575 2-6-2T to act as pilot. This type of formation was also noted several times on heavy evacuee trains at the start of the war. In contrast, the class was absent from the Barnstaple line except on summer Saturday relief workings.

Retention of some for purely stand-by duties was evidenced by snowplough-equipped Nos 2473 and 2534 standing in the Swindon Stock Shed in early January 1939. The latter coupled to two brake vans was seen at work in the Marlborough area on the 26th, and noted back in the stock shed by mid-February. Around this time, No 2490 was also snowplough-fitted and on stand-by at Machynlleth.

On 22nd July 1939, there was a foretaste of the fundamental changes in working patterns that were soon to come. An unidentified pair was seen working tender first between Taunton and Norton Fitzwarren, hauling a troop train of 12 coaches and five container trucks. The impact of transfers to the War Department was being felt at Oswestry by November 1939. A number of age-related withdrawals from this shed had occurred in the 1930s and with further departures on war service, four examples of Class 2251 were transferred in, including one with an ex-ROD tender.

Above - The oldest Dean Goods to work in France with the ROD was No 2303, seen here in 1934 having obviously received workshop attention.
PW Robinson

A favourite photographic location was Machynlleth depot and here is No 2450 in the late 1930s.
Lens of Sutton

No 2465 passing through Leamington Spa on a goods working in 1938.

Locomotives were still straying from their home turf. No 2462 had been overhauled at Wolverhampton in August 1939 and sent to Croes Newydd but was at Gloucester in October. That same month, No 2559 of Oswestry was seen at Winchester (Cheesehill). By the end of 1939, departures on war service were having a growing effect at some sheds with the arrival of 0-6-0s from other companies. However, Gloucester shed having lost Nos 2402, 2403 and 2450 which had been previously used for Kingham-Gloucester-Cheltenham-Honeybourne goods duties, mobilised Class 45xx/ 4575 2-6-2Ts in substitution. The small prairies had previously worked Cheltenham-Gloucester passenger services and in turn were replaced by Bulldog 4-4-0s.

Another Dean Goods (No 2422) departed Gloucester on war service in December 1939 leaving only Nos 2349, 2350, and 2517 in the district. Requisitions had a greater impact at Worcester where only Nos 2339 and 2458 remained at this one-time stronghold. The Taunton contingent had all left by late 1939, the last recorded working having been No 2578 on the Tiverton Junction goods on 17th November. Erstwhile duties were taken over by a variety of classes: Class 2251 on branch and shunting work; 0-4-2T No 4829 and 2-4-0T Metro Class No 3590 on carriage shunting. The Tiverton Junction goods was by then usually in the hands of Classes 2251 and 43xx, but even a Star

and a Castle were noted on this humble work. Apart from No 2418's brief excursion to Exeter, Taunton had long been the class's south-western outpost. However, as late as 1946, Bristol-Taunton goods trains regularly produced veterans such as Aberdares, Bulldogs, Dukes, Dukedogs, and quite often Dean Goods from St Philips Marsh.

For many years, transfer trips between Reading West marshalling yard and the Central Goods station had been the preserve of double-framed Dean 0-6-0 No 2369 but by Spring 1940, this work was covered by LMS 0-6-0s. The diminishing presence in the south was apparent in the disappearance of the class from the Weymouth area but they still appeared at odd locations elsewhere. On 10th April 1940, No 2513 was seen banking a train hauled by an LNER 0-6-0 up Old Hill incline between Stourbridge and Birmingham. Sightings were made around this time of several that had been requisitioned but lent back temporarily to the GWR.

Reports from this period are sparse but Nos 2340 and 2426 were noted at Swindon Works in September 1941 in company with some vintage pannier tanks, emphasising the importance attached to the availability of the whole fleet, regardless of age and size. Wolverhampton played an important role in servicing.

Swindon, 8th February 1939, with three withdrawals in line, from left to right: Ex-Barry Railway 0-6-2T Class No 63 as GWR No 254 (withdrawn January 1939), No 2313 (withdrawn December 1938), and Class 2361 No 2376 (withdrawn December 1938).

On 19th December 1941, the following were in the works: Nos 2452 (Oswestry), 2569 (Brecon), 2572 (Machynlleth) while Nos 2408 (Stafford Road), 2414 (Severn Tunnel Junction), 2458 (Worcester) were awaiting attention, indicating that those not called up were "doing their bit" for the war effort. No 2572 was even repainted before return to duty although the colour is not recorded. The habit of using ex-works engines on particular duties persisted with No 2578 (Newport) noted in late 1941 at Weymouth on the daily stores train from Swindon. This must have been one of the last visits of the class to that location.

There was still a propensity to roam with No 2452 (Oswestry) seen at Cardiff in January 1942. On 3rd March, No 2414 (believed to be a Worcester engine at the time) worked an Andover-Cheltenham passenger train. In March 1943, No 2322 (Stafford Road) was seen in the London area hauling a train of 40 wagons. The previous month, rather less strenuous work was given to 2573 (Reading) on the Lambourn branch and when not on that duty, it was used as a shunter at Newbury. Lambourn was something of a magnet when loadings were beyond the capacity of single diesel railcars; in the summer of 1944, Nos 2322 (Stafford Road on loan to Didcot) and 2532 (Didcot) were also seen there.

On 12th May 1943, No 2403 (Banbury) worked the morning passenger train from Bristol to Cardiff via the Severn Bridge. The heavy demands placed upon the railway system were evidenced by the size of passenger trains on the Cambrian coast route during the summer of 1944, typically loading to nine bogies. These services plus goods trains were worked by Class 45xx 2-6-2Ts, Collett 0-6-0s, Dukedog 4-4-0s, and some Dean Goods. On 18th July, No 2352 worked the afternoon Didcot-Southampton passenger service while on another occasion No 2568 (Swindon) was seen at Southampton. Nos 2532 (again) and 2350 were observed in the Southampton-Eastleigh area the next month.

At the other end of the operating scale, in 1944 the goods-only Shipston-on-Stour branch was open on Monday, Wednesday and Friday afternoons, worked by a Dean Goods from Worcester. The track was in poor condition with a line limit of 10 mph, except over two ageing timber bridges where speed was restricted to 5 mph. Traffic was quite heavy and with numerous level crossings operated by train staff, this was quite a tough duty.

By March 1942, locomotives deemed in need of repaint were turned out in plain black (except for

A post-war view of No 2386 at Moat Lane.   *Real Photographs*

No 2354 on post-war pick-up goods, cab awning erected and ex-private owner wagons in evidence.

4-cylinder 4-6-0s which were painted unlined green). Dean Goods known to have received the black treatment were Nos 2543 (Apr-42), 2411 (Jul-43), 2385 (Oct-43), 2323 (Nov-43), 2538 (Mar-44), 2343 (Apr-44), 2483 (Apr-46). However, in the company's closing days, Wolverhampton started to repaint engines in green with three pannier tanks so treated in December 1947 plus No 2431. At an earlier date, No 2532 had also been repainted green.

No 2356 (Machynlleth) was painted black after overhaul at Wolverhampton in the Autumn of 1944 when its top feed boiler was replaced with a standard B4 type. In December 1944, Wolverhampton might have re-cycled this boiler as No 2483 emerged from overhaul with top feed, believed to be the last with this feature. Despite age, it was evident that heavy repairs were considered justified in some cases, as with No 2543 which received new cylinders at Swindon in April 1944. With the exigencies of war receding, time was being called on some in rundown condition with 11 taken out of service that year. Dean Goods on Swindon "dump" were to be a continuing feature for the rest of the company's existence.

The class broke entirely new ground in early 1947 following track relaying on the Tanat Valley line. This rural route had been the last stronghold of ex-Cambrian Railways 2-4-0Ts Nos 1196 and 1197. At the other end of the spectrum, mainline duties still came the class's way as on 7th June 1947 when No 2349 (Hereford) worked a special train of Covcar wagons from Croes Newydd to Morris Cowley near Oxford.

Following the sale of 108 of the class for military service in 1940, withdrawals by the GWR were:

No	Date	No	Date	No	Date	No	Date	No	Date
2315	Nov-45	2348	Jul-45	2389	Jul-44	2525	Dec-45	2554	Nov-45
2320	Nov-44	2360	Feb-45	2395	Nov-45	2530	Oct-45	2564	Sep-45
2325	Nov-45	2381	Nov-45	2406	Nov-45	2535	Jun-46	2575	Feb-47
2345	May-47	2383	Aug-46	2424	Jul-46				

– which left 54 in service as at 31st December 1947 to be acquired by British Railways.

Chapter 7

OLD SOLDIERS

The official photograph of No 2533, WD No 101, the first Dean Goods to be lent to the War Department. ATC equipment and tender pick-up gear have been removed and WD number and insignia affixed. This was one of those sent to France without Westinghouse Brakes, which equipment was to be installed later by the Royal Engineers

At the outbreak of war in September 1939, it was expected that hostilities would repeat the static pattern warfare that had typified the years 1914-18. Based on the experiences of the earlier conflict, the War Department moved quickly to secure locomotives suitable to help supply a large army in the field. The superiority of the 2-8-0 tender goods locomotive had been recognised in World War I, and there was an early decision to rely once again on this type. However, the importance of simplicity and easy access to mechanical parts was also recognised, fostering a design evolution that culminated in Britain's last heavy freight type, the Class 9F 2-10-0 of 1954.

Acquisition and development of military motive power became the responsibility of R.A. Riddles who was appointed Director of Transportation Equipment, a new branch of the Ministry of Supply. Gresley of the LNER quickly offered Riddles a number of his Class O2 2-8-0s for immediate service overseas, subject to their being replaced by a like number of the same type to be built by the Government. This offer was rejected, as the O2 with its conjugated valve gear and three cylinders was considered too complex.

Instead, Riddles opted for the simpler LNER Class O4 (previously GCR Class 8K) and 300 were requisitioned for service with the British Expeditionary Force that was embarking for France. Overhaul of 36 locomotives had been completed by late November 1939 when this order was rescinded, although in 1941 a considerable number were to be requisitioned for service in the Middle East.

In due course, Class 8F 2-8-0s from the LMS were taken into military service and more built specifically for the War Department. Stanier had been responsible for this design and seemed to regard it as a logical modernisation of Churchward's Class 28XX of 1903; eventually a total of 852 were built. In 1943, through re-design and use of faster construction techniques, an austerity version known as the WD 2-8-0 was introduced. Markedly different in appearance, the WD 2-8-0 eventually totalled 835 examples and in the same year, a 2-10-0 version was introduced of which 150 were constructed.

Opposite page - The first 2-8-0 type to come under WD control was the Stanier LMS class 8F, and the history of these locomotives on military service was complex. Nos 508 and 512 were part of a batch of 143 built by Beyer Peacock and North British that were deployed in the Middle East from 1942 onwards. This pair was part of a shipment of five (engines only) recovered from the Egyptian State Railways in 1953; five tenders followed from the ESR two years later. The two engines are depicted in store at Longmoor in 1955, awaiting arrival of their tenders. They were built as oil burners and both acquired top feed stop valves while in the Middle East; they are carrying numbers in the post-war WD series. After overhaul they were little used by the WD; No 512 was converted to coal burning and sold to British Railways in 1957 (their No 48775) while No 508 saw out its time on the Cairnryan Military Railway.

RK Blencowe Negative Archive

Opposite, above - Stanier 8F WD No 70320 *Lt. W.O. Lennox VC, Royal Engineers* while serving with 10 Railway Squadron in Egypt. The engine is an oil burner and in a condition that reflects well the pride and enthusiasm of its owners. In 1952 it returned to the UK in poor condition and was overhauled by British Railways in 1954 for further WD service. It was bought by BR as their No 48774 in 1957.

Opposite, lower - WD 2-8-0 No 77030 (later BR No 90127) is seen in uncharacteristically clean condition in 1948 at what is believed to be Eastleigh. This design was developed from the Stanier 8F as being cheaper and faster to construct.   *W Gilburt*

Below - WD 2-10-0 No 73782 (later BR No 90758) stored in rundown condition. This design was similar to the WD 2-8-0 but more versatile in having a wider firebox and a lower axle loading. Reports state that this particular engine was one of 21 that stayed in the UK, six being stored and 21 lent to the home railways, mainly the LNER. It was at Longmoor from September 1946, later overhauled by the Southern Railway, and briefly used then in the Portsmouth area. It was one of a group of 25 lent for service in Scotland and purchased by BR as part of a block transaction in December 1948. However, the insignia on the cabside and tender are mysterious as they are both in positions favoured for engines serving in continental Europe. That on the cab seems to be a dark (red?) cross on a white shield while the tender insignia is different and might be that of the 21st Army Group (crossed swords superimposed on blue cross on red shield), although the image is indistinct. An exchange of tenders might have occurred but the uncertainty illustrates the risks of making definitive statements about the identity and deployment of locomotives on military service.   *W Gilburt*

This building programme anticipated increased demand for competent motive power. Except for the aborted plan to send Class O4s to France and for the later shipment of this type to the Middle East, the WD motive power programme largely reflected the latest in goods locomotive practice. Nevertheless, a type was also selected that was well into middle age when the GCR Class 8K (later LNER O4) appeared in 1911 and which preceded the introduction of Stanier 8F by no less than 52 years.

In 1917, sixty-two of the Dean Goods had been taken into military service on loan. Of this contingent, the age range was then between 18 and 34 years. In 1939-40,

the 108 engines that were lent by the GWR were between 41 and 50 years old. There can be few cases in military history where equipment of such antiquity has been used in the prosecution of contemporary warfare.

There were sound reasons for choosing the Dean Goods. The class was a "known quantity" that had done well 20 years earlier in France, Greece and Turkey. Further, it was a versatile machine that could operate over lightly or poorly laid trackwork, with the advantage of a low axle loading. With 180 examples still in traffic or recently stored, it was an obvious choice to be called up again for service.

WILLIAM DEAN

Later members of the class were favoured. Nine that had been withdrawn during 1939 were re-instated in anticipation of a growth in traffic, and five of these were pressed into military service. All of the class remaining in 1939 had been superheated and most were ATC equipped i.e. thoroughly modernised. The initial requisition was for 100 locomotives (ROD Nos 101 to 200) and in late 1940, a further eight locomotives (ROD Nos 93 to 100) were called up. Twenty-nine had served overseas with the Railway Operating Division in World War I.

Transfers of the 100 locomotives on loan to the Government started in the autumn of 1939 – nine were noted at Swindon as early as September, painted

black with yellow WD numbers in substitution for the brass number plates. This programme was completed in early 1940. The transfer of the further eight locomotives is thought to have commenced later that year.

Consequent upon the fall of France, by which time 79 of the class were in that country, the possibility of recovery in the foreseeable future was remote and the loan of 100 locomotives was converted into a sale to the government in October 1940. The remaining eight were recorded as being transferred on loan to WD service around October 1940 and then sold the following December. The numbers of the locomotives that legally became government property were:

GWR No.	WD No.	GWR No.	WD No.	GWR No.	WD No.	GWR No.	WD No.	GWR No.	WD No.
2392	187	2432	134	2465	162	2512	107	2548	168
2393	113	2433	93	2466	179	2514 §	180	2549 §	165
2399	94	2434	164	2467	158	2517 §	199	2550	153
2400	126	2435	188	2469 §	161	2518 §	104	2552	200
2402	181	2436	108	2470 §	95	2519 §	144	2553	130
2403 §	182	2437	191	2471	121	2520 §	140	2555	149
2404	190	2438	160	2472	189	2521	100	2557 §	151
2405	152	2439 ¥	102	2473 §	192	2522 §	146	2558	176
2410	183	2440	185	2475	157	2524 ⊖	112	2559	198
2412	122	2441	120	2476 §	163	2526	132	2560	129
2413	137	2442	97	2477	143	2527	150	2561	110
2415 §	98	2443	141	2478	172	2528 §	99	2562	124
2416	135	2446 §	178	2479	169	2529	156	2565	109
2418	119	2447 ±	128	2480 § µ	111	2531 §	195	2566 §	147
2419 #	106	2451	174	2481	125	2533 §	101	2567	116
2422	193	2454 §	133	2485	173	2536	170	2571	139
2423	145	2455 ¶	127	2486	103	2539	105	2574	166
2425	96	2456	114	2487	159	2540	197	2576	196
2427	117	2457 §	148	2488 §	194	2544	123	2577 §	136
2428	155	2459	154	2489 §	142	2545	171	2580 §	186
2429	131	2461 §	184	2490	118	2546	138		
2430 §	177	2463 §	167	2511	175	2547	115		

§ Served overseas during World War 1   ¶ Withdrawn Aug-39; re-instated Nov-39   ± Withdrawn May-39; reinstated Nov-39

\# Withdrawn May-39; reinstated Oct-39   µ Withdrawn May-39; re-instated Nov-39

¥ Withdrawn Apr-39; re-instated Oct-39   ⊖ Withdrawn Aug-39; re-instated Oct-39

An official photograph of No 156 (GWR No 2529) fully tooled up and ready for action with Westinghouse equipment in place. This engine was the only one of the number series WD101-166 not to be sent to France being retained at Longmoor for training purposes. It never served overseas but was later embellished with the name *Flying Fortress* (after the American bomber aircraft) and at another period *Alexander* (British General). *British Rail*

The WD number, followed where appropriate by the old GWR number, is used in the rest of this chapter.

On leaving the GWR, the 100 locomotives of the first loan were reconditioned and modified. This work included: removal of the ATC gear; substitution of a direct acting steam brake for the original valve working from the vacuum ejector; removal of tender water pick-up gear; and the fitting of continental-style side coupling chains on the buffer beams. Nos 183/119/189/150 (GWR Nos 2410/2418/2472/2527 respectively) had been Taunton engines and would have lost the staff exchange appartus fitted in 1938.

The position with installation of Westinghouse brakes is less clear. Photographs of locomotives from the early batches reconditioned at Swindon and Eastleigh show no sign of this equipment. It is understood that around 20 of the first engines sent overseas were not fitted until after arrival in France, and all may not have been so treated there. This would have restricted their sphere of activities. Also, there does not seem to have been consistency in the type of equipment used as some had the single air reservoir type and others the triple reservoir type usually found on continental engines. The pump was mounted on the smokebox, most usually the right-hand side although there were exceptions. Curiously, the photograph of No 156 shows triple reservoir equipment with pump mounted on the right hand side.

Ten were fitted with pannier tanks, and with condensing gear for exhausting steam back into the tanks in rather similar fashion to that applied to No 2578 in 1917:

WD No.	GWR No.	WD No.	GWR No.	WD No.	GWR No.
177	2430	195	2531	198	2559
178	2446	196	2576	199	2517
179	2466	197	2540	200	2552
180	2514				

WILLIAM DEAN

The purpose was to extend the operating range where water supplies might be limited, and to reduce the need to open the fire doors in locations where the firebox glow might reveal the locomotive's position. In the event, all remained in the UK during the war and this equipment was not used. Some lost their pannier tanks and condensing equipment towards the end of the war; certainly Nos 177 to 179/198 would have been so treated before despatch to China in 1946/7.

Swindon prepared 94 while the following 14 were processed at Eastleigh:

WD No.	GWR No.	WD No.	GWR No.	WD No.	GWR No.
181	2402	186	2580	191	2437
182	2403	187	2392	192	2473
183	2410	188	2435	193	2422
184	2461	189	2472	194	2488
185	2440	190	2404		

The eight locomotives (WD Nos 93-100) taken over in October 1940 were little, if at all, modified beyond affixing WD numbers and insignia. There is no photographic evidence of their being fitted with Westinghouse brake equipment. Only No 100 (GWR No 2521) went overseas, being one of six shipped to North Africa in 1943 and later sent to Italy. Presumably it received this equipment before departure. The only later modification for UK service was the fitting of an extended cab roof – at least No 94 (No 2399) was so treated.

Sundry modifications were made subsequently by different owners/operators, the most distinctive being cab improvements. This feature prominently betrayed the Class's late 19th Century origins and its Spartan

Top - A single example (No 2578) had been fitted with pannier tanks and condensing equipment for service in France in World War 1 and the concept was revived with WD Nos 177-180/ 195-200. No 198 (renumbered as 70198 and originally GWR No 2559) at Longmoor in November 1945 shows the Westinghouse brake mounted on the right-hand side of the smokebox in front of the pannier tanks. It is believed that the condensing equipment was never needed and that some engines lost this gear and the pannier tanks before the end of the war. No 70198 was one of the UK-based locomotives added to the group from France and sent to China. Before despatch to the Far East, the panniers and condensing equipment were removed.   *R Tourret*

Above - The other side of the pannier tank version is shown in this view of No 179 (GWR No 2466) at Canterbury East in September 1940. There is little room for the two Westinghouse reservoirs in front of the tank, which stands proud of the cabside, and which must have significantly impeded the fireman's forward view. The cab awning is fully extended, presumably as a black out precaution.   *AG Wells*

Left - Preparation of the eight engines in number series WD 93-100 was minimal. No 70099 (GWR 2528) at Kinnerley on the Shropshire and Montgomeryshire Railway in February 1946 appears to be in unchanged Great Western condition, except for the stencilled number on the cabside and removal of ATC gear.   *R Tourret*

WD No 167 (GWR No 2463) at Algiers (Agha) shed in 1943. The Westinghouse brake pump has been removed but the mounting brackets remain in place. The name *Margaret* can just be discerned in white on the centre splasher. The engine is standing in front of the shed's briquette store – a form of fuel compacted out of poor quality coal or slack and held together by a combustible bonding agent. This was usually the best quality fuel available under war conditions. Often crews had to cope with materials that were very much worse. *R Tourret Collection*

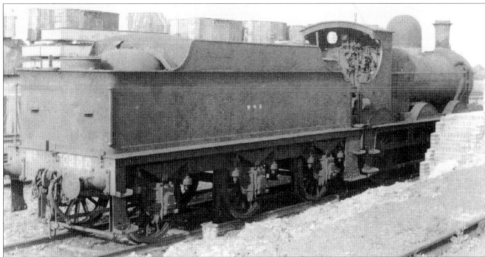

WD No 70200 (GWR No 2552) was another example that had lost its Westinghouse brake pump but not the mounting brackets. Standing at Stonor in June 1946, there is a light colouring to the centre splasher that might be the name *City of Birmingham* that was bestowed upon this engine while in military service. *AG Wells*

level of protection would have been unacceptable in climatically inhospitable regions. Changes generally involved roof extensions and extra side sheeting, often made of timber, with glazed/sliding windows.

The WD livery was initially plain dull black; GWR number plates were removed from the initial contingent and the WD numbers painted in dull yellow or white figures on the cabside. In the case of the additional eight engines, although allocated WD Nos 93-100, these were apparently not affixed until 1942. In the interim they must have carried their GWR numbers and their original livery – at least one still had its GWR buffer beam number post-war. Later, the official livery was changed to a shade of khaki and in some cases, a form of dark camouflage green. Those sent to North Africa acquired light brown "desert" livery. Lettering on the tender was "W ↑ D". It seems unlikely that there was ever a standard livery and with minimal external maintenance, accumulated dirt and grime made the issue rather academic.

In 1944, those under British control were renumbered by the addition of 70000 in the WD system. Also, a few acquired names that were changed in some cases; more may have been so adorned than have been recorded:

WD No.	GWR No.	Name
94	2399	*Monty*
100	2521	*Virginia*
103	2486	*Troy*
108	2436	*Casablanca*
156	2529	*Flying Fortress* later *Alexander*
167	2463	*Rosemary* alternatively *Margaret*
168	2548	*Margaret* alternatively *Rosemary*
169	2470	*Gert*
171	2545	*Betty* later *Francis*, alternatively *Volara*
172	2478	*Wavell* later *Margaret*
173	2485	*Alexander*
174	2451	*Jean Barbara* later *Wavell*, alternatively *Jean Ann*
178	2446	*Fagan*
197	2540	*Daisy*
200	2552	*City of Birmingham*

WILLIAM DEAN

Nos 169/171/172/197 were first named while serving in Kent. A source states Nos 100/167/168/171/172/174 received their names in North Africa. Usually, the names appeared on the centre splasher face in white paint but *Flying Fortress* (156) and *Alexander* (173) carried theirs in an arc on the upper part of the smokebox door. The named members of the African contingent apparently reverted to numbers only when receiving their first workshops attention.

Further adornment was applied to two while stationed at Canterbury, Kent in 1941. Already in sparkling condition, they had their coupling rods painted scarlet and all paint scraped off any part that had originally been brass, which was then vigorously polished. It was hardly surprising that glistening Great Western brass domes were soon judged to be unmilitary and all decoration was covered up with dull camouflage paint. The story of the 108 War Department locomotives is complex and records are incomplete. The individual

histories, where known, are categorised by geographic regions.

Northern & Eastern Europe

Locomotives were shipped to France in ten batches:

WD Nos	Month	WD Nos	Month
101-105	Oct-39	136-141/ 185-189	Feb-40
106-108	Oct-39	142-148/ 190-194	Mar-40
109-118/ 181-184	Nov-39	149-154/ 157/ 158	Mar-40
119-126	Jan-40	155/ 159-161	Mar-40
127-135	Feb-40	162-166	May-40

WD No 128 (GWR No 2447) at Bethune in June 1946 displaying evidence of rugged use. As this engine was allocated to the Nord system during the occupation of France, it retained its WD identity throughout the war. It was recovered in 1948 but not surprisingly its condition was such that it was judged too decrepit to move over British rails. On its return home, it travelled no further than Dover.

RJ Tredwell

WD No 188 (GWR No 2435) was captured by the enemy during the retreat to Dunkirk and retained by the Germans rather than left with the French railway operators during the Occupation. This view was taken at Wien Huttledorf shed (Austria) in 1948 while under Russian control. Despite having passed through several hands, this engine remains unmistakably Great Western, as modified for WD use, except with regard to the cab. The original front seems to have been retained but the sides have built up to provide better protection and an extended roof has been fitted. Perhaps foreign enginemen were not as tough as the GWR variety, or perhaps the Dean Goods under foreign "ownership" was used in locations where the weather was harsher than in the Welsh Marches. The wording just below the cabside window states "German Armed Forces OKH"   *F Kraus*

Above - At D-Day and in the weeks following, only a small proportion of the French railway network was still operating due to the heroic efforts of the French resistance movement in sabotaging track and equipment. Also locomotives and trains were prime targets for attack from the air in daylight. WD No 123 (GWR No 2544) is seen here at Bethune in June 1946, having been damaged by RAF cannon fire. This engine returned to the UK in 1948 and although its scrapping details are unknown, it seems unlikely that it moved beyond Dover.   *RJ Tredwell*

Below - WD No 188 from the other side, this time on Breitenlee dump in 1951. The British authorities had no interest in recovering this engine so the Soviet forces sent it to the blast furnaces at Enzesfeld an der Triesting, south west of Wien for disposal.
                                                                                                              Othmar Bamer

WILLIAM DEAN

They were used in Brittany, Picardy and Flanders as shunters, on ballast trains, and also in hauling materials to the sites of RAF airfields under construction. Records following the fall of France are sparse but 21 were taken over by the SNCF Nord Division, retaining their existing WD numbers. Thirty-five were acquired by the Ouest Division and renumbered in the series 030W001-020/028-041/045. The class was popular with French crews who described them as "small but very strong", predictably nicknaming them "Churchills". With the liberation of France, those still in operable condition changed sides for the second time and were employed by the Allies.

Of the remaining 23, the post-1940 existence of 14 can be confirmed but there is no definite record of the remaining nine. Because of the run-down and damaged condition to which some were reduced, identification with certainty is questionable. Some engines might have been cannibalised and it is known that tenders were sometimes exchanged. Those that returned had their numbers increased on paper by 70000 but it is unlikely that any were physically renumbered.

Information traced:

WD No.	SNCF No.	Locations/ sightings	Final disposal
101	030W028	Chateaubriant 1947 §	To UK Mar-49; scrapped at Cox & Danks, Park Royal Apr-49
102	030W029	Batignolles (Paris) 1944	Shipped to China 1946
103	030W030	Batignolles (Paris) 1944 §	Shipped to China 1946
104	030W031	Auray 1947	To UK May-49; scrapped at G Cohen, Canning Town Jul-49
105	030W032	Auray 1948 §	To UK May-49; G Cohen, Canning Town May-49;
106	n/a	Bruges 1940; Poland 1941	No information
107	n/a	German Democratic Republic post 1945	No information
108	030W033	La Folie 1944 §; Versailles-Matelots 1947 §	To UK 1948; scrapped at Dover Mar-49
109	030W034	Auray 1947 §; Landerneau, Brest 1948 §	To UK 1949; scrapped at TW Ward, Grays, Essex Apr-49
110	030W045	Savenay 1947	To UK 1949; G Cohen, Canning Town Apr-49;
111	n/a	Minden 1945	To UK May or Jun-49; scrapped at Dover Jun-49
112	030W035	Landerneau, Brest 1946-8 §	Scrapped in France, date unknown
113	030W036	Savenay 1946	Shipped to China 1946
114	030W001	Landerneau, Brest 1947-8 §	To UK 1949; British Iron & Steel Corp
115(a)	(Nord)	Lille 1945; Lezennes Works 1946; Lille 1947	To UK Sep-48; still extant at G. Cohen Canning Town Apr-49
116(b)	030W037**	Rennes 1947 §	To UK Jan-49; scrapped at G Cohen, Canning Town Mar-49
117	n/a		No information
118	n/a		No information
119	(Nord)	No information	Shipped to China 1947
120	(Nord)	Lille Fives 1945-47	Shipped to China 1947
121	(Nord)		Shipped to China 1947
122	(Nord)	Douai 1944; Mons 1944	Scrapped in Belgium, date unknown
123(c)	(Nord)	Bethune 1946 §	To UK Sep-48; scrapped at Dover, date unknown
124	(Nord)	Lille Fives 1945-47	Shipped to China 1947
125(d)	(Nord)	Lille Fives 1945-47	Shipped to China 1947
126(c)	(Nord)	Lille Fives 1947	To UK Sep-48; scrapped at Dover, date unknown
127	030W002	Chateaubriant 1947 §	To UK May-49; TW Ward, Grays, Essex May-49
128±	(Nord)	Bethune 1944-46 §	To UK Sep-48; scrapped at Dover Nov-48
129	(Nord)		Shipped to China 1947
130¥	(Nord)	Lille Fives 1947	To UK Sep-48; scrapped at Dover Feb-49
131	(Nord)		To UK Sep-48; scrapped at Dover Nov-48
132	n/a	Hassfurt 1945	No. "OKH-TN10" (Polish); believed to have ended in Russia
133	n/a		No information
134	030W003		Shipped to China 1946
135	n/a	Antwerp 1946	To UK May or Jun-49; scrapped at Dover Jun-49
136	030W004	Brest 1947 §; La Rody, Brest 1948-49 §	To UK Apr-49; TW Ward, Grays, Essex May-49
137	030W038	Dol 1947 §	To UK Mar-49; scrapped at TW Ward, Grays, Essex Apr-49
138	030W020	Savenay 1947	Believed scrapped in France

WD No.	SNCF No.	Locations/ sightings	Final disposal
134	030W003		Shipped to China 1946
135	n/a	Antwerp 1946	To UK May or Jun-49; scrapped at Dover Jun-49
136	030W004	Brest 1947 §; La Rody, Brest 1948-49 §	To UK Apr-49; TW Ward, Grays, Essex May-49
137	030W038	Dol 1947 §	To UK Mar-49; scrapped at TW Ward, Grays, Essex Apr-49
138	030W020	Savenay 1947	Believed scrapped in France
139	030W005		Shipped to China 1946
140	030W006	Brest 1947 §; La Rody, Brest 1948 §	To UK 1948; scrapped at Dover Feb-49
141	n/a		No information
142	n/a	German Democratic Republic post 1945	No information
143	030W007		Shipped to China 1946
144	030W008	Rennes 1947-49 §	Scrapped in France, date unknown
145	n/a		No information
146	n/a		No information
147	030W009		Shipped to China 1946
148	n/a	Czechoslovakia 1945	No information
149	n/a	Roosendaal 1948 §; Tilburg 1949 §	Scrapped 1949 at Tilburg
150	030W010	Brest 1947 §	Scrapped in France, date unknown
151	030W011		Shipped to China 1946
152	030W012	Auray 1947 §	To UK Apr-49?; G Cohen, Canning Town May-49
153	(Nord)		Shipped to China 1947
154	(Nord)	Valenciennes 1947 §	Shipped to China 1947
155	n/a	Unconfirmed report seen in Germany	No information
157	n/a	Minden 1945	To UK May or Jun-49; scrapped at Dover Jun-49
158(e)	(Nord)	Lille Sud 1944; Lille Fives 1945	Shipped to China 1947
159	030W013		Shipped to China 1946
160	n/a	Minsk, USSR – date unrecorded	No information
161	(Nord)		Shipped to China 1947
162	030W014		Shipped to China 1946
163	(Nord)	Lille Fives 1947-48	To UK 1948; scrapped at Dover Feb-49
164(f)	(Nord)	Lille 1945-47	To UK Sep-48; scrapped at Dover Dec-48
165	n/a		No information
166	(Nord)		Scrapped in France, date unknown
181	030W015		Shipped to China 1946
182	(Nord)	Lille 1944; Mons 1944	Scrapped in Belgium, date unknown
183	030W039	Landerneau 1947-48 §; Brest 1947	To UK 1949; G Cohen, Canning Town Apr-49
184	030W040	La Rody 1947-49 §; Brest 1948	To UK Apr-49; scrapped at G Cohen, Canning Town May-49
185	n/a	German Democratic Republic post 1945	No information
186	n/a		No information
187	030W016	Batignolles (Paris) 1945; Angers 1946	Shipped to China 1946
188(g)	n/a	Cottbus, Austria 1944; Vienna Nord 1949§	Scrapped in Austria, date unknown
189	030W017	Brest 1947; La Rody 1948 §	To UK 1948; scrapped at Dover Mar-49
190	030W018	Dol 1947 §	To UK Jun-48; scrapped at Cox & Danks, Park Royal Feb-49
191	n/a	Minden 1945	To UK May or Jun-49; scrapped at Dover Jun-49
192	030W019	Quimper 1947-48	To UK Jan-49; scrapped at Cox & Danks, Park Royal Feb-49
193	030W041	Rennes 1947 §	Scrapped in France, date unknown
194	n/a		No information

§ Denotes seen stored or in derelict condition
(a) No 115 was seen at Lille Jun-45 with tender from No 120
(b) No 116 (SNCF No 030W037) was seen after the war with tender numbered 030W0004
(c) Nos 123 and 126 were damaged by RAF cannon fire during an air attack on Bethune in Apr-44
(d) No 125 coupled to tender No 120 was seen at Lille Jul-47, both painted SNCF green
(e) No 158 was repaired Oct-44 by British Railway Mobile Workshop Coy, Royal Engineers; seen at Lille Oct-45 with tender from No 125
(f) No 164 seen at Lille Jun-45 with tender from WD No 120
(g) No 188 was used by the Germans in France and then transferred to Cottbus in Silesia. It was stored at Breitenlee marshalling yards (Austria) 1945 -1948, ownership being claimed by the Russians who affixed the letters "C C C P" to the tender; later restored to service. In 1952, it was returned to Austrian authorities and offered for sale before being scrapped. Like others marooned in Eastern Europe, this engine was still British government property but there was no interest in recovery in view of its distant location.

Thus, fourteen of the abandoned 79 locomotives did not come under French control but were sighted after 1940. They were apparently operated directly by the German authorities, specifically:

WD No.	GWR No.	WD No.	GWR No.	WD No.	GWR No.
106	2419	142	2489	160	2438
107	2512	148	2457	185	2440
111	2480	149	2555	188	2435
132	2526	155	2428	191	2437
135	2416	157	2475		

There seems to be no indication of the fate of nine engines after May 1940:

WD No.	GWR No.	WD No.	GWR No.
117	2427	146	2522
118	2490	165	2549
133	2454	186	2580
141	2443	194	2488
145	2423		

This suggests that they were either permanently disabled or destroyed by retreating British forces and/or captured by German forces and destroyed in later actions. Beyond these broad suppositions, no specific conclusions can be drawn.

Post-war return might seem unwarranted in view of their general condition but they remained UK government property and demand for scrap metal was high. Commercial breakers handled the final disposal with some too decrepit to move beyond Dover.

These were not the only small steam locomotives left in France. Fourteen of LMS Class 3F 0-6-0T ("Jinties") were transferred to the War Department in March 1940, and eight had been sent to France for shunting duties at the channel ports:

LMS No.	WD No.	
7613	8	Believed destroyed by British forces
7611	9	Allocated SNCF No 030TW042
7607	10	Allocated SNCF No 030TW043
7660	11	Allocated SNCF No 030TW044
7659	12	Allocated SNCF No 030TW026
7663	13	Believed destroyed by British forces
7589	14	Allocated SNCF No 030TW027
7617	15	Believed destroyed by British forces

WD No 157 (GWR No 2475) at Dover in June 1949. This was another example that was retained in German use; the only record of its activities concerns its sighting at Minden in 1945. From this angle it is possible to see how the cab was modified. The line of the original swept "cut away" can just be discerned through the grime and small plates appear to have been butt-welded to support the side-window frames and the extended roof. The engine looks virtually complete but being too sick to be moved, it was broken up at Dover in the month this photograph was taken.
AG Wells

Above - WD No120 (GWR No 2441) was allocated to Lille from 1945 until 1947. In this view taken at Lezannes carriage works, three miles south east of Lille, it looks in good condition. The cab roof has been extended, and the engine has been repainted in SNCF green with white driving wheel rims. In company with rolling stock of matching vintage, carrying an ornate headlamp on the buffer beam and equipped with the Westinghouse plumbing, No 120 has a slight continental air about it.

Below - SNCF (Est) No 030 O02, previously WD No 127, previously GWR No 2455 was one of those brought home from France that was fit enough to move beyond Dover. In more or less complete condition, it is standing behind a GWR tender in the yard of Breakers TW Ward, Grays, Essex in the summer of 1949. The Westinghouse brake pump has disappeared, possibly because it was much younger than the engine and someone wanted it for further use.   *T Jones*

Destruction was reportedly achieved by driving them off the docks at the channel ports with the secondary objective of their becoming a hazard to shipping. Remarkably, the remaining five survived the war and were returned to the UK between October and December 1948. After attention at Derby, they took up service with British Railways and were finally withdrawn between 1961 and 1966. WD No 14 (7589) lost its most attractive feature while at Derby – a Dean Goods chimney that it had acquired in France.

United Kingdom

After the fall of France, 29 locomotives remained in WD service in the United Kingdom. These comprised 21 of the original requisition plus the eight sold to the government in December 1940:

WD No.	GWR No.	WD No.	GWR No.	WD No.	GWR No.	WD No.	GWR No.	WD No.	GWR No.
93	2433	99	2528	170	2536	176	2558	196	2576
94	2388	100	2521	171	2545	177	2430	197	2540
95	2470	156	2529	172	2478	178	2446	198	2559
96	2425	167	2463	173	2485	179	2466	199	2517
97	2442	168	2548	174	2451	180	2514	200	2552
98	2415	169	2479	175	2511	195	2531		

With minimal immediate military need for all these engines, Nos 167 to 176 were lent back to the GWR in May 1940 while Nos 156/177/178/196/197/199 were also seen working on traditional duties later in the summer. No 156 had arrived at Longmoor by April 1940 but was noted at Swindon in July. This led to confusion among observers over their precise status as they were mainly painted black with WD running number and insignia on the tender, but with the original GWR number painted on the cab sides. By September, all had returned to military use forsaking ordinary GWR service for good.

The situation was also confused with Nos 93-100. Some reports state that they were lent by the GWR in October 1940 with an implication that this transaction actually occurred earlier. Others indicate that the loan transaction was more or less concurrent with legal sale in December 1940. As they retained GWR livery, remained in original condition, and did not receive their WD numbers for another two years, there was certainly scope for muddle.

To help face the invasion threat, several rail-mounted heavy artillery guns of World War I vintage were brought out of store and deployed in the southeast. The barrels could be elevated within the carriage frames but only minimal lateral movement was possible in traversing the barrel left or right of the centre line of the carrying vehicle. Greater adjustment in line was achieved by moving the whole assemblage along a curved length of track specially laid and

Opposite page - One of those that served on the home front was GWR No 2399, by now WD 70094. It is seen hauling a troop train comprising eight ageing coaches at Port Meadow near Oxford on a service from Piddington (Bicester Military Railway) to Oxford (Rewley Road). The engine, which carries express passenger headlamps and BMR Target No 1 at the base of the chimney, was crewed by sappers who had the necessary route knowledge, and who were trained in civilian and military railway operating rules. The GWR Bicester-Worcester line is to the left. Apparently it was normal for engines stationed on the BMR to be sent to Oxford GWR depot for boiler washouts. The class was very popular on the BMR for their steaming and haulage capacities, and for their operational reliability over hastily laid lines with poor quality ballast.   *RHG Simpson*

Below - WD 70094 again, this time in a yard on the SMR with the name *Monty* clearly visible on the centre splasher face and with two WD 0-6-0STs in the background. This engine was another of the eight that were passed to the War Department in October 1940. As seen here, No 70094 was coupled to a small 2000 gallon Dean tender which would have been unacceptable overseas in areas where water supply was uncertain. This engine has acquired another variety of cab with sides unchanged but with an extended roof, supported by pillars at the rear. This addition is believed to have been installed while this engine was at Cairnryan in Scotland. This feature would also have been useful as an air raid precautionary measure for black out purposes during the period 1942-44 when it was at Bicester Ordnance Depot.

suitably calibrated. Thus, there had to be an attendant locomotive in steam to position the gun carriage as required.

These duties were covered by Dean Goods at most locations except the Martin Mill Military Railway near Dover where Nos 180 and 197 were unsuccessful because of their inability to cope with a gun on this railway's 1 in 50 incline. Diesel shunter locomotives from the LMS, and later the Southern Railway, were substituted.

The class proved satisfactory with all other rail-mounted guns. They were deployed on these duties at a number of locations in Kent and Sussex, plus East Anglia and Lincolnshire. In the summer of 1940, Nos 169 to 172/179/180/195 to 197 were in Kent, Nos 173 to 176 in Essex and Nos 198/199 in Lincolnshire. By the end of the year they had been joined by Nos 94/95/100 (Kent) and 93/96 to 99 (Essex). There were several re-locations and No 156 came from Longmoor to participate. Only Nos 96/97 are thought never to have been posted to Kent. Apart from artillery duties,

they sometimes undertook shunting work.

Nos 195 to 197 (GWR Nos 2531/2576/2540) were deployed on the Kent & East Sussex Railway between 1941 and 1943, attending railway guns stationed at Rolvenden and Wittersham. The use of the heavier condensing pannier tank version might have been questionable but the light trackwork is likely to have suffered more from the weight of the guns. Railway artillery was also stationed on the East Kent Light Railway and both condensing and ordinary Dean Goods were used there – identities are unconfirmed.

By mid-1942 Nos 100/167 to 172/174 and possibly others had reverted to vacuum brakes for use on a broader range of duties. No 171 was machine-gunned from the air in October 1942 while hauling empty stock on the Elham Valley line; the fireman was killed and the engine damaged. The next month, No 167's tender was damaged by enemy fire at Elham, and in December No 168 was machine-gunned from the air while on the East Kent Railway.

WILLIAM DEAN

In November 1940, construction was approved for two deep-water military ports on the west coast of Scotland at Faslane and Cairnryan. Priority was given to the former as it could accommodate ships with draughts up to 33 feet and work on Cairnryan did not commence until mid-1942. Located in a remote area, this port placed a great strain on the rail routes to nearby Stranraer and extensive works were necessary to create sidings and other facilities. The first locomotives drafted in to help were Dean Goods Nos 93 to 95/170/171/177/199. No 171 left the area and was shipped from Faslane to North Africa in early 1943.

In August 1941, the War Department took over the defunct Shropshire & Montgomeryshire Railway. This system ran from Llanymynech (on the GWR Welshpool-Oswestry route) eastwards to Shrewsbury with a branch from Kinnerley to Llandrino/ Criggion. Approximately 23 square miles of land were requisitioned for ammunition storage and the SMR was substantially up-graded. Track was re-laid with 75 lb/ yard rail; marshalling yards constructed; the route was re-signalled; several new halts were installed; an engine shed was built at Kinnerley.

Under WD control, the SMR was used as a training railway as well as serving the extensive storage facilities. Over a million tons of military traffic were handled, in addition to passenger troop trains and a small number of civilian goods trains. These demands were far beyond the capacity of the five small antique locomotives owned by the SMR at the time of requisition. In due course, 12 engines were required to be in steam every day and significant numbers of requisitioned locomotives were imported plus, at a later stage, WD standard 0-6-0STs.

The Dean Goods were popular on the SMR with the following in use at different times: 93 to 99/169/170/ 175/176/180/196/197/200. The SMR continued in military use after the war and in late 1947, the class was still much in evidence with Nos 169/ 170/ 180/ 196 at Kinnerley in company with some of the ubiquitous WD 0-6-0STs. Nos 93-99/197 were stored at nearby Hookgate sidings. Most of these engines were there the following summer with No 98 still carrying its original GWR No 2415 brass number plates; No 175 was in course of being broken up. By September 1948, Nos 94-96/ 98/ 197 had also been disposed of on site while Nos 169/ 180/ 196/ 197 were awaiting their fate. An inspection of No 180 (GWR No 2514) revealed that it contained parts stamped with GWR Nos 2398/ 2478/ 2479. This supports the contention that there had been cannibalisation – although No 2398 was not a WD engine (possibly mis-reported for No 2399).

No WD 70093 on a scrap siding at the SMR in company with two other Dean Goods. No WD number is visible but the original GWR No 2433 is easily identifiable on the front buffer beam. Being another of the separate batch of eight, again there is little evidence of modification under WD ownership.

They also served - an unknown warrior crosses the River Severn on the Shropshire & Montgomeryshire line during its military occupation with a freight consisting mainly of ex-private owner wagons, themselves 'called up' for service during the conflict. The WD built the Central Ammunition Dump at Nesscliffe, close to the Severn and continued to run trains on the line for a considerable time after the War. It never returned to peacetime use and closed completely in 1959, some 10 years after the last Dean Goods were taken out of military service.

WILLIAM DEAN

Known deployments in the UK:

WD No.	GWR No.	Locations and dates
93	2433	CMR Nov-41; Old Dalby 1942; MMR 1943; SMR 1943; SRD Works Oct-43 to Dec 43; EKR 1944; SMR 1944; SRD Works Sep-46; SMR 1946
94	2399	Faslane Apr-41; CMR 1941; Bicester Aug-42; collided with WD 95 Dec-44 & sent to Swindon for heavy repairs Feb-45; SRD Works Sep-46; SMR Dec-46; Scrapped 1948
95	2470	CMR 1941; Kent 1943; Bicester 1943; EKR/LMR/Bicester 1944; collided with WD 94 Dec-44 & sent to Swindon for heavy repairs Feb-45; SMR 1946; Scrapped 1948
96	2425	LMR 1940; SMR 1941; SRD Works Jul-43 to Aug-43; LMR Oct-45; SMR 1945; Scrapped Sep-48
97	2442	SMR 1941; SRD Works Oct-42 to Dec-42; SMR
98	2415	Bicester; SMR May-42; SRD Works Mar-44 to Jun-44; Scrapped Sep-48
99	2528	SMR; Burton Dassett Jan-43; Melbourne Jul-43; SMR 1944; SRD Works AUG-42 to Sep-42; SRD Apr-43; SRD Works Jun-43; MMR Jul-43; SMR 1944
100	2521	Kent 1941; MMR 1943; Shipped from Faslane to Algiers, North Africa Feb-43
156	2529	LMR Jun-40; Swindon Jul-40; Kent 1940/1; Bicester Dec-41; to Swindon for heavy repairs Mar-43
167	2463	Shipped from Faslane to Algiers, North Africa Feb-43
168	2548	Shipped from Faslane to Algiers, North Africa Feb-43
169	2479	Kent 1940; Burton Dassett Oct-42; Long Marston Sep-43; SMR 1944; Burton Dassett Oct-43; SMR 1944
170	2536	Burton Dassett Oct-42; SMR Mar-44; CMR 1945
171	2545	EKR Nov-40; MMR 1943; Shipped from Faslane to Algiers, North Africa Feb-43
172	2478	Kent 1940; Shandon 1941; Burton Dassett 1942; Shipped from Faslane to Algiers, North Africa Feb-43
173	2485	Burton Dassett; Bicester Apr-42
174	2451	Kent/Burton Dassett 1942; Shipped from Faslane to Algiers, North Africa Feb-43
175	2511	SMR 1942; SRD Works Dec-42 to Jan-43; Kent 1943; SMR 1946; Scrapped Aug(?)-48
176	2558	SMR 1942; SRD Works Oct-42 to Nov-42 & May-43 to Jun-43; badly damaged in accident Oct-43 and scrapped Jan-44
177	2430	LMR 1940; CMR 1941; SRD Works Mar-42 to Apr 42 & circa Mar-43; Kent 1943; EKR (stored) 1944; Longmoor 1945; Shipped to China Nov-47
178	2446	MMR 1940; CMR 1941; Burton Dassett Aug-42; Kent 1943; LMR Apr-44; Bicester Nov-45; LMR 1946; Shipped to China Nov(?)-47
179	2466	Kent 1940; EKR 1943; STN 1944; LMR Apr-44; shipped to China Nov-47
180	2514	Kent 1940 to 1944; SMR 1946
195	2531	Kent 1943/4; Longmoor 1945 and later used there for locomotive re-railing practice; scrapped Apr-1959
196	2576	Kent 1943/4; SMR 1946
197	2540	Kent 1943; KESR 1943/EKR (stored) 1944; SMR 1946; Scrapped Sep (?)-48
198	2559	Kent 1943/4; LMR 1945; shipped to China 1947
199	2517	Kent 1943; LMR May-44; STN 1944; CMR 1946
200	2552	LMR 1940; SMR 1941/2; Kent 1942/3; Richborough (stored) 1946-7; Ramsgate (stored) Apr to Aug 47

Key to locations:

Bicester = Bicester Central Ordnance Depot, Oxfordshire

Burton Dassett = Junction for Edge Hill Light Rly on LMS Fenny Compton to Stratford-on-Avon line

CMR = Port built by the military on Loch Ryan, linked by military railway to nearby Stranraer

EKR = East Kent Railway

Faslane = Military port and supply depot on Gare Loch near Glasgow

KESR = Kent & East Sussex Railway

Kent = sundry locations in that county, mainly where heavy rail-mounted guns were stationed

Long Marston = Military supply depot in Warwickshire

LMR = Longmoor Military Railway, Hampshire

MMR = Melbourne Military Railway, part of line from Derby to Ashby de la Zouch

Old Dalby = On line between Melton Mowbray and Edwaldton, Leicestershire

Richborough = Military port built in WW1 near Sandwich, Kent; connected to EKR

SMR = Shropshire and Montgomeryshire Railway

STN = Southampton

SRD = Stafford Road, Wolverhampton

Right - No 156 (GWR No 2529) *Flying Fortress* on the Bicester Military Railway in December 1941. If the reported date is correct, then it is likely that the name recognised the RAF's acquisition of the B17 bomber earlier that year, this being the first air force with which this famous bomber saw active service.   *Jimmy Higgins Collection*

Below - No 2531 was a distinguished member of the class, having served in France with the Railway Operating Division in the First World War. In that capacity, coupled to a Caledonian 0-6-0, it worked the first Army Staff train over the Rhine into Cologne following the Armistice, making it the first (but not the last) Dean Goods to work in Germany. As WD No 195 (later 70195) it served again in the Second World War but this time entirely on the home front. When the surviving examples (either from the WD's UK contingent or recovered from continental Europe) were scrapped, No 2531 was retained at Longmoor for training sappers in re-railing techniques. It is seen here in good condition at what must have been the start of this final phase of its chequered career, on the rails but in a lifting sling with railway crane adjacent. By 1959 when it was finally withdrawn, it was in very battered condition. The photograph can also be dated by what must be a sapper officer in splendid plus fours showing his son in short trousers around the facilities.   *RK Blencowe Negative Archive*

No 70094 (GWR No 2399) forming part of a special train on its way to Swindon for repair in 1945.

A rather less clear view of the same train as shown above. No 70095 (GWR No 2470) was also part of the consist, which is being hauled by No 5010 *Restormel Castle*.
Both - RHG Simpson

Of the 29 locomotives requisitioned in 1940 that had not been shipped to France, one (No 176) had been scrapped and six despatched to North Africa during the War, leaving 22 at work in the UK. After the war, four (Nos 177 to 179/ 198) were selected for use in China (see below) because of a shortfall of sound locomotives in France. There was little need for the remaining 18 and all but one had been scrapped by 1949. No 195 (2531) remained at Longmoor for re-railing training. It was non-operable and in battered condition by the 1950s; in this role it gained the doubtful distinction of being the last "in service" when scrapped in 1959.

North Africa and Italy

In February 1943, six were despatched from Port Faslane to Algeria. These were numbers: 100 (2521); 167 (2463); 168 (2548); 171 (2545); 172 (2478); 174 (2451). They were initially employed on shunting at Algiers and in trip working to the marshalling yards at Maison Carrée. In March, Nos 172 and 174 were lent to the Americans for a short period before returning to the British forces at Bône. In June, Nos 100/ 167/ 168/ 171 were transferred to Medjez-el-Bab in Tunisia on the Tabarka – Tunis line where they were used on banking duties between Mastouta and Mateur. This section commenced with an incline of 1 in 100, continued to climb steadily for the next 30 miles and concluded with 2 miles at 1 in 50. Trains over this route were normally handled by S160 2-8-0s of the United States Army Transportation Corps, and banked by a Dean Goods up the incline. However, one memorable night a 300-ton train arrived at Mastouta hauled by No 168 (2548). Banked by No 171 (2545), the task was thought impossible by several observers but after a Herculean struggle that was the stuff of legend, No 171 returned to Mastouta eight hours later, job done.

Left - WD No 70169 (GWR No 2479) withdrawn from service and stored in the exchange sidings at Hookagate near Shrewsbury after the war. The cab roof has been extended and is supported by pillars.

Below - A Dean Goods in trouble, having become derailed at Griggs' Green on the Longmoor Military Railway. The date and identity is unknown, but the locomotive is looking rather tatty; it might be WD No 70195, serving out its time on re-railing training. This view is useful in showing details of the mounting bracket for the Westinghouse pump.

WILLIAM DEAN

In November 1943, No 168 was moved to Bône and was joined there by Nos 100/ 167/ 171 in January 1944. At that location they were used on services from Mateur to Bizerta and Ferryville. All six are believed to have passed through the workshops at Sidi Mabrouk near Constantine in Algeria but judging by their later reported condition, the overhauls must have been superficial.

In March 1944, they were landed at Taranto, being the first WD locomotives in Italy. They worked the harbour branch at Bari for a short period, and then the harbour branch and local services at Barletta. By August all were at Falconara (Ancona). Nos 171 and 172 closely followed the northward allied advance, being used at Pesaro in October and shortly later, Rimini where they were joined by No 100 in March 1945.

Italian footplate men held the class in high regard although by then their condition was appalling, despite having received some workshop attention at Foggia. The best in terms of steaming capacity reputedly was No 171 (by then renumbered 70171) but the reversing gear was so worn that on starting the driver could not be sure which direction the engine would take. Some drivers, apparently alarmed at No 70171's directional unpredictability, preferred No 70172 even though two of its superheater elements had been blanked off because of leaks.

Recognising their worth through the grime and wear, the Italians overhauled them at Foligno and repainted them in the official Ferrovie dello Stato (FS) livery of unlined black with red-brown wheels and frames. At least one received an extended cab roof with supporting pillars and all were fitted with FS Friedmann injectors. A particular problem that afflicted British locomotives in Europe was their use of imperial standards; the Italian Dean Goods acquired many metric threads to keep parts properly bolted together,

reducing repair costs and improving their utility.

From mid-1945 they were exclusively worked by Italian crews and in July 1946, they were formally taken over by FS. Allotted Nos 293.001 to 293.006, they were all based at Falconara where they were used as shunters. They also undertook these duties at Ancona, Faenza, Forli and Rimini and in addition worked local freight trains between these points. Two were regularly sub-shedded at Rimini. By March of the following year three were in store at Rimini and three at Ancona, but none were officially withdrawn until 1953.

An entertaining account of events leading up to a surprise meeting with one of the Italian contingent hard at work at Barletta appears in *Gone With Regret* by George Behrend. It seems that the class made an especial impact in the Bari and Barletta areas, as local enginemen believed they were the biggest and best Britain had to offer. This view was based on comparison with 50 Midland Railway outside-framed 0-6-0s that had been sold to FS years earlier. It was not until the arrival of some Stanier 8Fs from the Middle East in late 1944 that this view was corrected.

China

In November 1943 in Washington DC, the representatives of 44 countries signed an agreement to form the United Nations Relief and Rehabilitation Administration (UNRRA), an organisation that pre-dated the formation of the United Nations proper, with the intention of providing aid to Jews and displaced persons in Europe in the post-war world. After the Japanese surrender, UNRRA's responsibilities were expanded to China to provide aid to liberated territories on the mainland including provision of assistance to the Nationalist Chinese government.

Those sent to China were:

WD No.	French No.	To China	WD No.	French No.	To China	WD No.	French No.	To China
102	030WO29	1946	134	030WO03	1946	161	(Nord)	1947
103	030WO30	1946	139	030WO05	1946	162	030WO14	1946
113	030W036	1946	143	030WO07	1946	177	From UK	1946?
119	(Nord)	1947	147	030WO09	1946	178*	From UK	1946?
120	(Nord)	1947	151	030WO11	1946	179	From UK	1946?
121	(Nord)	1947	153	(Nord)	1947	181	030WO15	1946
124	(Nord)	1947	154	(Nord)	1947	187	030WO16	1946
125	(Nord)	1947	158	n/a	1947	198	From UK	1946?
129	(Nord)	1947	159	030WO13	1946			

WILLIAM DEAN

It is believed that the French locomotives were sent directly to China after receiving workshop attention. Most had been in use with SNCF from the liberation of France until 1946/7 but there were too few in sound condition to meet the request for 25. Three or four from the UK, all allocated to Longmoor from 1945, made up the numbers.

They were classified as XK3 in China and two blocks of numbers were allocated: 61 to 65 and 66 to 90. These obviously conflict with the information that 25 locomotives were ordered. It has been suggested that actually 26 might have been selected, an extra unidentified engine (possibly No 178 whose reported inclusion in the list is uncertain) filling the role of donor for spares. Alternatively, it is possible that Nos 61 to 65 were allocated to a separate locomotive type, the

identity of which remains unknown.

The selection of small, ageing locomotives for transportation over such a long distance is a noteworthy endorsement of the authorities' opinion of the Dean Goods. It would be a fitting conclusion to the story of their overseas adventures to report on how they fared on the far side of the world. However, their career in the hands of the nationalists was short as by 1949, the communists had assumed control of the Chinese mainland. In the aftermath of that conflict, China was effectively a closed country to westerners and nothing has been recorded about their activities or how long they survived. It has been speculated that they were used in industrial service rather on main line work, but it is unlikely that details of their life in the Orient will ever be known.

Above - No 181 as SNCF Est system No 030W015. Date and location are unknown but it is on shed in company with another Dean Goods and what appears to be a Belgian locomotive. This was the first to be processed at Eastleigh before despatch to France and the intention had been to fit Westinghouse brake after it had left the UK. Unless the fitting is on the other side, it would seem that the Royal Engineers never had time to complete the task. Modifications have been effected in the form of a cab extension with what seems to be rudimentary black-out protection plus chimney attachment that might be for spark arresting. Beyond this view, there is apparently no record of this engine being sighted post-1940 in Europe but it was one of the contingent despatched to China after the war.

Previous page - No 179 in an intriguing view that shows the pannier tanks and related equipment from an unusual angle. The engine is shunting wagons of US origin or ownership on to an American Landing Craft (Tank), somewhere in the UK. The wagons are in pristine condition but empty – presumably an LCT destined for continental Europe would have made the crossing with loaded wagons. Perhaps this photograph was taken during a test of loading procedures or for training purposes. No 179 spent the earlier part of the war in Kent, but was later at Longmoor which suggest that the location is one of the English channel ports. It was one of those sent to China direct from the UK after the war.

Chapter 8

DERIVATION AND ANNEXATION

The success of the Dean Goods was an influence on the GWR's motive power policy generally. Although the class underwent little change beyond the modernisation that the company applied to its fleet, as a standard design it formed a basis for development of other types. Those introduced or acquired that owed something to the presence of the Dean Goods are reviewed more or less chronologically.

Class 2361

The first derivative appeared early with Lot 67 of 1885-6, the purpose for which rested on the need for a fleet of locomotives that could be readily converted for Broad Gauge use. The background to this exercise is discussed in **Chapter 3**.

Above the running plate, these engines resembled Class 2301 although there were dimensional differences. The fitting of under-hung springs to the outside frames made them particularly distinctive and this helped disguise the slightly shortened wheelbase compared with the inside-framed engines. As built, they carried a slightly larger version of the S2 type boiler that had first appeared on the second batch of Dean Goods (Lot 63).

Subsequent boiler changes were complex, following the general pattern applied to the inside framed engines. The round-topped firebox with dome on the front boiler ring (type S2) gave way to the later version with dome on the rear ring (S4). Later, the Belpaire firebox with dome on the front ring (B2) appeared before all acquired the B4 version that was so

characteristic of the Dean Goods. However, there were marginal dimensional variations among the S2/ S4/B2 type boilers before standardisation with those fitted to the inside-framed engines. Details of types, dimensions and changes are recorded in **Appendix A.2**.

Progressive modernisation paralleled that applied to the Dean Goods. Boiler pressure was up-rated to 150 lbs/ sq in and later to 180 lbs/ sq in as the S4 and later B4 boilers were fitted. Four (Nos 2361/ 2368/2369 and 2380) are known to have carried B4 boilers with top feed, and only No 2371 was never superheated. The class was subject to the 1930/31 programme for installation of Automatic Train Control; Nos 2365/2371/2374/2377 and 2379 were never so equipped.

No	Built	Withdrawn	No	Built	Withdrawn
2361	Sep-85	May-22	2371	Jan-86	Mar-30
2362	Oct-85	Nov-46§	2372	Jan-86	Feb-38
2363	Nov-85	Oct-32	2373	Feb-86	Nov-34
2364	Nov-85	Aug-34	2374	Mar-86	Nov-30
2365	Nov-85	Oct-28	2375	Mar-86	May-38
2366	Dec-85	Feb-33	2376	Mar-86	Dec-38
2367	Dec-85	May-32	2377	Apr-86	Feb-31
2368	Dec-85	Mar-38	2378	Apr-86	Mar-45
2369	Dec-85	Nov-37	2379	Apr-86	Feb-31
2370	Dec-85	Mar-35	2380	May-86	Sep-43¥

§ First withdrawn Jun-39; re-instated Jan-40
¥ First withdrawn Aug-39; re-instated Nov-39

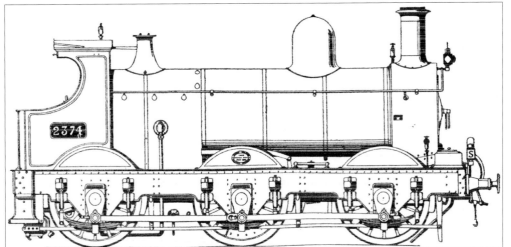

Figure VII - Class 2361 with Type S2C round topped boiler

Above -Class 2361 No 2377 shown in 1904 while on snowplough duty. This locomotive was fitted with a Type S4a boiler in January 1899 and replaced with the standard dimensioned Type S4 in February 1904.

Below - No 2362 on a goods working, the type of duty for which this class was originally intended. The date and location are unknown but it is likely to be a pre-Grouping scene. This locomotive carried a Belpaire firebox continuously from 1902; the smokebox is of the early dished variety.

L & GRP

No 2379 at Wrexham, 18th August 1920. This engine is also fitted with the original dished style of smokebox door and the brass safety valve cover has yet to be painted. The tender is pre-Dean with coal rails.
L & GRP

No 2375 at Worcester in July 1932. The engine, which is in final condition with ATC fitted, seems dwarfed by its tender. No 2577 is in the background.
Coltas Trust

WILLIAM DEAN

The departure of No 2365 preceded the first withdrawal of a Dean Goods for "natural causes". Withdrawals during the 1930s were slightly in advance of the life-expired programme applied to locomotives in the 2301-2360/2381-2400 number series.

Little can be traced of the work of these engines in the 19th Century although they seem to have shared duties with the Dean Goods. Official records exist for the pre-World War 1 period of the 20th Century and the following extract of allocations indicates a small class well dispersed throughout the system:

Later in their career, they were mainly associated with the Worcester, Wolverhampton and London divisions – in the latter case principally being used on trip working. After the Grouping, they do not appear to have been used at all in the West of England, or in the Neath division. They seem to have been regarded as goods locomotives although the late survivors assumed mixed traffic duties similar to those handled by remaining Dean Goods.

The outbreak of war led to the reinstatement of Nos 2362 and 2380, both of which were repainted at

	1902	1909	1913		1902	1909	1913		1902	1909	1913
Aberdare	1			Newton Abbot			1	Southall	1	2	
Banbury		2	3	Neyland		1	2	Swindon		1	1
Bristol	3	2	5	Oxford	1	1		Swindon Works	3		
Didcot	3	3		Paddington		1	1	Trowbridge		1	1
Exeter	1			Pontypool Road	1	2	1	Tyseley			
Gloucester	1	1	1	Reading		1	1	Weymouth	1		1
Landore			1	Salisbury	1			Wolverhampton	2	2	
Newport	1			Severn Tunnel Jct			1				

Several of the class were to be found at work in the London area in the 1930s. Here is No 2376 at Southall shed on 22nd May 1935.
RS Carpenter Photos

Above - Class 2361 was reputedly used mainly on goods trains and rarely in Wales until World War 2 when two reinstated engines were allocated to Oswestry. However, this pre-war but undated photograph depicts an unidentified class member on a local passenger train of vintage stock at Fishguard & Goodwick. *Transport Treasury*

Below - Class 2361 No 2371 on shed at Fishguard. Location of stains on this locomotive suggests that it might be the same engine as that in the previous photograph.

Above - On return of an engine to duty after overhaul, it was normal to couple the next available tender. In early BR days when engines were being repainted black, it was not uncommon for a black engine to be coupled to a green tender and vice versa. This practice made it futile to record pairings as changes were so frequent.

In this view taken at Wolverhampton Stafford Road on 3rd July 1937, the tender is in pristine condition; cleaning of engine No 2378 seems to have been limited to the front buffer beam.

CM & JM Bentley

Class 2361 No 2372 with Dean Goods No 2382 behind in this 1930s view. No 2372 was withdrawn in 1938 whereas the Dean Goods survived in to the BR era.

Two of a kind. No 2369 (left) facing No 2370.

Photomatic

Swindon in 1941. They were employed in the Central Wales Division, an area not previously penetrated by the class, replacing Dean Goods sold into military service. The other late survivor, No 2378, was shedded at Banbury in the 1940s up until its withdrawal. A report dated January 1946 refers to the esteem in which Oswestry shed held its older locomotives. In particular, No 2362 which was seen on a five coach train from Whitchurch was considered locally to be "a very fine engine".

Class 3901

Traffic growth in the Birmingham area in the 1900s led to a need for more powerful tank locomotives on suburban services. At the time, Swindon had a full order book and could not handle additional new build projects. To fill the gap, the 20 Dean Goods of Lot No

104 (built 1896) were earmarked for conversion to inside-cylinder 2-6-2Ts. Wheels and motion were retained but new frames were cut to carry the longer superstructure. Standard No 5 taper boilers as used on Class 45xx 2-6-2Ts were fitted. The long tanks, which held 1500 gallons, had oval holes cut into the sides above running plate level to allow access to the motion. The result had a rather awkward appearance that lacked the handsome lines of contemporary classes, the small Churchward prairies in particular. The superstructure certainly displayed no evidence of the design's antecedence.

Conversion started in February 1907 and by October 1908, 18 had been treated. Almost as an afterthought, the final two were converted in January 1910, underlining the secondary nature of the exercise. In rebuilt form, the class seems to have done its work

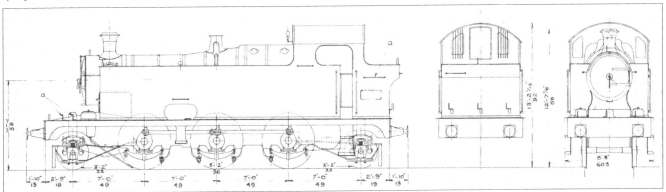

Figure VIII Class 3901 in later form withtop feed and extended bunker.

well – as would reasonably be expected of a machine that was fusion of existing components. Key dates for these locomotives in their post-Dean Goods phase:

Original number	Class 3901 number	Date converted	Super-heated	Final withdrawal
2491	3901	Feb-07	Mar-17	May-34
2492	3906	Oct-07	Sep-15	May-32
2493	3915	Jun-08	Nov-15	May-32
2494	3916	Jul-08	Jul-14	Nov-34
2495	3918	Oct-08	Jan-17	May-32
2496	3919	Jan-10	Jul-15	Mar-34
2497	3908	Nov-07	Jul-17	Sep-30
2498	3902	Feb-07	Aug-16	Aug-32
2499	3905	Oct-07	Jul-15	Aug-30
2500	3910	Feb-08	Jan-16	Apr-31
2501	3903	May-07	Dec-16	May-32
2502	3920	Jan-10	Jul-17	Feb-31
2503	3913	Apr-08	Jan-15	Jun-31
2504	3904	May-07	Aug-14	Oct-33
2505	3917	Jul-08	Jun-17	Oct-32
2506	3914	May-08	Jul-16	Jun-31
2507	3909	Dec-07	Jul-17	Oct-30
2508	3907	Oct-07	Aug-15	Sep-34
2509	3911	Apr-08	Apr-17	Jul-32
2510	3912	Apr-08	Oct-14	Apr-31

In view of the steaming qualities of the Dean Goods, use of the Standard No 5 boiler seems a luxury. This appears to be an early example of the fixation with tapered boilers where the benefits would have been so marginal as not to justify the greater capital expense. Also, the haste with which superheating was installed over three years contrasts with the 13 years it took to treat the first 40 members of Class 45xx.

The early pattern of allocations:

	1909	1913
Landore	2	3
Leamington		1
Swindon Works		3
Tyseley	12	11
Wolverhampton	4	2

The majority of the class continued to work on Birmingham suburban trains until displaced by 2-6-2T Class 51xx around 1929. Thereafter, they were dispersed to the London and Neath divisions. Post-war exceptions to the Birmingham concentration were noted from time to time including Nos 3911/3914/3916/3918 at Hereford, and Nos 3910/3915 at Aberdare. In the early 1920s, No 3908 was for a period at Westbury and No 3909 at Taunton. It is possible that the Aberdare pair were also allocated to Cardiff for a time.

2-6-2T Class 3901 No 3902 in photographic grey after conversion from Dean Goods No 2498 in February 1907.

F Moore's Railway Photographs

Their careers as tender engines ranged between 11 and 14 years, and as tank engines between 24 and 28 years – acceptable working spans by the standards of the time.

Leading dimensions of Dean Goods (second batch as built), Class 2361 and Class 3901:

	Class 2301 (Nos 2341-2360)	Class 2361	Class 3901
Wheel arrangement	0-6-0	0-6-0	2-6-2T
Cylinders	17" x 24"	17" x 26"	17 1/2" x 24"
Boiler - barrel	10' 3"	10' 6"	10' 6"
- outside diameter	4' 5"	4' 5"	4' 9 1/2" to 4' 2"
- pitch	7' 3"	7' 3"	8' 3"
Firebox - outside length	5' 4"	5' 4"	5' 10"
Tubes	230 x 1 5/8"	239 x 1 5/8"	255 x 1 5/8"
Heating surface - tubes	1023.8 sq ft	1095.1 sq ft	1178 sq ft
- firebox	103.3 sq ft	103.3 sq ft	93.9 sq ft
Grate	16.4 sq ft	15.2 sq ft	16.6sq ft
Boiler pressure	140 lbs/ sq in	140 lbs/ sq in	200 lbs / sq in
Driving wheels	5' 0"	5' 0"	5' 2"
Pony and trailing wheels	n/a	n/a	3' 2"
Wheelbase	7' 9" + 8' 3"	7' 9" + 8' 0"	7' 0" + 7'0" + 7' 0" + 7' 0"
Axle loading - leading pony	n/a	n/a	6 tons 7 cwt
- leading	11 tons 12 cwt	12 tons 6 cwt	14 tons 4 cwt
- driving	11 tons 12 cwt	12 tons 6 cwt	17 tons 4 cwt
- trailing	9 tons 17 cwt	12 tons 6 cwt	16 tons 11 cwt
- trailing pony	n/a	n/a	7 tons 18 cwt
Total weight	33 tons 1 cwt	36 tons 18cwt	62 tons 4 cwt
Tractive effort (85%)	13,313 lbs	14,420 lbs	20,155 lbs
Route colour	Uncoloured	Uncoloured	Blue

Left - Later in its career at Old Oak Common on an unknown date, No 3902 retains its "flower pot" shaped chimney but has received top feed. The bunker has been extended in similar fashion to that adopted with the earlier members of 2-6-2T Class 45xx.

Right - No 3915 was converted from Dean Goods No 2493 in June 1908. Condition is similar to that depicted in the view of No 3902 in later years except that this engine has acquired a parallel sided chimney.

No 3906 (ex-Dean Goods No 2492) in late condition

0-6-0 tender locomotives acquired at the Grouping

A total of 861 locomotives was acquired between 1922 and 1924 from the companies absorbed at the Grouping. Tender locomotives totalled 145, the most common wheel arrangement being 0-6-0, contributed by the following companies: Cambrian (34), Midland & South Western Junction (10), and Taff Vale (42).

The Grouping occurred at a difficult time as Swindon was engaged in redressing post-war maintenance arrears, and the assimilation of a heterogeneous collection of locomotives was a considerable task. Viewed in hindsight, there was little sign that there was much, if any, strategic assessment of the locomotive assets acquired in relation to existing traffic needs. Locomotives unlucky enough to be among the first called to Swindon for inspection and found to be in doubtful condition were summarily condemned. Later a more benign attitude prevailed, doubtless stimulated by recognition that continued mass withdrawals would engender a serious replacement problem. As a result, some less deserving cases were either repaired or extensively "Great Westernised" – a process that involved installation of a standard GWR boiler and other fittings on an original chassis. Sometimes, superficial modifications only were applied (eg chimneys, safety valve covers, and other boiler fittings) that gave a GWR look to an engine in otherwise original condition.

The ad hoc nature of the early inspection and

withdrawal regime could prove expensive. This is demonstrated by the destruction of three of the well-regarded Cambrian Large Belpaire Goods engines in 1922. These were only 19 years old (ie younger than any of the Dean Goods) and they could have put in another 30 years' useful service on their native system – as did the remainder of the class – working alongside their GWR counterparts. Even so, this action pales into insignificance compared with the treatment meted out to the splendid 0-6-4T Class L of the Barry Railway, all ten of which were scrapped in the autumn of 1926 when just 12 years old.

Once the initial assessment programme was completed, rebuilding and modifications proceeded, but not always in the most financially efficient manner. Standardisation was attractive for maintenance cost reduction but had no purpose where life expectancy was limited as with the Taff Vale 0-6-0s. Also, the case was slim for small classes; the ex-MSWJR fleet seems to have received disproportionate attention in this regard. Perhaps subjective views were at play in wishing to eliminate evidence that a lesser concern had once had the temerity to penetrate the GWR's mechanical heartland

Every class of absorbed 0-6-0 received attention from Swindon concerning the installation of GWR boilers. Dean Goods type boilers were only installed with examples of two classes but all are reviewed for the sake of completeness.

Cambrian Railways Small Goods No 14 as GWR No 898 at Oswestry on 28th August 1926. A moderate degree of Great Westernisation has been applied in the form of boiler fittings but the tender remains in pre-Grouping condition.
HC Casserley

Ex-Cambrian Railways

The 34 locomotives absorbed from the Cambrian comprised three classes – Small Goods (nine locomotives), Large Goods (ten) and Large Belpaire Goods (15).

Small Goods

The nine surviving members of this class (all built by Sharp Stewart) were taken over by the GWR but five were soon withdrawn on grounds of poor boiler condition:

Figure IX: Cambrian Railways Small Goods as GWR No 908 with class 2021 boiler and four-wheeled tender.

Cambrian No	GWR No	Makers No	Built	Withdrawn
40	899*	1446	Jun-63	Jul-22
45	900	1530	Aug-64	Sep-45
46	901*	1531	Aug-64	Jul-22
51	910	1590	Apr-65	May-35
52	911*	1597	May-65	Jul-22
4	897*	2232	Jun-72	Jul-22
14	898	2511	Sep-75	Nov-47
48	908	2339	Nov-73	Dec-38
49	909	2347	Dec-73	Jul-22

* GWR number allocated but not carried

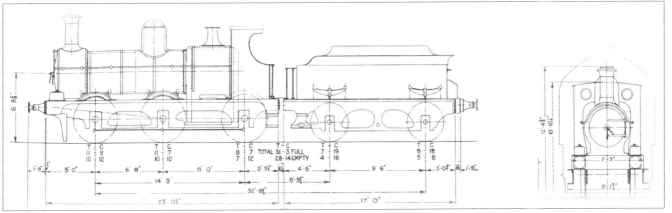

WILLIAM DEAN

Above - GWR No 898 at Oswestry. The ancient tender has been fitted with GW-style side fender and tool boxes, andhas acquired a shirt button roundel which dates this view as 1934 or later. This was the last of the Small Goods in service being withdrawn in November 1947 after a working life of 72 years.
Colling Turner Photos

Below - Cambrian Railways Small Goods No 48 as GWR No 908 and rebuilt with Class 2021 boiler, at Barmouth Junction on 1st September 1930. This successful rebuild was carried out in 1927 but with only three more of the type then remaining, repetition of the exercise was obviously not thought worthwhile. Oddly, despite this effort, No 908 retained its diminutive 4-wheeled tender until 1933. The passenger stock is of mixed style and age.
Ifor Higgins

For the last five years of its career, No 908 worked with a 3000 gallon tender which served to show how small was this engine.
LT George Collection

No 908 was fitted with a Class 2021 boiler at Swindon in March 1927 and retained the curiosity of a four-wheeled tender until 1933. During GWR days, the surviving five were allocated to Oswestry, Portmadoc and Machynlleth.

Large Goods (Figure IX)

Boiler replacement had commenced with these engines in 1915, and this programme was continued by the GWR using Dean Goods boilers. The first rebuilding of No 878 used a saturated type B4 boiler; six more received superheated versions of this boiler and No 878 was brought into line with them in 1933.

Cambrian No	GWR No	Built	Builder	Maker's No	Re-boilered	At	Withdrawn
73	875	May-94	Neilson & Co	4691	Jan-30	Oswestry	Dec-36
74	876*	May-94	"	4692	Aug-24	Oswestry	May-48
75	878	May-94	"	4693	Mar-24/ Nov-33	Swindon	Oct-38
76	879	Jun-94	"	4694			May-32
77	880	Jun-94	"	4695	Jun-29	Oswestry	Nov-38
78	881	Aug-95	Vulcan	1445	May-24	Swindon	Jul-32
79	882	Aug-95	"	1446			Jan-35
80	883	Aug-95	"	1447			Nov-26
87	884§	Jan-99	Neilson Reid	5401	May-31	Oswestry	Aug-47
88	885¶	Jan-99	"	5402	Jul-26	Oswestry	Aug-44

First withdrawn: * June-39; § Sep-39; ¶ Aug-39; all returned to service Dec-39

GWR No 875, formerly Cambrian Large Goods No 73, under repair in Oswestry Works on 28th August 1926. "Great Westernisation" has so far been limited to the safety valve cover and the number plates. This engine received a Dean Goods Type B4 boiler in January 1930 but was taken out of service in December 1936.

HC Casserley

The Large Goods remained in Wales, shedded mainly at Oswestry, Machynlleth and Brecon, working alongside Dean Goods transferred to the Central Wales Division. As rebuilt they looked very similar to the Dean Goods, except for the more commodious cab and their Cambrian tenders.

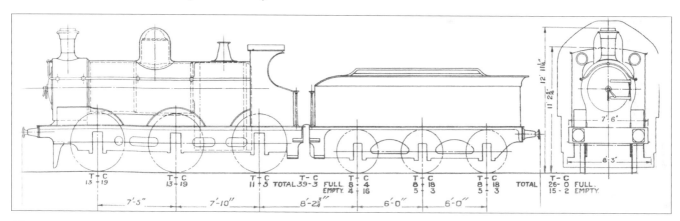

Figure X - Cambrian Railways Large Goods, fitted with saturated Dean Goods Type B4 boiler.

Above - Cambrian Large Goods No 87 as GWR No 884 in similar condition to No 875.

Below - GWR No 884 again, but by now it is carrying the Dean Goods Type B4 boiler that was first fitted in May 1931. It is on shed here at Portmadoc with an unidentified Dean Goods behind

Cambrian Large Goods No 88 as GWR No 885 at Swindon fitted with type B4 boiler.

Large Belpaire Goods

These were the Cambrian's largest and most modern goods engines, and were the first on the system to be built with Belpaire boilers. Soon after the Grouping, three that had been sent to Swindon for inspection were condemned on grounds of boiler condition, a decision that in retrospect seems premature.

The remainder were treated more sympathetically, receiving Standard No 9 boilers (Group 105). This was a superheated parallel Belpaire design created originally for ex-Barry Railway 0-6-2T Classes B, B1

and F. This was found to be suitable for the Cambrian engines and later, a saturated version was introduced (Group 106). The two types were indiscriminately rotated within the class with only No 873 always remaining in saturated condition. The first fitting of new boilers took place as shown below. After 1946, all boiler changes took place at Wolverhampton.

In re-boilered form, these engines bore a general resemblance to the Dean Goods. However while the boiler barrel had the same external dimensions, the firebox was deeper and longer. Thus the boiler had a pitch of 7' 8¼" compared with the 7' 3" of the final form

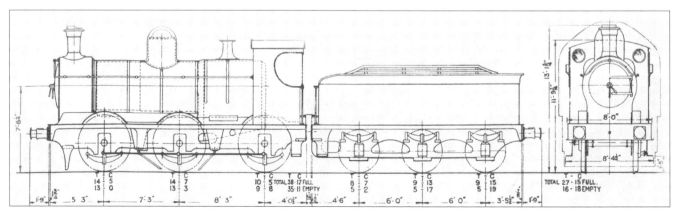

Figure XI - Cambrian Railways Large Belpaire Goods as fitted with GWR Standard No 9 boiler

Cambrian Large Belpaire Goods No 54 as GWR No 874 at Oswestry, 28th August 1926. Obviously fresh out of the shops, GWR boiler fittings have been added but the original Cambrian boiler fitted when built in June 1919 remains *in situ*. A Standard No 9 boiler was fitted three years later but apart from the three premature withdrawals (Nos 888/ 889/ 891), No 874 was the first to be taken out of service in March 1993 following its involvement in a fatal accident at Vriog.   *HC Casserley*

of Dean Goods with type B4 boiler. In this respect, together with their larger cabs, they looked like an enlarged and modernised version of William Dean's classic:

Cambrian No	GWR No	Built	Builder	Makers No	Re-boilered	At	Withdrawn
15	844	Oct-18	Beyer Peacock	5944	Sep-28	Swindon	Aug-54
29	849	Nov-18	"	5945	Apr-31	Oswestry	Oct-54
31	855	May-19	"	5946	Oct-24	Swindon	Oct-54
38	864	Mar-03	"	5031	Feb-36	"	Nov-52
42	873	Jun-19	"	5947	Mar-33	"	Mar-54
54	874	Jun-19	"	5948	Sep-29	"	Mar-33
89	887	Apr-03	R Stephenson & Co	3089	Mar-32	"	Nov-52
90	888*	May-03	"	3090	n/a	n/a	Mar-22
91	889*	May-03	"	3091	n/a	n/a	Aug-22
92	891*	May-03	"	3092	n/a	n/a	Aug-22
93	892	Jun-03	"	3093	Mar-30	Swindon	Apr-53
99	893	Mar-03	Beyer Peacock	5029	Nov-24	"	Feb-53
100	894	Mar-03	"	5030	Jul-33	"	Apr-53
101	895	Mar-03	"	5032	Jun-24	Oswestry	Oct-54
102	896	Mar-03	"	5033	Sep-32	Swindon	Apr-53

* GWR number allocated but not carried

WILLIAM DEAN

The remaining twelve were well-regarded, being considered good strong engines that worked satisfactorily in tandem with the Dean Goods. No 874 was condemned in 1933 having sustained heavy accident damage. Final withdrawals were part of the general cull of older 0-6-0s in Wales in the period 1952-4.

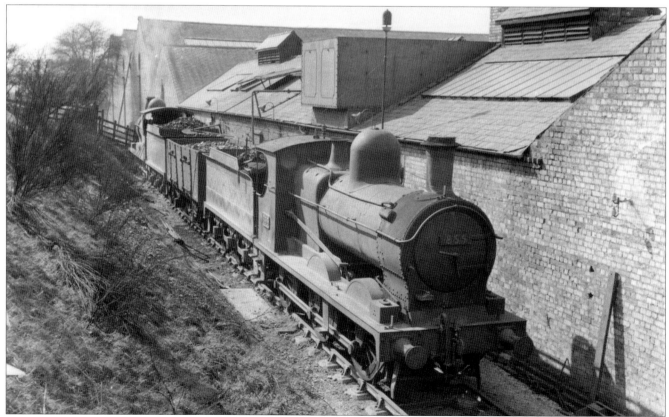

Opposite, above - GWR No 892 (ex-Cambrian Large Belpaire Goods No 93) with Standard No 9 boiler. The date is unknown but the location appears to be Machynlleth.

Opposite, below - Cambrian Large Belpaire Goods No 855 at Oswestry, 28th March 1954 with another example in rear.   *Coltas Coll'n*

Below - No 849 standing at Swindon, awaiting scrapping in October 1954

Ex-Midland & South Western Junction Railway

At the Grouping, the MSWJR 0-6-0s consisted of a single class of 10 locomotives being the company's first attempt at a standard type. They were built by Beyer Peacock and intended for goods work, particularly at the southern of the company's system where there had been a significant increase in military traffic around the end of the 19th Century. Following an early modification to the cab sides of the first six to make them conform with the remainder, they remained virtually unchanged until January 1925 when rebuilding commenced. A consistent appearance was resumed for the entire class by December 1927 with the conclusion of this exercise. In rebuilt form, they carried superheated Standard No 10 tapered boilers and new cabs with high-arched roofs. In this state they resembled a primitive version of Class 2251 that was to be introduced in 1930.

MSWJR No	GWR No	Built	Maker's No	Reboilered	Withd'n	MSWJR No	GWR No	Built	Maker's No	Reboilered	Withd'n
19	1003	1899	4097	Jun-26	Oct-36	24	1008	"	4102	Mar-27	Dec-36
20	1004	"	4098	Dec-25	Dec-34	25	1009	Aug-02	4440	Dec-25	Jan-35
21	1005	"	4099	Jan-25	Mar-38	26	1010	"	4441	Oct-26	Dec-34
22	1006	"	4100	Jan-26	Dec-34	27	1011	Sep-02	4442	Sep-25	May-37
23	1007	"	4101	Aug-25	Jun-37	28	1013	"	4443	Dec-27	Jun-37

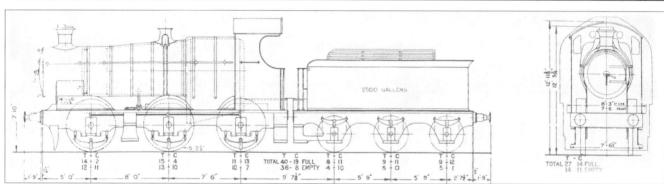

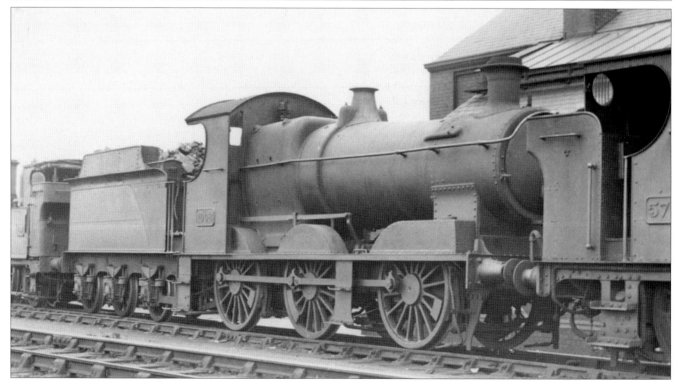

Opposite, above - Midland & South Western Junction Railway No 25, later GWR No 1006 in March 1923 at Cheltenham (High Street) which was the northern limit of that company's operations.

Opposite, middle - Figure XII - Midland & South Western Junction Railway 0-6-0 rebuilt by the GWR with Standard No 10 boiler.

Opposite, bottom - GWR N0 1008 (ex-MSWJR No 24) as rebuilt with Standard No 10 boiler, at St Philips Marsh Bristol. This view is undated but this locomotive was withdrawn soon after moving to Bristol. The tender has also been included in the Great Westernisation process by having its coal rails replaced with side fenders and by having GW-style tool boxes installed. *L&GRP*

Below - GWR No 1011 (ex-MSWJR No 27) on shed. *Real*

This was another class where the case for installation of tapered boilers was marginal. Presumably the originals were approaching the end of their working lives thus warranting replacement. However, having modernised the entire class by December 1927, Nos 1004/1006/1010 survived for nine years or less. Further, mileages averaged around 16,000 pa, compared with 22,000-24,000 pa achieved with the ex-Cambrian Large Belpaire Goods – a marked disparity given that both types did the same sort of work over lengthy rural routes.

Under GWR control, their allocation was split between Cheltenham and Swindon until 1936. In that year, Nos 1008/1011/1013 were moved to Bristol from where they were withdrawn. It seems regrettable that work could not be found for them elsewhere.

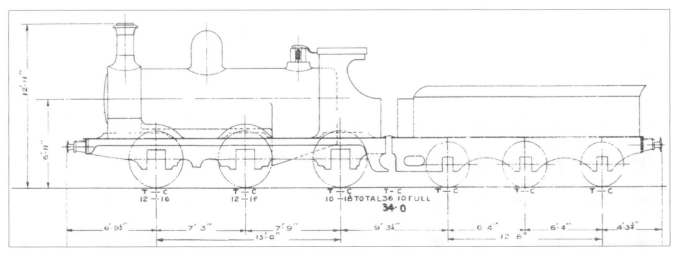

Figure XIII - Taff Vale Railway Class K as GWR Diagram A. 17

WILLIAM DEAN

Ex-Taff Vale Railway

This was the most significant of the absorbed railways, and overwhelmingly a tank engine company at the Grouping. Only 42 of its fleet of 274 were tender locomotives, all of the 0-6-0 wheel arrangement.

Classified as either "K" or "L", rebuilding, cannibalisation and boiler exchanges had made the distinction irrelevant by the 1920s. They were mainly built by Kitson, except for a few constructed by the Taff Vale itself (denoted by the prefix "TV" in the Makers No column below):

TVR No	GWR No	Built	Makers No	Withd'n	TVR No	GWR No	Built	Makers No	Withd'n
219	912	Mar-84	TV -169	Oct-26	302	933	Oct-75	2031	Apr-23
253	913	Dec-82	TV -168	Jun-25	304	935	Oct-75	2033	Jun-23
259	914	Aug-84	2658	Jun-25	313	936	Jul-80	2346	Dec-25
261	915	Jul-74	1976	Oct-26	314	938	Jul-80	237	May-25
281	916	Feb-85	2842	Apr-22	316	939	Oct-80	2351	Jun-24
284	917	May-74	1974	Aug-27	320	941	Sep-81	2443	Oct-23
288	918	Jan-75	1978	May-22	322	942	Nov-83	2584	Dec-23
298	919	May-75	2027	Feb-30	325	943	Jan-84	2587	Apr-23
337	920	Sep-84	2664	Dec-27	327	944	Jan-84	2589	Feb-23
210	921	Oct-81	2444	Jun-23	328	946	Feb-84	2590	Sep-23
217	922	Nov-80	2354	Oct-28	333	Not allotted	Aug-84	2660	Feb-22
220	923	Mar-84	TV - 170	Sep-23	335	948	Sep-84	2662	Jun-25
235	924	Dec-80	2352	Feb-27	336	968	Sep-84	2663	Mar-23
236	925	Dec-80	2353	Oct-23	339	969	Sep-84	2666	Feb-23
239	926	Oct-75	TV - 151	Mar-23	340	970	Sep-84	2667	Aug-23
242	927	Oct-83	2581	Sep-23	354	974	Jan-85	2841	Apr-23
245	928	Nov-83	2582	Oct-23	356	978	Feb-85	2843	Jul-25
252	929	Nov-83	2583	Apr-23	357	984	Feb-85	2844	Feb-24
283	930	Dec-74	TV - 150	Mar-23	358	1000	Feb-85	2845	Jan-23
297	931	May-75	2026	Jun-22	359	1001	Feb-85	2846	Dec-26
301	932	Oct-75	2030	Dec-25	360	1002	Feb-85	2847	Jun-25

This class was already in decline at the Grouping and all had been renumbered in the TVR's surplus stock list by 1921. The TVR's withdrawal programme had accounted for more than half the 85 that had been originally built. A further 22 were condemned in 1922/23 and the class would deserve no more than a passing reference, were it not for the case of GWR No 917 (previously TVR No 284).

This engine had been the prototype, built as No 43 in May 1874. It was renumbered 284 in 1905 on transfer to the surplus stock list, but was fitted in 1914 with a boiler from an 0-6-2T. In July 1923 it was inspected at Swindon and after thirteen months appeared with the boiler from sister engine GWR No 984 (ex-Taff Vale

No 357), withdrawn February 1924. This boiler was extensively Great Westernised with a standard smokebox, parallel chimney and GWR safety valve cover with dimensions: Tubes 232 x 1 5/8"; Heating surfaces – tubes 1064 sq ft, – firebox 98.5 sq ft; Grate -17.7 sq ft. The slotted splasher faces were replaced with solid sheets. Externally, it resembled a Dean Goods with Type S4 boiler, except for the smaller driving wheels and the wider cab.

The treatment accorded this engine was strange in view of the work schedule that had caused more deserving cases to be condemned. When it entered Swindon, there were 25 of the type in service but on its return, only 15 were left. Further, the TVR 0-6-0s had

Ex-Taff Vale Class K 0-6-0 No 337 as GWR No 920 in original condition except for safety valve bonnet and number plate at Penarth dock shed on 1st May 1929.

been built for mineral trains on which by 1922, the 0-6-2T type was preferred. When No 917 returned to service, the new 0-6-2T Class 56xx was under construction and by the year end, Nos 5600 to 5603 were available for work. There could have been little contest between a new example of a wheel arrangement favoured locally and the attempted

rejuvenation of a diminishing group of geriatric 0-6-0s whose origins were contemporaneous with the last Armstrong Goods.

No 917 lasted three years before withdrawal in August 1927. By then, only two other examples remained, the last (No 919) being condemned in February 1930.

Leading dimensions of absorbed locomotives modified with GWR or GWR-style boilers

Railway	Cambrian	Cambrian	Cambrian	MSWJ	Taff Vale
Class	Small Goods	Large Goods	Large Belpaire Goods	Nos 19-28	K/L (GWR No 917)
Number	1	7	12	10	1
Driving wheels	4' 6"	5' 1 1/2"	5' 1 1/2"	5' 2 1/2"	4' 6"
Wheelbase	6' 9" + 8' 0"	7' 5" + 7' 10"	7' 3" + 8' 3"	8' 0" + 7' 6"	7' 3" + 7' 9"
Boiler type	2021/ Group 13b	Dean Goods groups 20/ PA & 21/ Pl	Standard No 9 Groups 105 & 106	Standard Type D3 Group 22	Modified TVR Class K See dimensions above
Cylinders	16" x 24"	18" x 26"	18" x 26"	18" x 26"	17.25" x 26"
Engine weights	11t 9c + 11t 7c + 8t 7c	13t 19c + 13t 19c + 11t 5c	14t 5c +14t 7c + 10t 5c	14t 2c +15t 4c + 11t 3c	12t 16c + 12t 16c +10t 18c§
Diagram	A26	a20/21	A23/28	A24	none
Route availability	Uncoloured	Yellow	Yellow	Yellow	Uncoloured

§ As built

WILLIAM DEAN

Class 2251

The total number of Dean Goods in service at the Grouping was 232; withdrawals determined by age and/or condition did not commence until 1929. By then the class had been displaced from front line freight duties, but was still much in demand for pick-up goods, branch and secondary passenger duties ie a genuine mixed traffic role. Further, the Grouping had added a network of routes in Wales where axle loading was an operating limitation. With the oldest Dean Goods approaching 50 years in service, there was a need for a replacement type and this appeared in 1930 with the construction of 0-6-0 Class 2251.

By the 1903s, the 0-6-0 type was increasingly viewed as obsolescent, notwithstanding that other companies continued to build more examples. The LMS turned out more of the Midland Railway-derived 4F 0-6-0s until 1941, a class that has been cited as prime evidence of proliferation not necessarily implying excellence (772 were built). The LNER grew a class of 289 locomotives in its J39 between 1926 and 1941, a group standard mixed traffic type in the North Eastern/ Darlington tradition. It was widely dispersed throughout the LNER but curiously had almost disappeared in the early 1960s before withdrawal of its preceding smaller wheeled version (Class J38) commenced.

Maunsell on the Southern Railway designed 20 members of Class Q, which appeared in 1938. This was conceptually closest to Class 2251 in being intended to replace 0-6-0s approaching the end of their normal life expectancy. Oliver Bulleid roundly condemned the Class Q as being out-dated but ironically had to produce for rather different needs an austerity 0-6-0 (Class Q1) in typically iconoclastic vein during World War II.

The combination of tapered boiler and side window cab gave Class 2251 the most modern appearance of the 1930s vintage 0-6-0s with considerably improved comfort and weather protection, particularly when coupled to the high-bodied ex-ROD 4000 gallon tender. Crews often referred to them as "Baby-Castles" and they were useful, well-liked engines. Leading dimensions were similar to those of the Dean Goods:

	2251	Dean Goods (late condition)
Cylinders	17.5" x 24"	17.5" x 24"
Boiler		
- barrel	10' 3"	10' 3"
- diameter	4' 5" To 5' 0.5"	4' 3"
- pitch	8' 0"	7' 3"
Firebox length	6' 0"	5' 4"
Heating surfaces		
- tubes	1049.4 sq ft	960.5 sq ft
- firebox	102.4 sq ft	75.3 sq ft
- superheater	75.7 sq ft	105.5 sq ft
Grate	17.4 sq ft	16.4 sq ft
Boiler pressure	200 lbs/ sq in	140 lbs/ sq in
Wheels	5' 2"	5' 2"
Wheelbase	7' 3" + 8' 3"	7' 3" + 8' 3"
Max. axle loading	15t 15c	14t 0c

Class 2251 No 2204 in a condition that suggests it had been recently out-shopped new from Swindon. This engine was built in August 1939; the tender is much older being of Dean or Churchward vintage.   *HMRS*

The most significant difference between the two designs lay in the axle loading which placed the new engines in the Route Colour yellow category. There did not appear to be any attempt to compare performance but it must have been questionable whether the tapered version offered any appreciable improvement over the older design. Further, it was more expensive to manufacture and added to the overall weight, and thus maximum axle loading.

With the new class unable to work over routes where the Dean Goods was the principal motive power, it was not a complete replacement for the 1883 design. The only way this could be achieved would be by track up-grading to elevate uncoloured routes to the Yellow status – hardly viable in areas with low traffic volumes.

The wartime installation of makeshift cab extensions unconsciously showed the way in which the Dean Goods could have been modernised while retaining its "all lines" availability ie as an alternative to Class 2251. Earlier engines were fitted with lever reverse, whereas later examples carried the screw type. A variety of tenders were used: Dean/Churchward 2500 and 3000-gallon types, the ex-ROD 4000 gallon type, and the continuous fender version of the 3000-gallon tender introduced by Collett. The final two locomotives, actually completed by British Railways, enjoyed the distinction of being the last 0-6-0s introduced in these islands, excluding Class UG Nos 145 to 149 delivered in January/February 1948 by Beyer Peacock to the Great Northern Railway (Ireland),

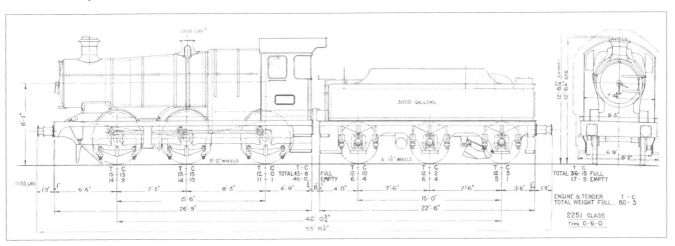

Figure XIV GWR Class 2251

Above - Class 2251 No 2227 in shabby condition, fitted with older style tall safety valve cover, and coupled to a modern Collett-vintage 3000 gallon tender.

HMRS

Below - Class 2251 No 2286 at Worcester shed on 12th March 1939. This engine displays a small feature typical of earlier class members – split hand rails adjacent to the cab side windows while on later examples, a single "L" shaped rail was fitted. This view displays a third option with a 4000-gallon tender that came to the GWR with an ROD 2-8-0 purchased in the 1920s. Bargain prices were paid for the ROD engines and tenders; after withdrawal of the less serviceable locomotives, the tenders mostly moved to Aberdare 2-6-0s and on their withdrawal, some passed to Class 2251.

RS Carpenter Photos

Above - Class 2251 No 2243 with ROD tender at Old Oak common in the 1950s. *Lens of Sutton*

Below - Class 2251 No 2244 leaving Aberdovey on 4th June 1952 with a Machynlleth-bound passenger train. *M Whitehouse Collection*

The construction of the 120 members of the class was accorded moderate priority:

Lot No	Engine Nos	Built	Lot No	Engine Nos	Built
261	2251-2270	1930	347	2231-2240	1944
283	2271-2280	1934		2241-2250	1945
298	2281-2290	1936	360	3200-3209	1946
312	2291-2299/2200	1938		3210-3217	1947
322	2201-2210	1939		3218/ 3219	1948
337	2211-2230	1940			

Above - Over four years into nationalisation and the new owners are still finding work for the class. It is September 1952 and No 2532 is hauling an up goods of over 40 wagons near Didcot.
SV Blencowe Collection

Below - The oldest surviving Dean Goods, No 2322.is seen here departing Bristol Temple Meads on a passenger train destined for Weston-Super-Mare.
City Photographic Collection

Chapter 9

THE LAST DEAN

With no unusual ceremony, No 5037 *Monmouth Castle* left Paddington on time with the 11.50 pm train to Penzance on 31st December 1947. Exactly 15 minutes later, No 5032 *Usk Castle* started out on its journey to Birkenhead to a fanfare of exploding detonators, this being the first British Railways (Western Region) train to leave the terminus. A few bangs in the night and an act of Parliament might have helped serve the needs of form; changing the substance was a different matter.

In January 1948, four locomotives were repainted at Wolverhampton after overhaul. Three – 0-4-2T No 1412, 2-6-2T No 3150, and 0-6-0PT No 3650 appeared in plain green; No 2323 (Machynlleth), the

second oldest 0-6-0 owned by BR(WR), appeared in green also but with the initials "GWR" on the tender, as if nothing had changed. A small gesture of defiance perhaps but resonant of Crewe in the 1920s when following an edict from the ex-Midland Railway politburo that engines were to be painted red once supplies of black had been used up, Beames and Co continued to find "surplus" stocks of the latter colour from somewhere for a surprisingly long time.

That the remaining Dean Goods were still fulfilling a useful role across the Western Region was evident in the GWR's official allocations as at 31st December 1947:

London Div (3)						Neath Div (3)					
Didcot	2532					Carmarthen	2409	2411	2431	2474	
Reading	2573					**Newport Div (8)**					
Oxford	2579					Cardiff Canton	2484	2537	2538	2570	
Bristol Div (9)						Newport (Ebbw Junc)	2407				
Bath Road	2444	2462				Pontypool Road	2385				
St Philips Marsh	2322	2340	2426	2534	2578	Severn Tunnel Junc	2414	2460			
Swindon	2563					**Central Wales Div (21)**					
Westbury	2445					Brecon	2343	2351	2386	2401	2468
Wolverhampton Div (2)						Builth Wells	2556				
Banbury	2408					Llanidloes	2382	2516	2569		
Chester	2513					Machynlleth	2356				
Worcester Div (7)						Moat Lane	2354	2449	2482		
Gloucester	2515					Oswestry	2327	2483	2523	2543	
Lydney	2350					Portmadoc	2323	2464	2572		
Hereford	2349	2541									
Worcester	2339	2458	2551								

Another Temple Meads view in BR days. This unidentified class member displays no evidence of new ownership unlike the ex-LMS Stanier Black 5 behind.

Details of their duties are incomplete and it is unclear why single locomotives were retained at locations such as Oxford, Westbury and Chester. It seems most probable that they were used on shunting, pilot duties or trip working i.e. tasks that could have been equally well covered by smaller pannier tanks and Class 2251. This is speculation but there might have been a policy of keeping a working reserve in the absence of any replacement type for Central Wales where the need for uncoloured route category engines remained.

There were specific roles for some engines such as at Reading where one was required as substitute for ex-MSWJR 2-4-0s on the Lambourn Branch. At that time Dean Goods were limited to 25 mph (passenger trains) and 15 mph (goods) on the branch. This restriction was lifted in May 1952 after track improvements that opened the route to yellow category engines, although No 2516 was seen on 3rd July 1953 hauling two coaches and four horseboxes. Once this work was finished it returned light engine to Reading.

Retention elsewhere seems to have been based in part on local esteem for popular veterans, rather in the vein of the respect enjoyed by No 2362, the final survivor of the double-framed Deans at Oswestry, its last shed. More definitive information is available for other areas.

In the summer of 1948, the class was filling a secondary role on the Cambrian Coast section. Machynlleth-Pwllheli services were mainly handled by Dukedogs and Class 45xx 2-6-2Ts, and to a lesser extent, Class 2251 0-6-0s. Dean Goods were working Machynlleth-Portmadoc freight trains, the favourites being Nos 2323, 2464, 2543 and 2572. Further south, Dukedogs and Dean Goods were sharing Moat lane-Brecon services. On 10th November 1948, No 2556 emerged from Wolverhampton Works with "British Railways" on its tender, the first of the class to be so decorated. Another typical duty then was the Kington branch goods, which was usually worked by No 2349.

Thus the class was on remote routes in Wales, minor branch line duties, shunting and trip working – as might be expected with a nationalised system planning a range of standard steam locomotives while flirting with diesel and gas turbine power sources. This environment was one where small 0-6-0s of the previous century should have had no role on front line duties, but once again the class served to surprise. On Sundays, the Severn Tunnel was regularly closed for maintenance work and London-South Wales services were diverted to alternative routes. Rather than take the hike up through Gloucester, most trains used the line over the Severn Bridge between Sharpness and Lydney, some miles upstream from the Severn Tunnel.

Above - The ex-Midland & South Western Junction Railway 2-4-0s Nos 1334-1336 class were associated with the Dean Goods in the final years. These engines were retained for working the Lambourn branch when traffic was too heavy to be handled by diesel railcars (usually No 18). A Dean Goods would substitute if a 2-4-0 was not available. No 1334 is seen here at Swindon on 22nd May 1952; it was withdrawn the following September.
EW Fry

Below - Another veteran 0-6-0 class that saw out its time with BR in Wales was ex-Cambrian Large Belpaire Goods. No 895 is seen at Machynlleth – at the Grouping this was an Oswestry engine while it had moved to Builth Wells at nationalisation. By withdrawal in October 1954, it was back at Oswestry.
HMRS

Above - In their final years, the Dean Goods were mainly associated with Wales as in this case with No 2572 at Brecon. This engine later reversed the prevailing trend by leaving Wales for England; it last allocation was Bristol St Philips Marsh.

City Photographic Collection.

Below - The "Dukedog" or Class 32xx (later 90xx) introduced between 1936 and 1939 by fitting Duke boilers on Bulldog chassis also spent their final years in Central Wales. No 9012 was a Machynlleth engine at nationalisation, and was still allocated there when withdrawn in July 1957.

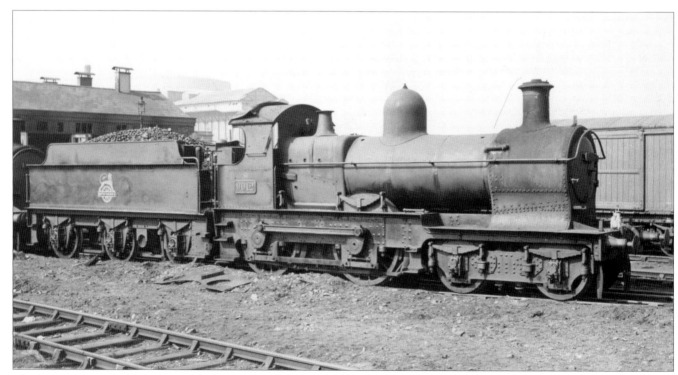

Above - No 2401 departing from Barmouth Junction on a passenger train.   *RK Blencowe Negative Archive*

Below - No 2407, seen here at Oswestry, was one of the Central Wales contingent that was withdrawn in January 1952, well ahead of the 1953 massacre. In this view from early BR days, this engine appears to be in reasonable external condition.

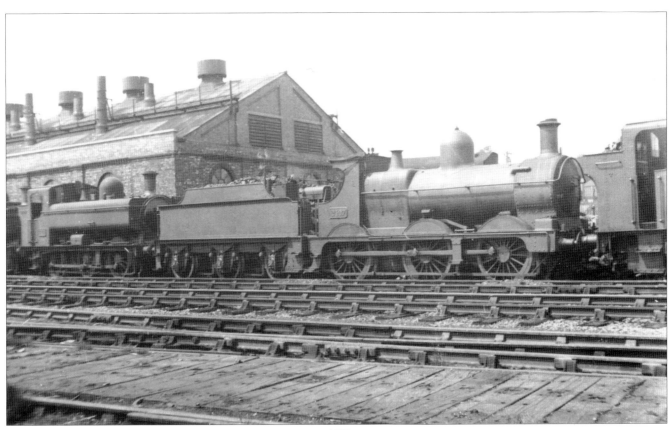

Above - No 2340, then of Bristol appears to be standing in the down goods loop at Uphill Junction near Weston-Super-Mare on 21st April 1950.

Below - No 2340 now has the road and is pulling out of Uphill junction loop on its way towards Taunton. From this angle, the significant length of the train is evident. By the date of this view (21st April 1950), only 12 members of the 23xx series remained in service but age obviously was considered no deterrent to hard work.   *Both; CM & JM Bentley*

Above - Eight days later, No 2340 is on shed at Bristol St Philips Marsh, apparently in dirtier state than in the previous two views.
HC Casserley

Below - And No 2340 yet again… in this case passing the Bristol Temple Meads Loco Yard Signal Box *circa* 1951. The engine now looks rundown but in fact was not withdrawn from Westbury shed until June 1954.
PJ Gartland Collection

Above - No 2579 on a secondary passenger working south of Wolvercote Junction.

Below - No 2350 at Leamington in 1948 or 1949 on a goods working from Gloucester. The engine is in smart condition having had a smoke number plate fitted but the tender has yet to display any sign of new ownership.   *PJ Gartland Collection*

No 2409 in the presence of royalty at Swindon on 3rd June 1951, almost two years before withdrawal from Oswestry in April 1953.

This 22 span cast iron bridge, completed in 1879, was a rather flimsy affair necessitating limits on locomotive weight and train speeds. Jointly owned by the GWR and LMS from the Grouping, at nationalisation most services were hauled by ex-GWR engines. (There were quaint working instructions that no train should cross the bridge in less than three minutes and that only Classes 2021, 74xx, 14xx and non-condensing (?) Dean Goods Nos 2322-2346/2382-2484/2513-2579 were permitted). Mainline passenger trains were therefore hauled on Sundays over this route by Dean Goods which proudly and legitimately carried express passenger train headlamps.

Nationalisation allowed the class to break new ground. Responsibility for operating the Hereford-Brecon route, which had been mainly part of the LMS, passed to BR (WR) and ex-GWR engines were gradually drafted in. Nos 2401 and 2451 were seen at work in May/June 1951 on both passenger and goods trains. At that time, Newport-Brecon trains were being shared between Dean, Collett and ex-Cambrian 0-6-0s.

The class still showed a propensity to wander when No 2568 (Swindon) made a surprise appearance at Plymouth on 6th July 1949 on a fish train working. This was believed to be the first appearance that far west in over 10 years – and almost definitely the last.

Under military control, the class had enjoyed a strong affinity with the Shropshire and Montgomeryshire Railway but civilian No 2483 (Oswestry) was seen on the line in May 1949 with a 20-ton breakdown crane in connection with the dismantling of a bridge. This is believed to have been the only example still fitted with top feed.

Although several remained concentrated at Bristol (on 24th July 1949 No 2444 was at Bath Road while St Philips Marsh was hosting Nos 2322/2462/2578), the critical mass resided at Oswestry. On 3rd September 1949, Nos 2327/2382/2452/2482/2516 were on shed in company with ex-Cambrian 0-6-0s Nos 893/896. The continuing need for the class was demonstrated by No 2483 in Wolverhampton Works in March 1949 for overhaul and the fitting of new cylinders. In September, No 2322 (built 1884) was in for heavy repairs, and two months later Nos 2349/2452/2538 were there for the same purpose.

A significant observation was that of ex-LMS 2MT 2-6-0 No 46413 which was at Swindon Works in November 1949 together with No 2579. The latter was being prepared for the Test Plant. On 24th November, the LMS engine hauled a Stoke Gifford-Didcot train comprising a dynamometer car and 39 loaded wagons on a Class 1 freight working. Comparative running then took place with No 2579 on the Test Plant, and further road testing by No 46413 between Swindon and Gloucester on 10th/11th December. The 2-6-0 was back on the Test Plant on the 16th. It would have been preferred to conduct the road testing between Neath and Brecon but there were no suitable freight workings over that route. In June 1950, No 46413 was undergoing yet more evaluation on the Test Plant, and did not return to the LM Region until September that year.

The future of the remaining Dean Goods was a matter of debate. Despite the steady stream of withdrawals, five were repaired during 1950, as there was official concern that the class had become so depleted that there were not enough to handle its traditional duties.

The repair programme and the recognised need for retention of the survivors was at odds with the announcement of withdrawals planned for 1950/51: all remaining Bulldogs, Dukes, Saints, Stars (except Nos 4061/4062), the seven oldest Class 43xx, sundry other classes, and all remaining 0-6-0s (including the ex-Cambrian engines) up to No 2411. The younger Dean

Goods were to be concentrated in areas where heavier classes were prohibited. One such preserve was removed when after trials in November 1949, ex-LMS Class 2MT 2-6-0s were passed to work over the Severn Bridge; by March 1951 Class 63xx were also working the Sunday trains.

Work was still available where axle loading was not an issue. During 1950, one of the Bristol allocation was regularly used on Lawrence Hill-Portishead services. Other work came the way of the Bristol engines in the summer of 1951 when No 2456 (Bath Road) was regularly stabled overnight at Barrow Road shed (ex-LMS) while engaged on local freight work from Westerleigh yard to Yate. On 13th June 1950, No 2407 (Cardiff) was derailed at Kidlington on the Hinksey-Banbury goods. On 18th April 1951, No 2340 was at Taunton, thought to have arrived with a pick-up goods from Bristol. An extraordinary sight on 2nd May 1951 was of Class 2251 No 2241 departing Hayes Loop double headed by No 2340 on a down goods comprising 68 wagons. The pair had the train well under control on what could have been the last working of a Dean Goods in the London area.

Above - No 2401 waiting for the unloading of the brake third of its train to be completed.

Opposite page - The 1953 withdrawals of Dean Goods were made possible by the introduction of 25 Ivatt 2MT 2-6-0s of LMS design. This batch was built that year at Swindon and No 46256 was the penultimate member of that class.

By June 1950, nine had been withdrawn since nationalisation but the distribution pattern had not changed:

condemned on the 19th. How different from the grotesque condition to which steam was reduced at its final demise, and how reminiscent of those rows of

London Div (3)		
Didcot	2532	2579
Reading	2573	
Bristol Div (8)		
Bath Road	2445	2534
St Philips Marsh	2322	2340	2462
	2578	
Westbury	2426	2444
Wolverhampton Div (4)		
Chester	2513	
Hereford	2349	2515	2541
Worcester Div (2)		
Worcester	2339	2458
Neath Div (3)		
Neath	2411	
Carmarthen	2431	2474

Newport Div (5)		
Cardiff Canton	2407	2537
Pontypool Road	2385	
Severn Tunnel Junc	2414	2469
Central Wales Div (20)		
Brecon	2343	2351	2401
	2409	2452	2468
Machynlleth	2323	
Oswestry	2327	2354	2386
	2408	2449	2482
	2483	2484	2516
	2538	2543	2556
	2572	

Four years into nationalisation, with affection for the GWR remaining strong, there was widespread recognition that a motive power era was rapidly passing. This is no better demonstrated than with one of the few remaining Saints, No 2933 *Bibury Court*. This engine was specially cleaned at its home shed, Leamington Spa, on 16th January 1953 before its last journey to Swindon the following day; it was

sparkling broad gauge engines standing at Swindon in 1892.

By April 1952, the arrival of LMS-design 2-6-0s was obviously anticipated as the 1953 condemnation programme included 10 Dean Goods. It was also expected that Class 57xx 0-6-0PTs would soon replace the class on the Hereford-Brecon line. These

Above - Apart from war-related withdrawals, the greatest number of condemnations occurred in 1953. No 2543 was one of this group and was recorded at Swindon on 10th May. Apart from removal of the smokebox number plate, there are no other signs that dismantling has started.

Below - The date is 15th June 1954 and No 2340 has also reached the end of the road at Swindon.   *RK Blencowe Collection*

Above - No 2532 was one of the last dozen in service. This engine, withdrawn in 1954, is seen here on a down engineers train at Didcot in British Railways days – a classic ageing goods locomotive with a classic clerestory coach coupled behind the tender. This view poignantly reminds that elements of BR(WR) formed a working museum in the 1950s and that many enthusiasts (like the author) failed fully to appreciate how many treasures could still be witnessed in every day service.   *Amyas Crump*

Previous page, top - Final role call for Nos 2449, 2401, 2468, 2408 – all victims of the 1953 cull – on the scrap road at Swindon in February of that year.   *Eric Sawford/ Railway Modeller*

Previous page, middle - Another of the casualties of 1953 at Swindon – No 2537. The engine in front would appear to be 2-6-2T Class 44xx No 4403 which was withdrawn in January 1953, displaying the distinctive distance piece between old and new buffer beams to support extended bunkers fitted to that class from 1924 onwards. The engine behind is a Class 2021 pannier tank.
                                                                                Eric Sawford/ Railway Modeller

Previous page, bottom - No details have been traced of works attention to No 2516 but in this early BR view, the engine is in poor external condition.

In the 1950s, survivors were in demand for rail tour duties. On 24th April 1955, No 2474 was near the site of Longdon Road station on the freight only branch from Morton-in-Marsh to Shipston-on-Stour.

intentions notwithstanding, they were still making their presence felt in odd locations. In August, No 2460 was seen in the sidings at Severn Tunnel Junction while a month later, No 2352 substituted for the usual Class 14xx 0-4-2T on the Wallingford auto train.

The new 2-6-0s had become well established in Central Wales by March 1953 and crews were appreciative of their comforts, particularly during inclement weather. A driver aboard one of the new steeds remarked to an observer, with pride and sincerity "The old Great Western was a good company to work for …but they thought their enginemen liked to have plenty of fresh air".

No 2516 had become something of a rail tour celebrity by 1955, as at Minsterley on 23rd April.   *HF Wheeler Collection*

Above - No 2516 also visited Wellington on the rail tour of 23rd April 1955.

Below - By 21st May 1955, further efforts had been made to heighten the illusion that nationalisation had never happened. The BR smokebox number plate remains in place but the figures have been over-painted so as to camouflage its presence. Very likely as part of the same subterfuge, the number has been returned to the buffer beam. No 2516 makes a fine sight carrying express train headlamps at Birmingham Snow Hill.

Also on 21st May 1955, No 2516's rail tour penetrated the Oldbury branch, a line that had not seen a passenger train in over 40 years. The engine is running round its train.
RK Blencowe Collection

At the end of 1955, only No 2516 and 2538 remained in service, both allocated to Oswestry. They seemed to lead a charmed life, especially as early in 1956 it was announced that Class 2251 Nos 2251/2252 were to be included in the 1957 condemnation programme. Remarkably, No 2538 went to Wolverhampton Works in January 1956 for heavy repairs, returning to duty on 18th February.

The good companions. The final pair seen together – No 2516 with No 2538 behind.
SV Blencowe

WILLIAM DEAN

The two old engines were retained for working the Abermule-Kerry branch. This line had lost its passenger trains in 1931 but an attenuated goods service remained on Mondays, Wednesdays and Fridays. This comprised the engine and guards van from the pick-up goods that left Oswestry at 9.30 am, due at Abermule at 1.30 pm plus whatever wagons were offering for the 3½ mile branch. The 5 mph speed limit was regularly ignored to avoid stalling on the climb up through the Mule Gorge. On return to Abermule, the remainder of the train was recovered and taken on to Newtown. Then the engine went light to Moat Lane Junction to haul the 8.13 pm passenger train to Llanidloes where it stabled overnight. The next day it returned home on the 6.30 am Llanidloes-Oswestry passenger train. This cycle was repeated three times a week by the same engine while the other rested at Oswestry.

The need to keep the pair ceased on 7th May 1956 with closure of the Kerry branch and No 2516 was

withdrawn later that month, arriving at Swindon in June. Not long after came the welcome news that this engine was to be officially preserved, and that it was safely stored in the Swindon Stock Shed.

Sole survivor No 2538 was in good mechanical fettle following its repairs at Wolverhampton, matched by smart external condition. In June 1956 it was noted engaged in shunting and on the occasional trip working to Gobowen. By 12th September it was more active, being seen on the Moat Lane-Brecon goods. After stabling overnight it worked back to Oswestry the following day. Later that year it was regularly working goods trains to Whitchurch and reportedly was to be fitted with a snow plough for the coming winter. Whether this took place is not known but on 15th May 1957 came the final call to Swindon. On the evening of the 22nd, it was seen en route at Stafford Road, marked "condemned". On 16th June, a boiler was noted in the dismantling shed at Swindon with "The Last Dean" chalked on the side of its smokebox.

Above - No 2538 looks in good fettle at Oswestry shed on 30th August 1953. Extra weather equipment in the form of a cab roof tarpaulin looks ready to be fixed up.
Initial Photographs

Opposite, above - In this view of No 2538 at Oswestry dated 30th June 1956, rain was clearly forecast – unless the crew required protection from the savage Welsh tropical sun.
HC Casserley

Opposite, below - No 2538 is seen here, resting at Llanidloes.
WA Brown

The newly formed British Railways inherited a heterogeneous collection of reminders of the Dean era. This comprised Class 2021 0-6-0ST/PT (120 examples); Aberdare 2-6-0 (12); Bulldog 4-4-0 (45); Metro 2-4-0T (10); Class 3571 0-4-2T (3); Duke 4-4-0 (11), and their age meant that the continued presence of most was to be short. The Dukedogs, whose numbers were intact at the beginning of 1948, could

be added to this list although their "modernity" ensured their existence until the end of the 1950s.

The comprehensive pre-war construction programme had rendered this interesting group redundant, except for the 2021s which were soon to make way for the new Class 16xx. The remaining Dean Goods were different in that so far, they had no substitute over

WILLIAM DEAN

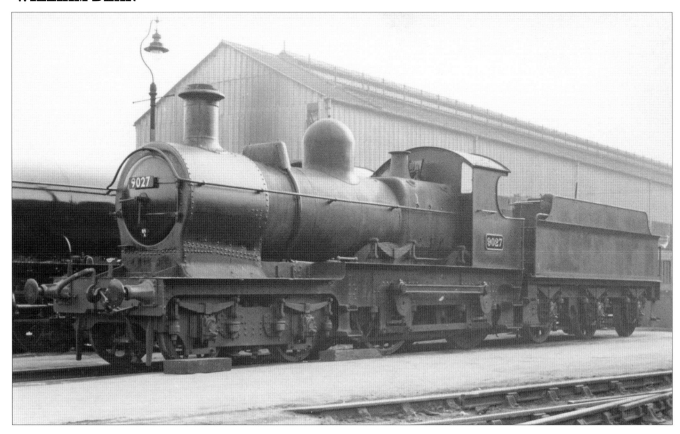

A 'modern' Dukedog, No 9027 was also a long-term Welsh resident. It was a Machynlleth engine at nationalisation but was withdrawn from Oswestry in August 1957. It is seen here at Swindon fitted with a top feed boiler.

those routes denied to Class 2251 0-6-0s. This omission was very likely caused by the same exigencies of war that had extended the working lives of the other older classes, but there is evidence to suggest that consideration might have been turning in the 1940s to a new strain of lightweight tender engines.

Speculation about "what might have happened" can be dangerous territory invoking contentious debate but there are grounds for believing that Hawksworth's thoughts could have been turning to this vintage niche in the motive power spectrum. In 1945, plans were prepared for an outside cylindered 2-6-0PT with 4' 7½" driving wheels that had a number of modern features.

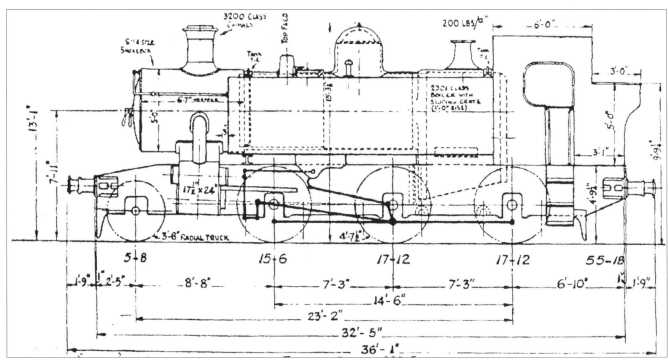

The last route over which only the Dean Goods was permitted was the freight-only branch from Abermule to Kerry. In its last years, the branch saw a goods train on Mondays, Wednesdays and Fridays. No 2538 is shunting at Kerry and as can be seen, loads could be substantial. Working the branch with its gradients therefore required some skill. After the branch closed in May 1956, the need to retain the final pair fell away and No 2516 was withdrawn that month, leaving No 2538 as the sole representative in normal service.

Opposite - Figure XV- Outline drawing of proposed 2-6-0PT of 1945.

Below - Figure XVI - Diagram of the final new Great Western design of all, Class 15xx, which were never GWR engines, being built by British Railways.

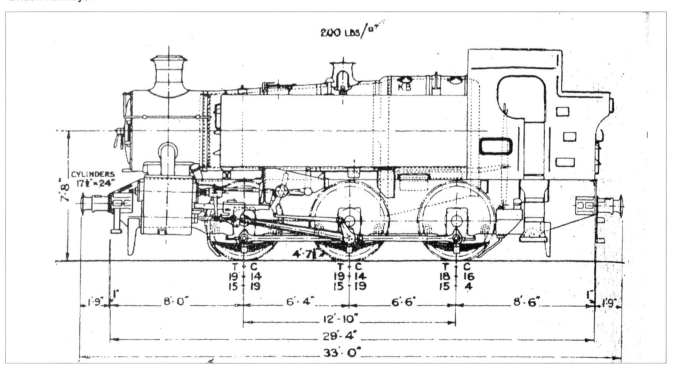

WILLIAM DEAN

That this was not a draughtsman's flight of fancy is borne out by the Class 15xx 0-6-0PT that actually appeared in 1949. The two designs bore a clear familial resemblance with extensive use of welded construction, outside motion, no running plate or splashers, excellent accessibility and inclined cylinders – the last feature a marked departure from the Churchward tradition.

The principal drawback with the proposed 2-6-0PT lay in the restricted space at the back end, limiting coal capacity and thus operating range. However, in the tradition of Swindon producing tank versions of tender locomotives and vice versa, removal of pannier tanks and bunker, and addition of a tender would have provided a template for Dean Goods replacement. Resultant savings of 12-15 tons would have been partially offset by 5' 2" driving wheels and installation (perhaps) of a running plate but a lightweight mogul tender engine could have been created with an acceptable axle loading. It would be nice to think that Swindon had this notion in mind, especially as a slightly modified Class 2301 boiler was incorporated in the plans.

Nationalisation brought new GWR-derived design initiatives to a close but the Dean Goods had a role to play in the evolvement of the next generation. In the expectation that steam would remain the principal power source for the foreseeable future, the new owners were keen to explore the potential offered by the design and construction practices of the Big Four. The first outward expression of this intent was in the Locomotive Exchanges of 1948, an exercise that yielded limited useful information. The idea of comparing designs on the road was notionally attractive but the results were distorted by differing driving styles. Some crews strove to exact maximum haulage performance while others were intent on minimising coal consumption.

To Swindon's chagrin, none of their participants (King, Modified Hall and Class 2884) demonstrated any consistent distinction, and although further tests run on home territory yielded better results, the episode highlighted the inconsistences possible with sole reliance on road testing. It is perhaps with this experience in mind that considerable effort was expended in evaluating the type proposed as the Dean Goods' replacement.

An important omission in Stanier's re-stocking programme of the LMS had been provision of a modern tender locomotive in that company's Type 2/ 3/ 4 power categories. After the war HG Ivatt had set about filling this gap and his Type 2MT 2-6-0, later affectionately nicknamed "Mickey Mouse", became the basis for the BR standard type in this category. As noted above, one was lent to the Western Region in 1949/ 50 and underwent extensive evaluation. It would appear that Swindon was keen to make up for its earlier indifference towards a modern all-lines tender engine.

Perhaps with the inconsequential conclusions of the 1948 Exchanges in mind, the Swindon stationary testing plant played an important role in the exercise – an approach that later proved valuable in modifying the Manors and doubling their maximum steaming rate. With regard to the Mickey Mouse, stationary testing in comparison with Dean Goods No 2579 established that the old engine had a superior steaming capacity. Resultant modifications to the modern design made a good engine even better. Then over 52 years old, the Dean Goods had been painted in lined BR mixed traffic black for the occasion and looked very fine in this neo LNWR livery.

No 2579's triumph was a fitting valediction to a fine class, and to the GWR's greatest Locomotive Superintendent.

Previous pages - 'The Last Dean'; No 2538 is approaching Abermule on the Oswestry-Moat Lane goods, a train that is at least 25 wagons long so the old engine is still earning its keep. The bulk of the train will be left at Abermule while the engine takes its three-times-a-week excursion up to Kerry and back before proceeding to Moat Lane. The signalman has his arm out to collect the train staff, standing in front of Abermule Signal Box which like the station appears to be immaculate. Ignore the car waiting at the level crossing gates, the smokebox number plate, and the BR "cycling lion" on the tender and the scene is almost timeless. The year could be 1946 or 1936, but the date is actually 29th April 1956.

The Kerry branch closed a few days later and with it passed the *raison d'être* for keeping representatives of the class in service. Nonetheless, Oswestry was able to find employment for the Last Dean for a further 13 months.   *JA Peden*

Chapter 10

A CASE PROVEN?

We are like dwarfs on the shoulders of giants, so that we can see more than they, and things at a greater distance, not by virtue of any sharpness of sight on our part, or any physical distinction, but because we are carried high and raised up by their giant size.

- attributed by John of Salisbury to Bernard of Chartres, 1159

Reflecting upon William Dean as an individual and upon what he achieved for the Great Western Railway induces overwhelming impressions of loneliness, duty and courage.

Elevation at the age of 23 from apprentice to the rank of chief assistant to the divisional superintendent was a meteoric advancement that isolated him from his peer group and sat him directly in the world of senior management, an arena from which he did not escape for 39 years. Even responsibility limited to that of "assistant" was destined to be short-lived. Following Joseph Armstrong's move to Swindon after little more than a year, the ex-apprentice found himself with a new boss and the added responsibility of Works Manager. Financial stringencies caused the doubling up of responsibilities but for Dean this went further in his assumption of the Chief Clerk's duties – three important positions concurrently held by one man.

Confronting the key challenge of how to manage the rundown and extinction of the Broad Gauge, Joseph Armstrong called Dean – barely five years out of apprenticeship – from Wolverhampton to serve once again at his side. The future must then have appeared set fair as the protégé of a business leader cast in the finest mould of benign Victorian patriarch. The company's finances were gradually improving and motive power issues would hopefully soon be simplified by eradication of the broad gauge incubus.

Yet within nine years, the complexion of Dean's career had changed radically. The shock of Joseph Armstrong's death in office was compounded by the nightmare revelation that the Severn Tunnel project would be more difficult and costly than had ever been expected. The corollary was twofold – continuation of the cost and operating inconvenience of the broad gauge and deferment of much-needed infrastructural investment west of Exeter. In broad terms, the company struggled under this yoke for around 30 years from the financial crisis of the mid-1860s.

Such constraints would have daunted any locomotive superintendent in charge of a conventional motive power fleet but William Dean's obligations were far from conventional. Broad gauge services had to be maintained with an ageing and archaic fleet for an indeterminate period. The motive power of the newly acquired companies from Bristol westwards needed assimilation and rationalisation. Narrow gauge machines required development to meet longer-term traffic requirements. The diverging needs of the two gauges had to be accommodated by a separate locomotive breed that could be readily adapted to operate on either.

In sum, Dean's task at Swindon meant responsibility for four discrete groups of locomotives with all their associated idiosyncrasies – burdens enough without taking into account the Wolverhampton anomaly. George Armstrong might have felt cause for frustration at being passed over for his late brother's job but the prevailing circumstances demanded a man with rare qualities. His obstreperous reaction to Dean's advancement shows a lack of understanding of those demands; the late Joseph Armstrong had preferred wisely and Daniel Gooch chose well.

Dean's response to this petulance suggests flexibility and astuteness. Rather than enter a trial of strength, he left George to his own devices and over time reached a professional relationship that suited both, and above all the company's best interests. Wolverhampton played a vital role through those difficult years in providing many locomotives whose modest duties kept them out of the limelight but in the forefront of revenue generation. The company was blessed in having two men capable of coping with the demands exerted by their respective locomotive works. The achievement of this effective partnership says much for the manner in which Dean managed personal relationships.

Little has been recorded of his way of handling people but the evidence suggests that his competence was also effective in this area. For 12 years, his work –

particularly his failed experiments – was under the scrutiny of a chairman who was himself an accomplished locomotive engineer. He sponsored and supported WH Stanier's spirit of scientific enquiry into metallurgy, which demonstrated a visionary approach to locomotive construction. He pioneered investigative work into alternative construction methodologies including bogie design, tandem compounds, locomotive brake systems, valve gear, and boiler construction. Pursuit of so many lines of enquiry called for courage in being prepared to accept and learn from failure plus tenacity and determination. It also meant that he had to lead effectively, and to gain the loyalty of, his subordinates.

Above all, one relationship stands out from the rest. Dean obviously had an eye for talent and in 1882 recognised that a 25-year-old member of the drawing office team was especially gifted, elevating him to the role of Inspecting Engineer for materials. It could be speculated that this was a reflection of Dean's continuing interest in matters metallurgical but it was more significantly the first step up the ladder for GJ Churchward.

The multiple challenges that Dean had to confront, and the senior executive burden that he bore from a young age would have inevitably detached him in a social sense from his fellows. The antagonistic nature – at least in the early stages – of his relationship with George Armstrong might have been repeated with other older colleagues as a young man's rapid rise can engender envy and enmity among co-workers. A usual response to the isolation imposed by such situations is to seek solace in family life but there he was cruelly served by twice becoming a widower and by both his daughters predeceasing him, prior to his retirement.

Against the background of corporate difficulties and personal tragedy, William Dean did so much to lead the GWR's locomotive affairs out of confusion and into confidence and self-assurance at the eve of the company's brilliant Edwardian phase. Along the way, he fostered a locomotive story of infinite variety and interest. The delicate beauty of 2-2-2 No 157, the mysteries of 4-2-4T No 9, the pragmatic simplicity of the convertibles, the unparalleled elegance of *Achilles* et al, and the dogged reliability demonstrated by his 0-6-0 goods engine on distant shores all form part of the story of William Dean

His memorial was the pioneer 4-6-0 that bore his name but in the creation of which he might not have been much involved. His epitaph was the finest locomotive family the world has seen, created by his successor in an extraordinarily short space of time, in large part due to his pioneering and experimental efforts.

This extraordinary individual has yet to receive the full acclamation that is his due. Perhaps, in a world where re-creation of long-lost locomotives is now an accepted practice, proper recognition might in due course take the form of a working replica of one of William Dean's engines.

One can but hope.

Appendix A.1
Boiler histories - Dean Goods

To help identify boiler styles, the RCTS (the Railway Correspondence and Travel Society) devised a two digit code for different types. This system, although unofficial, has gained widespread acceptance as a convenient means of recording changes of boiler type.

All Dean Goods were fitted with parallel boilers, nominally of five different varieties, but with internal variations within each type. In all examples, the top of the boiler barrel was flush with the top surface of the firebox. The principal external differences concerned the firebox and the dome:

RCTS Code	Description
S0	Round-topped firebox; domeless
S2	Round-topped firebox; dome mounted on front ring of barrel i.e. "front dome" boilers
S4	Round-topped firebox; dome mounted on rear ring of barrel i.e. "back dome" boilers
B2	Early form of Belpaire firebox boiler rebuilt from type S2, with dome retained on front ring
B4	Built new in Belpaire form; dome on rear ring of barrel

In the early days, official records stated which boilers had been allocated to particular classes. With the 80 type S0 boilers built in 1881 to 1884 that were carried by the first Lot of Dean Goods and the remainder by two other classes, records were maintained of which boilers were fitted to which engines. This orderly approach soon broke down as boilers were exchanged during overhauls. For example, the S4 type (of which 348 were built new and others rebuilt to conform) was fitted indiscriminately to several tank and tender classes.

To identify boilers of different types, the GWR formally adopted a numerical system of Group classification. S2 boilers were recorded in Groups 16 and 18, each of which contained fireboxes of differing leading dimensions. The distinction between the two groups was based on the later category having slightly larger barrels; the increase of 2 inches resulted in a diameter of 4' 5" which was standard for all remaining boilers. All S4 boilers were in Group 19; B4 boilers were divided between Groups 20 (saturated) and 21 (superheated), although with further variations in firebox dimensions.

By 1912, an additional classification system had been introduced in the form of a two letter code, as subsidiary to the "Standard" classification system (i.e. Standard No 1 for Classes 28xx/29xx/40xx etc). Codes for Class 2301 were prefixed "P" with sequential letter suffixes. This system was used to identify variations in what became known as the "Class 2301" boiler which was fitted to the Dean Goods and to other classes. It is not possible to correlate these codes with the dimensional variations recorded within each Group. Thus, saturated RCTS Code B4 boilers came within Group 20 for which there were 12 recorded dimensional varieties but 14 different "P"-prefixed codes. The relationships between the various codes cannot be clearly reconciled but the following table summarises the situation as clearly as has proved possible:

Round-topped boilers, as originally fitted:

Boiler Group	Letter Codes	RCTS Code
15	None recorded - probably withdrawn before system introduced	S0
16	None recorded - probably withdrawn before system introduced	S2
18	PG, PH, PJ, PK, PL, PP, PT PU	S2
18X	None recorded	B2
19	PG, PH, PJ, PK ,PL, PP, PT PU	S4
20	PA, PB, PD, PE, PF, PQ, PS, PW, PE2, PF2, PH2, PJ2, PK2, PL2	B4
21	PC, PI, PR	B4

All members of Class 2301 were equipped with round-topped, flush fitting fireboxes when new. There were four distinct groups: domeless/ two types of visually identical front domed/ rear domed. Apart from the domeless variety which was exclusively used on Lot 61, the other styles were rotated throughout the entire class at subsequent overhauls. All but a small number eventually carried the rear domed (S4) variety; the exceptions moved straight from the S2 type to boilers with Belpaire fireboxes.

In a number of cases, engines that had carried S2 boilers when built, graduated to S4 and then reverted to S2. Also, there were examples of locomotives in the number series 2451 upwards that had been built new with S4 boilers later acquiring the S2 variety. Generally speaking, a locomotive once fitted with a Belpaire boiler remained so equipped until withdrawal but there were cases of reversion to round-topped boilers (Nos 2303/2304/2306/2319/2384/2421/2431/2474/2536).

The programme to install Belpaire boilers commenced in 1901 but some round-topped boilers had long lives, a few surviving into the 1920s.

WILLIAM DEAN

Lot 61 (Nos 2301 to 2320) Type S0 Group 15

Boiler type: two-ringed domeless
Firebox type: flush fitting round-topped
Barrel: 10' 3" x 4' 3"
Casing: 5' 4" long
Pressure: 140 lb/ sq in

This type was confined to the first 20 locomotives. The remaining 60 were fitted to 2-4-0T "Metropolitan" Class Nos 1445-1464 and the 40 members of 0-6-0ST Class 1813 as built. No more domeless boilers were built so

in the absence of spares, domed replacements were fitted commencing with No 2320 in July 1890. Apparently the boilers fitted to Nos 2301 to 2320 remained exclusive to that batch with the sole exception of one being carried by 2-4-0 "Stella" Class No 3520 between September 1900 and March 1904.

The last domeless boiler was removed from No 2310 in December 1905. All replacements were domed with round-topped fireboxes, except for No 2307 which received an early Belpaire firebox boiler. There were dimensional variations within the domeless boilers:

Built	Number	Firebox:			Tubes:		Heating surfaces:		(sq ft)
		length	width	height	no.	diameter	tubes	firebox	grate
Oct-81 to May-82	20	4' 8"	3' 7"	5' 2.5"	152	2"	836.8	92.5	16.4
Sep-82 to Oct-82	6	"	3' 6"	5' 6.5"	218	1 5/8"	973	105	"
Oct-82 to Jan-84	54	"	"	5' 10.5"	241	"	1079.1	113.6	"

Lot 62 (Nos 2321 to 2340) Type S2 Group 16

Boiler type: two-ringed front dome
Firebox type: flush fitting round-topped
Barrel: 10' 3" x 4' 5"
Casing: 5' 4" long
Pressure: 140 lb/ sq in

These were dimensionally identical with the last batch of the domeless type, the only difference being the dome which was mounted on the front boiler ring making them "front dome" engines.

Built	Number	Firebox:			Tubes:		Heating surfaces:		(sq ft)
		length	width	height	no.	diameter	tubes	firebox	grate
Jan-84 to Jun-84	20	4' 8"	3' 6"	5' 10.5"	241	1 5/8"	1079.1	113.6	16.4

Lots 63, 82, 87, 92 (Nos 2341 to 2360, 2381 to 2450)   Type S2 Group 18

Boiler type: two-ringed front dome
Firebox type: flush fitting round-topped
Barrel: 10' 3" x 4' 5"
Casing: 5' 4" long
Pressure: 140 lb/ sq in

There was significant dimensional variation within this Group resulting from later modifications in the number

and size of tubes; also boilers from other groups were rebuilt to conform with this type. In addition to being fitted to engines when new in the lots noted above, this type was installed in other engines when new: 0-6-0ST Class 1854 (except for the last 20 examples); 2-4-0 "Stella" Class 3201; Broad Gauge (later converted to narrow gauge) 2-4-0T Nos 3501 to 3510; and 2-4-0T Nos 3511 to 3520. (Last two types later rebuilt as part of the "Stella" 2-4-0 class).

Many of the S2 boilers built in 1884/ 5 had clack boxes fitted externally on the firebox sides.

Built	Number	Firebox:			Tubes:		Heating surfaces:		(sq ft)
		length	width	height	no.	diameter	tubes	firebox	Grate
Jul-84 to Dec-84	20	4' 8"	3' 4"	6' 2.5"	239	1 5/8"	1030	103.3	???
Dec-84 to Sep-85	25	"	"	"	268	1 1/2"	1107	"	???
Jan-90 to Oct-90	41	"	"	5' 11.5"	262	1 3/4"	1263	107.8	17.2
Jul-90 to Feb-91	21	"	"	"	"	"	"	103.3	"
Feb-91 to Jun-91	21	"	"	"	"	"	"	99.6	"
May-92 to Feb-93	40	"	"	"	245	"	1180.5	99.8	"
Oct-91 to Oct-95	65	"	"	"	"	"	"	108	"

Lots 99, 100, 104, 107,108, 111 (Nos 2451 to 2580) Type S4 Group 19

Boiler type: two-ringed back dome
Firebox type: flush fitting round-topped
Barrel: 10' 3" x 4' 5"
Casing: 5' 4" x 4' 6"
Pressure: 140-150 lb/ sq in

In addition to Class 2301, this boiler type was fitted to several classes of tender and tank locomotives.

Built	Number	Firebox: length	width	height	Tubes: no.	diameter	Heating tubes	surfaces: firebox	(sq ft) grate
May-95 to Aug-05	20	4' 8"	???	6" 0.5"	249	1 3/4"	1200	105.2	???
Oct-95 to Jul-01	308	"	3' 8"	"	"	"	1200	107.7	17.3
May-03 to Mar-04	20	"	"	"	245	1 5/8"	1096.6	"	"

Belpaire firebox boilers

Installation of Belpaire boilers commenced in 1901. Eventually they were carried by the entire class, except for 13 locomotives of Lot 104 (Nos 2491/2492/ 2494/2497/2498/2500/2501/2503/2504/2507 to 2510). These still retained round-topped fireboxes at the time of their withdrawal for rebuilding as 2-6-2Ts.

All lots except Nos 92 and 104 (locomotives Nos 2431 to 2450, 2491 to 2510) Type B2 Group 18X

Following the decision to change to Belpaire fireboxes, approximately 25 examples of S2 boilers (Group 18) were so modified. Overall dimensions were as for Group 20 described below but the dome was retained on the front boiler ring. Presumably it was later deemed more economic to construct new boilers than to modify existing types, the youngest of which had been constructed 7-8 years earlier.

All Lots Type B4 Group 20

Boiler type: two-ringed back dome
Firebox type: Belpaire
Barrel: 10' 3" x 4' 5"
Casing: 5' 4" x 4' 6"
Pressure: 160-200 lb/ sq in

Apart from the Dean Goods, this boiler type was fitted to several classes of tender and tank locomotives. Initially constructed in saturated form, from early 1929 onwards new boilers were built with superheaters (references L & M). Boilers of this type built at Wolverhampton were fitted with side-feed (refs F & G).

The distinction between Group 20 and Group 21 (next described) is confused as a number of boilers from other groups that were dimensionally modified to conform with Group 20. Further, some of Group 21 had their superheaters removed effectively making them part of this group.

Built	Ref.	No.	Firebox: length	width	height	Tubes: no.	diameter	Heating tubes	surfaces: firebox	(sq ft) grate
Feb-01 to Aug-01	A	6	4' 8"	3' 11"	6' 1"	235	1 7/8"	1218.9	110.5	15.5
Aug-01 to Dec-01	B	20	"	"	"	233	1 7/8"	1209.3	"	"
Jun-02 to Dec-02	C	17	"	"	"	116 + 117	1 7/8" 1 3/4"	1168	"	"
Mar-03 to Jul-03	D	7	"	"	"	233	1 3/4"	1128	"	"
Mar-03 to Jun-04	E	10	"	"	"	233	1 5/8"	1047.5	"	"
Oct-03 to Jun-04	F	6	"	???	"	237	1 3/4"	1147.3	111.6	???
Dec-04 to Sep-06	G	4	"	???	"	237	1 5/8"	1065.4	111.6	???
Aug-03 to Apr-06	H	40	"	3' 8"	6' 0.5"	245	1 5/8"	1100.4	106.3	15.5
Aug-06 to Jan-09	J	40	"	"	"	243	1 5/8"	1092.4	101.3	15.3
Aug-08 to Feb-15	K	154	"	"	"	"	"	1091.4	106.3	15.5
Jan-29 to Jul-31	L	310	"	"	"	2 + 233	5 1/8" 1 5/8"	1075.7	102.3	15.3
Sep-33 to Dec-50	M	603	"	"	"	2 + 219	5 1/8" 1 5/8"	1012.8	102.5	15.3

WILLIAM DEAN

All Lots, except Lot 104 Type B4 Group 21

These were constructed as a superheated version of Group 20 reference K with the same overall dimensions but with variations in heating surfaces as tabulated below. From the construction dates and the numbers built, it is apparent that Group 21 straddled the transition between selective application of superheaters and the later wholesale installation of this equipment in smaller locomotives.

Built	Ref.	No.	No. of tubes: 1 5/8"	5 1/8"	No. of s/ heater elements	Heating tubes	Surfaces (sq ft): superheater	firebox
Apr-11 to Aug-14	N	21	162	8	48	837.4	105.7	106.7
Mar-15 to Jun-17	P	110	201	6	"	937.8	97.3	106.4
Jun-17 to Dec-22	Q	135	195	"	"	960.9	"	"
Apr-21 to Oct-22	R	100	"	"	36	"	82.1	"
Dec-24 to 1928	S	120	"	"	"	"	75.3	"

Superheaters

The initial superheaters fitted to the class were of the 8-48 configuration with two groups of four flues set in the upper corners of the tube plate. Later superheaters had the normal 6-36 layout and it seems that the two types were rotated throughout the class during routine boiler changes. Locomotives known to have reverted for a period to saturated form are denoted § in the "Superheated" column below but this list is unlikely to be complete. No 2307 was unusual in receiving one of the earliest B4 boilers (Oct-03), and then one of the earliest with a superheater (Oct-12) before reverting to (saturated) B2 boiler (Dec-21).

Top feed

From 1913, top feed was fitted to about 40 B4 boilers; a couple of S4 boilers were also noted with this equipment but dates of fitting and removal, and the identities of the locomotives involved, have not been confirmed. The last top feed boiler appears to have survived into the early 1950s.

Changes of boiler type by locomotive - Lot 61

	S0	S2		S4	B2	B4		Superheated
2301	May-83	Mar-92		Jan-08		Nov-18		Nov-18§
2302	Jun-83	Oct-95				Nov-02		Feb-25
2303	Jun-83	Dec-96		May-10		Sep-03	May-16	Aug-23
2304	Jun-83	Aug-95	Jan-05		Sep-02	Dec-07		Nov-15
2305	Jul-83	Jun-92		Nov-06		Mar-14		Dec-24
2306	Jul-83	May-92		May-05		Nov-01	Nov-11	Mar-26
2307	Jul-83				Dec-21	Oct-03	Oct-27	Oct-12§
2308	Aug-83			Jul-01	Jan-05	Jan-07		-
2309	Aug-83	Feb-91			Feb-02	Jun-10		Mar-22
2310	Aug-83			Dec-05		Oct-14		-
2311	Aug-83	Jun-00				Jun-04		Jan-16
2312	Sep-83	Oct-90	Aug-07	Apr-00	Feb-11	Apr-21		-
2313	Sep-83	Jul-92		Jul-04		May-10		Jan-17
2314	Sep-83	Mar-05		Jun-99	Jun-12	Apr-15		Apr-15
2315	Oct-83	Mar-01		Jun-96	Nov-06	May-04	May-10	Jan-19
2316	Oct-83	Jan-99				Jun-16		Jun-26
2317	Oct-83	Jun-93		Aug-02		Feb-13		Aug-24
2318	Nov-83			Jun-97	Feb-12	Sep-03	Sep-14	May-21
2319	Nov-83	Jun-93	Apr-01¶	Feb-07		Oct-03	Oct-10	Oct-15
2320	Nov-83	Jul-90		May-03		Jan-07		Mar-34

¶ Recorded as an experimental boiler – details not available.

Changes of boiler type by locomotive - Lot 62

	S2			S4	B2	B4		Superheated
2321	Jan-84			Jul-99		Dec-27		Dec-27
2322	Jan-84					Nov-01		May-25
2323	Jan-84	Dec-04		Aug-07§		Mar-14		Aug-21
2324	Feb-84			Mar-00		Feb-15		-
2325	Feb-84			Feb-00		Jan-26		Jan-26
2326	Feb-84					Sep-01		Feb-16
2327	Feb-84			May-00	Jun-03	Apr-06		Nov-29
2328	Mar-84	Nov-09		Nov-04		May-14		Apr-32
2329	Mar-84	Jun-08		Sep-05		Aug-12		Aug-26
2330	Mar-84			Nov-98		Nov-12		Oct-28
2331	Mar-84	Apr-00§				Nov-08		Jan-27
2332	Apr-84			Oct-99		Nov-12		Nov-29
2333	Apr-84	Feb-09		May-04		May-14		-
2334	May-84			Feb-99		Sep-13		-
2335	May-84	Feb-04§		Sep-09		Jun-24		Jun-24
2336	May-84					Apr-03		Apr-27
2337	May-84	Feb-03		Jun-96	Mar-06	Oct-08		Oct-20
2338	Jun-84					May-02		Sep-26
2339	Jun-84	Oct-93§		Jan-06		May-14		May-14
2340	Jun-84	Aug-01§		Jun-04		Oct-13		Dec-26

§ The consecutive fitting of S2 type boilers to these locomotives suggests replacement of Group 16 (as built) with Group 18 types.

Changes of boiler type by locomotive - Lot 63

	S2			S4	B2	B4		Superheated
2341	Jul-84			May-06		Mar-20		-
2342	Aug-84					Mar-04		Apr-12
2343	Sep-84					Mar-16		Oct-20
2344	Aug-84			Nov-07		Mar-17		Nov-23
2345	Sep-84	May-13		Apr-04		May-18		May-18
2346	Sep-84			Jun-98		Oct-08		Mar-22
2347	Oct-84			May-04		Apr-21		Dec-27
2348	Oct-84	Aug-09		Dec-02	Jan-12	Sep-13		Jul-26
2349	Nov-84					Oct-03		Dec-26
2350	Nov-84	Apr-15		May-04		Jul-21		Jul-21
2351	Nov-84	Dec-03¶		Feb-01	Aug-06	Mar-15		Mar-15
2352	Nov-84			Feb-06		Sep-17		-
2353	Nov-84	Dec-04		Jan-03	May-07	Aug-14		Apr-20
2354	Nov-84	Nov-11		Nov-02	Dec-13	Sep-20		Sep-20
2355	Dec-84	Nov-02		Aug-99	Jun-05	Mar-10		Apr-16§
2356	Dec-84			Jan-03		Dec-20		Mar-26
2357	Dec-84			Jun-99	Jun-06	Dec-02	Nov-09	Jan-16
2358	Dec-84			Feb-05		Jul-08		Jul-15
2359	Dec-84			Apr-98	Nov-06	Jul-02	Nov-11	-
2360	Dec-84	Jan-04	Dec-14	May-96	Apr-07	Jun-21		Jun-21

¶ S2a type – for details refer to Appendix A.2 which covers boilers built primarily for use with Class 2361

WILLIAM DEAN

Changes of boiler type by locomotive - Lot 82

	S2		S4		B2	B4		Superheated
2381	Jun-90		Apr-07			Apr-15		Apr-15
2382	Jun-90					Dec-03		Sep-30
2383	Jun-90		Oct-06			Feb-09		Apr-15
2384	Jun-90		Nov-08			Nov-03	Aug-10	Sep-24
2385§	Jul-90					Jun-06		Jun-15§
2386	Jul-90		Nov-08			Apr-11		Apr-11
2387	Jul-90		May-07			Feb-12		-
2388	Jul-90	Jun-03	Dec-00	May-07		Feb-12		Feb-34
2389	Aug-90					Aug-06		May-31
2390	Aug-90		Nov-03			Oct-07		Sep-11
2391	Aug-90				Mar-02	Jun-06		Nov-15
2392	Aug-90					Nov-01		Jul-25
2393	Sep-90		Jan-06			Sep-15		Sep-15
2394	Sep-90				Feb-05	Sep-07		Aug-15
2395	Sep-90	Feb-09	Aug-06			Oct-11		Jul-21
2396	Sep-90		Jun-06			Aug-15		Aug-15
2397	Oct-90				Apr-02	Mar-08		Jun-11
2398	Oct-90		Dec-02			Mar-14		Mar-31
2399	Oct-90		Nov-99			Mar-10		Aug-20
2400	Oct-90	Feb-04	May-01			Feb-07		Nov-18

Changes of boiler type by locomotive - Lot 87

	S2		S4		B2	B4		Superheated
2401	Oct-91		Jun-01			Aug-04		Mar-33
2402	Oct-91		Jan-01			Apr-18		Apr-18
2403	Oct-91		May-02			Oct-10		Mar-27
2404§	Oct-91	Dec-05	Feb-03	Feb-10		Jun-15		Jun-15§
2405	Nov-91		Oct-09			Feb-16		Feb-16
2406	Nov-91	Mar-04	Jun-10	Jun-01	Nov-06	Dec-12	Oct-21	Jun-25
2407	Nov-91		Jan-03			Oct-18		Oct-18
2408	Nov-91	Feb-09	Nov-05			Nov-11		Mar-21
2409	Nov-91		Sep-04		Jul-07	Jan-11		Jan-19
2410§	Nov-91					Jan-03		Jul-17§
2411	Nov-91	Apr-06	May-03	Aug-11		Aug-14		Feb-25
2412	Nov-91		Nov-00			Nov-21		Nov-21
2413	Nov-91	Jan-06	Nov-02	Jan-10		Feb-14		Sep-17
2414	Dec-91	Nov-02	Aug-00	Feb-05		Jun-14		Jun-14
2415	Dec-91					Mar-08		Apr-25
2416	Dec-91					Sep-02		Nov-25
2417	Dec-91		Oct-05			Jun-15		Jun-15
2418	Dec-91	Oct-10	Jun-03			Sep-14		Sep-17
2419§	Dec-91					Apr-06		May-23§
2420	Dec-91	Jun-08	Nov-05	Apr-11		Jan-17		-

Changes of boiler type by locomotive - Lot 87 - continued

	S2		S4		B2	B4		Superheated
2421	Dec-91		Oct-05			Sep-02	Jun-15	Jun-15§
2422	Jan-92				Apr-13	Dec-02	Mar-17	Mar-17§
2423	Jan-92		Dec-09			Mar-15		Mar-15§
2424	Jan-92		Nov-08			May-12		Feb-19
2425	Jan-92		Mar-11			Jul-14		Dec-23
2426	Feb-92	Sep-05	Apr-03	May-08		Sep-11		Mar-15§
2427	Feb-92		Jan-06			Mar-15		Mar-15
2428	Feb-92		Aug-03			Feb-07		Jan-29
2429	Mar-92		Dec-01		Mar-11	Sep-04	Aug-18	Oct-21
2430	Mar-92		Jun-04			Jun-10		Jan-17

Changes of boiler type by locomotive - Lot 92

	S2			S4		B4		Superheated
2431	Feb-93	Feb-04		Dec-00	Jan-11	Jun-07	Mar-20	Mar-20
2432	Mar-93			Dec-05		Jul-07		May-22§
2433	Mar-93					Sep-03		Nov-18
2434	Mar-93					Feb-03		Jan-18
2435§	Mar-93	Aug-10		Aug-02	Sep-13	Mar-15		Mar-15§
2436	Mar-93					Mar-03		Oct-21
2437§	Apr-93	Mar-05		May-02	Feb-09	Jul-15		Jul-15§
2438	Apr-93			Sep-03		Jan-07		Apr-27
2439	Apr-93			Jul-12		Oct-21		Oct-21
2440	Apr-93			Oct-03		Feb-07		Jul-21
2441	Apr-93	Jun-03	Jan-13	Sep-01	Mar-08	Sep-17		Jul-21
2442§	May-93			Jan-06		Jul-21		Feb-28§
2443	May-93			Oct-02		Sep-04		Jun-21
2444	May-93			Feb-06		Nov-22		Sep-28
2445	May-93	Nov-09		Jun-07		Nov-14		Apr-27
2446	Jun-93			Aug-07		Oct-11		Oct-29
2447	Jun-93			Apr-04		Nov-17		Nov-21
2448	Jun-93					Nov-02		-
2449	Jul-93			Nov-02		Aug-08		Mar-15
2450	Jul-93			Feb-02		Mar-07		Jun-25

Changes of boiler type by locomotive - Lot 99

	S2	S4	B2	B4		Superheated
2451		Oct-95	Jul-10	Sep-02	Jul-13	Nov-27
2452		Oct-95	Sep-09	Jan-07	Feb-13	Oct-28
2453		Nov-95		Feb-07		-
2454		Nov-95		Nov-03		Sep-34
2455	Oct-04	Nov-95		Jul-08		Oct-15
2456	Sep-07	Dec-95	Aug-09	Oct-18		Oct-18
2457	Feb-06	Dec-95		Apr-10		Aug-16
2458		Dec-95		Nov-11		Jan-16
2459		Dec-95		Aug-14		Nov-35
2460	Aug-07	Dec-95	Dec-11	Apr-15		Apr-15

WILLIAM DEAN

Changes of boiler type by locomotive - Lot 99 - continued

	S2		S4		B2	B4	Superheated
2461	Nov-02	Aug-09	Dec-95	Jul-05		Nov-11	Jan-17
2462			Dec-95			Sep-15	Oct-26§
2463			Dec-95			Sep-06	May-23
2464	Jun-03		Jan-96			Oct-08	May-11
2465			Jan-96			Aug-15	Aug-15
2466	Dec-02		Jan-96			Mar-09	Jul-23
2467	Apr-13		Jan-96			Aug-15	Aug-15
2468			Feb-96			Mar-09	Oct-18§
2469			Feb-96			Jan-07	Oct-30
2470	May-07		Feb-96			Aug-12	Oct-16

Changes of boiler type by locomotive - Lot 100

	S2	S4	B2	B4	Superheated
2471		Feb-96		Jun-21	Jun-21
2472	Mar-03	Mar-96		Sep-06	Mar-29
2473		Mar-96		Oct-03	Jun-11
2474	Dec-04	Mar-96	Mar-02	Jan-07	Jun-21
2475		Mar-96		May-06	Apr-22
2476	Jul-10	Apr-96		Mar-14	May-16
2477	Oct-02	Apr-96		Mar-07	Feb-16§
2478		Apr-96		May-24	Mar-29
2479		Apr-96		Jun-07	Apr-25
2480		May-96		Jun-02	Sep-22
2481	Apr-03	May-96	Nov-05	Jun-11	Jun-11
2482	Apr-01	May-96		Sep-03	Feb-29
2483		May-96	Sep-02	Oct-07	Mar-33
2484	Jun-03	Jun-96	Nov-08	Jul-14	Nov-25
2485	May-05	Jun-96	Jan-09	Aug-11	Mar-31
2486		Jun-96	Oct-02	Mar-07	Jul-11
2487	Sep-04	Jul-96		Mar-09	Sep-35
2488		Jul-96		Apr-14	Jul-38
2489		Jul-96		Sep-04	Nov-11
2490		Jul-96		Aug-03	Feb-21

Changes of boiler type by locomotive - Lot 104 (None superheated)

	S2	S4	B4
2491		Aug-96	
2492		Aug-96	
2493		Aug-96	Nov-02
2494		Aug-96	
2495		Aug-96	Aug-06
2496		Sep-96	May-06
2497	Oct-02	Sep-96	Feb-05
2498		Sep-96	
2499		Sep-96	Sep-03
2500		Sep-96	

Changes of boiler type by locomotive - Lot 104 (None superheated) - continued

	S2	S4	B4
2501		Oct-96	
2502		Oct-96	Aug-03
2503	May-05	Oct-96	
2504		Oct-96	
2505		Oct-96	Nov-02
2506		Nov-96	Jun-02
2507		Nov-96	
2508		Nov-96	
2509		Nov-96	
2510		Dec-96	

Changes of boiler type by locomotive - Lot 107

	S2			S4			B2		B4		Superheated
2511				Feb-97					Jun-14		Jan-24§
2512	May-03			Feb-97	Aug-07				Nov-10		Jun-14
2513				Feb-97			Dec-09		Jun-02	Dec-12	Jan-24§
2514				Mar-97					Oct-02		Sep-16
2515				Mar-97					Oct-01		Apr-31
2516	May-06			Mar-97	Sep-08				Oct-13		Oct-35
2517				Apr-97					Apr-06		Nov-15
2518				Apr-97					May-10		Oct-27
2519	Apr-12			Apr-97					Jul-16		Feb-30
2520	Dec-01			Apr-97	Jul-04				Sep-06		Feb-17
2521				May-97					Feb-12		Feb-12
2522				May-97					May-06		Nov-16
2523	Sep-00	Jan-08	Dec-12	May-97	Nov-05	Sep-09			Nov-15		Dec-20
2524	May-06			May-97					Nov-08		Jan-19
2525	Oct-06			May-97					Apr-10		Mar-15
2526				May-97					Aug-08		Nov-20
2527				Jun-97					Sep-15		Sep-15
2528	Jun-04			Jun-97					Jan-07		Apr-22
2529				Jun-97			Jan-02	Sep-11	Sep-06	May-15	May-15
2530	Mar-03			Jun-97					Feb-06		May-11

Changes of boiler type by locomotive - Lot 108

	S2	S4			B2	B4		Superheated
2531	Mar-10	Jun-97				Jan-13		May-30
2532	Jan-15	Jun-97				Mar-20		Jan-31
2533		Jul-97				Nov-06		May-21
2534		Jul-97				Aug-15		Sep-25
2535		Jul-97				Jul-04		Dec-24
2536		Jul-97	May-05	Feb-18		Nov-02	Jan-22	Jul-32
2537	???-03	Jul-97	Nov-05	Dec-14		Dec-17		Nov-19
2538	Oct-05	Aug-97				Jul-10		Apr-32
2539		Aug-97				Nov-21		Nov-21
2540	Aug-01	Aug-97				Sep-04		Jul-21

WILLIAM DEAN

Changes of boiler type by locomotive - Lot 108 - continued

	S2	S4	B2	B4	Superheated
2541	Oct-02	Aug-97		Sep-06	Feb-19
2542		Aug-97		Oct-14	-
2543		Aug-97		Nov-03	Sep-15§
2544		Sep-97		Aug-20	Aug-20
2545		Sep-97		Jun-14	Jan-20
2546		Sep-97		May-12	Jan-14
2547		Sep-97		Nov-21	Nov-21
2548		Sep-97		Jun-07	Mar-29
2549		Sep-97		Apr-10	Aug-16
2550		Sep-97		Nov-12	Nov-12

Changes of boiler type by locomotive - Lot 111

	S2	S4	B2	B4	Superheated
2551	May-17	Nov-97		Jul-21	Feb-27
2552		Nov-97		Aug-08	Nov-29
2553		Nov-97		Apr-07	Jul-20§
2554		Nov-97		Feb-21	Jul-34
2555		Nov-97		Feb-25	Feb-25
2556	Jun-10	Nov-97	Sep-13	Mar-17	Mar-17
2557		Nov-97		Jul-03	Apr-32
2558	Apr-09	Dec-97		Mar-15	Mar-15
2559	Feb-06	Dec-97	Sep-09	Jan-16	Jun-23
2560		Dec-97		Feb-07	Jul-26
2561	May-05	Jan-98	Dec-08	Jul-13	Jun-18
2562	Mar-06	Jan-98		Oct-08	Nov-11
2563		Jan-98		Jun-14	-
2564		Jan-98		Feb-15	Jul-23
2565		Feb-98	Mar-07	Jul-09	Nov-19
2566		Feb-98		Dec-11	Aug-28
2567	May-02	Feb-98	Jun-03	Aug-15	Aug-15
2568	Mar-08	Feb-98		Nov-14	Aug-21
2569		Apr-98		Dec-09	Jul-25§
2570		Apr-98		Apr-14	May-30
2571	Apr-08	Oct-98	May-10	May-13	May-22
2572	Aug-07	Nov-98	Aug-10	Sep-13	Nov-15
2573		Nov-98		Jul-08	Aug-15
2574	Nov-07	Nov-98	Aug-09	Jul-20	Nov-27
2575		Dec-98		Jun-02	Mar-30
2576	Sep-07	Dec-98	Nov-09	Oct-14	Sep-20§
2577		Jan-99		Oct-16	Oct-16
2578		Jan-99		Jul-08	Dec-33
2579	Jun-09	Jan-99	Apr-14	May-18	May-18§
2580		Jan-99		Sep-06	Mar-29

Appendix A.2

Boiler histories - Class 2361

For a class of only 20 locomotives, the boiler history was surprisingly complex with nine different variants. In some respects, recorded information appears contradictory. Variations on standard types were denoted by addition of a suffix:

RCTS Code	Description
S2/S2a/ S2b/S2d	Round-topped firebox; dome mounted on front ring of barrel i.e. "front dome" boilers
S4/S4a	Round-topped firebox; dome mounted on rear ring of barrel i.e. "back dome" boilers
B2/ B2c	Early form of Belpaire firebox boiler rebuilt from type S2, with dome retained on front ring
B4	Built new in Belpaire form; dome on rear ring of barrel

Round-topped boilers

In the early days, official records stated which boilers had been allocated to particular classes. This system applied to the 60 boilers of Group 37 (installed in Nos 2361-2380 and 0-6-0ST Nos 1661-1700). This orderly approach soon fell into disuse as varieties multiplied, and as boilers were distributed among other classes. Three Letter codes were allocated (PN/PO/PX) which actually embraced boilers of different styles – Groups 37 and 27

The suffixes denoted variations in barrel dimensions.

All those without suffixes had dimensions as for corresponding types fitted to Class 2301: Thus:

a = 10' 5" x 4' 5"; **b** = 10' 6" x 4' 5"; **c** = believed to be 10' 5" x 4' 5"; **d** = 10' 3" x 4' 5"

Type S2b Group 37

These boilers were slightly larger than those of the contemporaneous Group 16 (barrel – 10' 3" x 4' 3") and Group 18 (10' 5" x 4' 5") fitted when new to Dean Goods Nos 2321-2360 and 2381-2450. A few were renewed in 1902, usually with 249 x 1¾" tubes, which probably account for examples of the S2b type surviving quite late on some engines (e.g. Nos 2361 until Jun-10; 2365 until May-19; 2368 until Aug-11; 2376 until May-19).

> Boiler type: two-ringed front dome
> Firebox type: flush fitting round-topped
> Barrel: 10' 6" x 4' 5"
> Casing: 5' 4" long
> Pressure: 140lb/ sq in

Built	Number	Firebox: length	width	height	Tubes: no.	diameter	Heating surfaces: tubes	firebox	(sq ft) grate
Sep-85 to Jun-87	29	4' 8"	3' 4"	5' 2.5"	239	1 5/8"	1095.1	103.3	15.2
Jun-86 to Feb-87	31	"	3' 6"	5' 6.5"	241	1 5/8"	1058.8*	103.3	"

* Believed to be incorrect in records

Type B2 Group 37X

Two (some records state three) S2b boilers were rebuilt in 1902 as type B2, and allocated Letter code PX. There are references to up to five Type S2 boilers in Group 37X but it is not clear why round-topped and Belpaire fireboxes should be placed in the same group designation.

> Dimensions as for Group 37 (S2) except:
> Tubes 116 x 1 7/8" and 117 x 1¾".
> Boiler pressure: 165 lbs/ sq in

WILLIAM DEAN

Type S4 Group 27

In the late 1890s, a programme was started to fit S4 boilers to Dean Goods that had been built with the S2 type. In parallel, a programme commenced to fit back-domed round-topped boilers (Type S4a) with barrels two inches longer than the normal S4 type to Class 2361. Only three were built before it was decided in 1899 to cease fitting non-standard sized boilers and to use standard Dean Goods boilers instead.

Boiler type: two-ringed back dome
Firebox type: flush fitting round-topped
Barrel: 10' 5" x 4' 5"
Casing: 5' 4" long
Pressure: 150lb/ sq in

Built	Number	Firebox: length	width	height	Tubes: no.	diameter	Heating tubes	surfaces: firebox	(sq ft) grate
Jun-97 to Oct-99	10	4' 8 1/16"	3' 8"	6' 1/2"	249	1 3/4"	1219	107.7	17.3

Top Feed -Nos 2361/ 2368/ 2369/ 2380 are known to have carried top feed; dates unknown.

Changes of boiler type by locomotive

	S2b	S2a	S2d	S2	S4	S4a	B2	B2c	B4		Superheated
2361	Sep-85	May-07			Sep-98			Jun-10	Jan-14		Dec-22 §
2362	Oct-85			Nov-99				Jul-02 Dec-04			Jun-28
2363	Nov-85			Mar-00					Sep-06		Oct-27
2364	Nov-85						Mar-06		Oct-01 Sep-09		Jul-21
2365	Nov-85		Mar-06	Nov-00				Jul-10	May-19		May-19
2366	Dec-85	Jul-01							May-04		Oct-22
2367	Dec-85	Feb-02		Oct-04					Apr-19		Apr-19
2368	Dec-85	Feb-03	May-00						Aug-11		Jun-20
2369	Dec-85			Oct-00	Jan-03		Dec-07	Oct-05	Jun-11		Dec-24
2370	Dec-85		Feb-01	Aug-02					Nov-07		May-23
2371	Jan-86		Mar-06	Nov-99	Dec-09				Aug-17		n/a
2372	Jan-86						May-17	Apr-02	Sep-10 Mar-26		May-29
2373	Feb-86							Mar-02	Sep-04		Apr-19
2374	Mar-86								Apr-04		Jul-11
2375	Mar-86	May-05		May-00					Oct-10		Dec-18
2376	Mar-86	Dec-02	Apr-09			Dec-99 Mar-06			May-19		May-19
2377	Apr-86	Dec-10		Feb-04	Jan-99			Mar-14	Aug-21		Jul-24
2378	Apr-86				Aug-07				May-12		Sep-29
2379	Apr-86								Sep-06		Dec-19 §
2380	May-86								Aug-01		Apr-28

Appendix B
William Dean's experimental and "one-off" designs

The experimental designs introduced under the auspices of William Dean are so numerous and diverse as to warrant a separate study in themselves. The table set out below summarises the different locomotives; more information appears in Chapters 2 and 5.

There was evidence of Churchward's growing influence from Lot 114 forwards but Dean held the ultimate responsibility for motive power up until the middle of 1902.

Lot No	Running No	Type	Built	Withdrawn	Comments
46	1	4-4-0T	1880	1882	
		2-4-0T	1882	1924	Rebuilt from 4-4-0T
54	9	4-2-4T	1881	1881	
		2-2-2	1884	1905	Rebuilt from 4-2-4T
n/a	10	4-2-4T	n/a	n/a	Construction stopped early; parts used in No 1833
58	1833	0-6-0T	1882	1884	
		0-6-0	1884	1906	Rebuilt as tender locomotive
66	10	2-2-2	1886	1906	Second No 10; built as new engine similar to No 9 rebuilt as 2-2-2
68	7	2-4-0	1886	1887	Tandem compound
		4-4-0	1894	1928	Rebuilt as member of "Armstrong" Class
70	8	2-4-0	1886	1892	Broad Gauge tandem compound; never in regular service
		4-4-0	1894	1929	Rebuilt as member of "Armstrong" Class
72	13	2-4-2WBT	1886	1897	Conventional design with many non-standard dimensions: purpose unclear
		4-4-0T	1897	1926	Rebuilt from 2-4-2WBT
74	14	2-4-0	1888	1892	Broad Gauge convertible
			1894	1928	Rebuilt as member of "Armstrong" Class
74	16	2-4-0	1888	1892	Broad Gauge convertible
			1894	1930	Rebuilt as member of "Armstrong" Class
81	34, 35	0-4-2ST	1890	1906/8	Changed to 0-4-4Ts in 1895; no unique features; purpose of design unclear
106	36	4-6-0	1896	1905	First GWR 4-6-0 and first attempt at heavy goods engine
114	1490	4-4-0PT	1898	1907	First pannier tank; too heavy and unstable to replace Metros; sold
116	2601	4-6-0	1899	1904	Experimental design incorporating several novel features (the "Kruger")
116	2602	2-6-0	1901	1907	Mogul version of No 2601 ("Mrs Kruger")
116	2603-2610	2-6-0	1903	1906	Similar to No 2602 but with detail modifications
128	33	2-6-0	1900	1936	Prototype of successful Aberdare Class 26xx - extinct 1949
130	11	2-4-2T	1900	1933	Prototype of successful "Birdcage" Class 36xx - extinct 1934
132	100	4-6-0	1902	1932	Named "William Dean"; design attributed to GJ Churchward; start of a new era
136	101	0-4-0T	1902	1911	Experimental oil-burner; novel boiler design - several later modifications

Appendix C

William Dean's convertible designs

Joseph Armstrong initiated the convertible principle with the first 10 locomotives of the final batch of Buffalo 0-6-0STs, which were built new as Broad Gauge locomotives in 1876. Five more of this class were so built in 1878 by Dean and a further 35 were converted later. The final 20 examples of the Standard Class 388 0-6-0 locomotives were later converted to Broad Gauge but Dean designed all the other convertible types.

Class	Built	Type	Lot No	Nos	Conversion history
1076 ("Buffalo")	1876	0-6-0ST	43 (part)	1228 -1237	Built as BG; converted to NG 1892/ 3
	1878		48 (part)	1561 -1565	Built as BG; converted to NG 1892/ 3
	1878/ 9		48 (part)	1566 - 1580	Built as NG; ran as BG from 1884; converted to NG 1892/ 3
	1876/ 7		43 (part)	1238 - 1247	Built as NG; ran as BG from 1887/ 8; converted to NG 1892 /3
	1877		44 (part)	1248 - 1257	Built as NG; ran as BG from 1887/ 8; converted to NG 1892/ 3
388 (Standard Goods)	1876	0-6-0	42 (part)	1206 - 1215	Built as NG; ran as BG from 1884; converted to NG 1892/ 3
	1876		42 (part)	1196 - 1205	Built as NG; ran as BG from 1887/ 8; converted to NG 1892
3201 ("Stella")	1884/ 5	2-4-0	65	3201 - 3205	Built as NG; never converted to BG
3501	1885	2-4-0T	64 (part)	3501 - 3510	Built as BG; Nos 3501/ 2/ 5/ 7/8 converted to BG 2-4-0 in 1890/ 1 All converted to NG 2-4-0 in 1892; became part of Class 3201
	1885	2-4-0T	64 (part)	3511 - 3520	Built as NG; never converted to BG; rebuilt as 2-4-0 in 1894/5 as part of Class 3201

Class	Built	Type	Lot No	Nos	Conversion history
2361	1885/ 6	0-6-0	67	2361 - 2380	Built as NG; never converted to BG
1661	1886	0-6-0ST	69	1661 - 1680	Built as NG; never converted to BG
	1886/ 7		71	1681 - 1700	Built as NG; never converted to BG
8	1886	2-4-0	70	8	Built as BG tandem compound; withdrawn 1892: rebuilt 1894 as NG 4-4-0
14/ 16	1888	2-4-0	74	14, 16	Built as BG; stopped work 1892 but not withdrawn; rebuilt as NG 4-4-0 in 1894
	1887/ 8	0-4-2T	73	3521 - 3540	Altered to 0-4-4T 1891/ 2; never converted to BG; rebuilt as 4-4-0 1899-1902
3521	1888/ 9	0-4-2ST	76 (part)	3541 - 3559	Built as BG; converted to 0-4-4T 1890/ 1: converted to NG 1891/ 2; converted to 4-4-0 1899-1902
	1889	0-4-4T	76 (part)	3560	Built as BG 0-4-4T; converted to NG 1892; converted to 4-4-0 1899
3001 ("Achilles")	1891	2-2-2	86 (part)	3021 - 3028	Built as BG; converted to NG 2-2-2 in 1892

Appendix D

The Railway Operating Division and its Motive Power Fleet

The scale of the Great War of 1914-1918 was unprecedented in human history. Through its "Schlieffen Plan", the German high command intended a swift invasion of Belgium and Luxembourg in August/ September 1914. This was to be followed by a flanking movement through northern France to capture Paris in the hope of a decisive war and complete victory in about six weeks. The plan's failure led to a stalemate that lasted four years as opposing armies assumed entrenched and largely static positions known as the Western Front, which stretched from the English Channel to the French/ Swiss border.

Britain's land forces in the summer of 1914 were modest compared with some countries. There had been no pre-war conscription and the regular army comprised 247,000 volunteer soldiers, half of whom were stationed overseas throughout the British Empire. A reserve force numbering 224,000 and the Territorial Army, which was 269,000 strong, supported the professional army. In response to Field Marshall Kitchener's famous poster "Your country needs you!" and in a wave of patriotic fervour, 2.6 million volunteers had joined the army by January 1916. A further 2.3 million were conscripted between then and the end of the war. The size of the British Army in the field is reflected in the grim statistics of 662,000 killed in action and 1.65 million wounded between 1914 and the Armistice.

With the establishment of the trench system, the division of responsibility for the 200 miles Western Front was split between three allies. The Belgian army held the northern section from the English Channel to a few miles north of Ypres. From there over a distance of around 100 miles, the British held the frontline while the French covered the remaining sector south to the Swiss border.

A feature that distinguished this from earlier wars was logistical mobilisation to a degree never before witnessed. In the Napoleonic Wars, the last major military campaigns of the pre-railway era, it had been calculated that an army of 60,000 men and 40,000 horses consumed 450 tons of food and forage every day. The limited capacity to meet these demands by horse- and oxen-hauled wagons, especially as supply lines became extended, fashioned the nature of warfare. Periods of physical confrontation between opposing forces were of finite duration as armies had to keep moving to find new supplies in the process of living off the land.

In contrast, the static trench war meant that a vast body of men had to be housed, fed and watered on a continuous basis. Further, enormous numbers of horses were used thereby making the provision of forage a matter of great consequence. In earlier conflicts the consumption of munitions was small in relation to the volumes of food and forage required, but in World War I protection of the front line required transportation of massive tonnages of heavy guns and ammunition.

Motor vehicles were primitive, unreliable, and available only in restricted numbers. Their effectiveness was also limited by poor road surfaces, which quickly broke up under heavy traffic and became impassable. Wagons hauled by horses or oxen could only move slowly and usually could cover no more than 20 miles in a day. Use was made of the inland waterways of northeast France and heavy tonnages were moved by barge, but only at slow speeds. Thus the main burden of logistical support fell on the railways, which basically assumed two forms.

The civilian standard gauge network was taken over for military use, and many miles of additional track were laid to increase the capacity of existing routes, and as temporary lines. Understandably, many of these new routes were hastily graded and laid, necessitating the use of smaller locomotives. The standard gauge lines supplied railheads typically near the Front. At these railheads, loads were transhipped to 60 cm gauge networks built specifically for military purposes. These narrow gauge lines could be quickly laid and removed as circumstances dictated, and they reached close to front line positions. Demands on the railway systems increased substantially during offensive actions; for example, it was necessary to run 160 standard gauge trains every day to support the British forces during the height of the Battle of Passchendaele.

Efficient exploitation of railway systems had proven vital in earlier conflicts. During the American Civil War, an engineer called Herman Haupt had established the United States Military Railroads. This organisation managed the railroads of the northern states, and followed principles devised by Haupt for the efficient operation of trains supporting fighting troops. Adherence to these principles ensured that the northern states made better use of railroads than did their Confederate opponents. This was a vital element in the North's military successes in the later stages of the war. The importance of Haupt's principles was further reinforced when they were successfully employed by Prussian forces, proving a decisive factor in the Franco-Prussian War of 1870-71.

To provide an effective administration of rail services within the military command structure, the Railway Operating Division (ROD) was created in 1915 as an arm of the Corps of Royal Engineers, and eventually grew to comprise 76,000 skilled railwaymen. Full operational control of complete sections of the French standard gauge network commenced in the summer of

1916, the first being the important Hazebrouck-Ypres route. In addition, the ROD installed and operated over 800 km of 60 cm gauge railways. From modest beginnings, the ROD became a highly effective transport organisation. This was particularly apparent in the skilful working of purpose-designed hospital trains. For example, the battle at Messines Ridge commenced before dawn on 7th June 1917 yet the first wounded arrived at Charing Cross in London at 2.15 pm the same day.

Although in 1914 the British Army was under-resourced in manpower, in contrast the railway companies were generously equipped to cope with added demands. Years of competitive over-investment in routes, motive power and rolling stock had yielded surpluses compared with other European nations. At the outbreak of hostilities, the broad statistics of the railway systems of the main combatants were:

	Route miles	Total number of locomotives	Locomotives per 100 route miles	Total number of carriages	Carriages per 100 route miles	Number of wagons
Austria-Hungary	28,400	10,000	35	21,000	74	245,000
Belgium	5,400	4,300	80	10,000	186	90,000
France	31,200	14,500	47	33,500	107	364,000
Germany	39,000	28,000	72	60,000	154	600,000
Russia	45,000	17,200	38	20,000	44	370,000
United Kingdom§	23,700	23,000	97	73,000	308	1,300,000*

§ The UK statistics are the more remarkable in that they included the extensive but sparsely stocked Irish network
* Approximate figures which included around 600,000 private owner wagons

However, the UK's numerical advantage was largely illusory. Many of the locomotives were small and under-powered compared with those of foreign operators. The size disparity was more acute when British locomotives were called upon to handle heavy trains overseas.

The better use made by Germany of its wagon fleet was striking. In Britain before the war there had been no pooling arrangements for wagons (unlike Germany) and for many years the railway companies had, for no obvious or logical reason, resisted all attempts to introduce the "common user" principle. Return working of empty wagons resulted in mileage accumulation in non-revenue-earning movements, a situation accentuated by the hopelessly inefficient use of private owner wagons. These operating methods led to chronic congestion at key locations. Although

improvements were progressively introduced from February 1915 onwards, it was not until World War II that universal pooling was established through the abolition of private wagon ownership. Such surpluses as were rendered by improved traffic management were of limited benefit outside the UK as many British wagons were too small and primitive for overseas service. Despite the vast size of the UK wagon fleet, only about 29,700 were actually used in France.

During 1914-1915, the bulk of the ROD's motive power needs was covered by approximately 225 engines, mainly of the 0-6-0 wheel arrangement. These had been evacuated in advance of the German invasion and were hired from Etat-Belge. Despite including some antique-looking but nonetheless effective specimens, much of this fleet was essentially British, being derivations of Caledonian Railway 0-6-0 Class

812, designed by McIntosh. The first pure British locomotives to serve overseas were a pair of South Eastern & Chatham Railway Class P 0-6-0Ts sent in 1915 to shunt the docks at Boulogne, which effectively had come under SECR control.

During 1916, sundry locomotives were sent to France including 14 requisitioned 4-6-4T's built by Beyer Peacock for the Dutch State Railways, plus 28 0-4-0STs from Baldwin and some petrol "tractors" from Manning Wardle. However, there were continuing disputes with the Belgian authorities over hire of their locomotives and the French became increasingly reluctant to lend engines from their diminishing serviceable fleet. Therefore by late 1916 the requisition of locomotives from the domestic UK companies became unavoidable. This process was aided by control of the railways having been vested in the UK Government through the Railways Executive Committee at the outbreak of hostilities. In November/ December 1916, 44 London & North Western Railway 17" coal engines and one Great Northern Railway Class J4 arrived in France.

During 1917 there was a rapid escalation in shipments from the UK. An estimated 501 locomotives arrived in France that year including 10 2-8-0s originally intended for the New South Wales Government Railways, 32 of the newly-built ROD 2-8-0s based on the Great Central Class 8K, and 8 industrial 0-6-0STs by Kerr Stuart originally ordered by the Directorate of Inland Water Transport. The remainder were supplied by the British Railway companies.

Apart from the diminishing ability of the French and Belgians to help cover the British Army's locomotive needs, the motive power situation had become critical for two additional reasons. Firstly, Britain and its allies were also fighting the Central Powers on the Eastern Fronts in Macedonia, Palestine and Mesopotamia and support for these armies by sea was slow, and also hazardous in the face of the U-boat threat. At the beginning of 1917, the Allies therefore introduced a trans-European railway service to connect Cherbourg with Taranto in Italy by means of a circuitous 1500 miles route that went through western France. Intended to provide six trains a day that would require the availability of over 100 locomotives, this service never achieved more than 2-3 trains daily and was suspended following the defeat of the Italians at Caparetto in October 1917.

Secondly, the entry of the United States of America into the war greatly exacerbated the demands on the railway system. With the English Channel ports working at full capacity, American troops and materials had to be landed at the French Atlantic ports and then transported overland to the Front. These services were operated jointly by the French and American authorities without direct ROD involvement. Considerable numbers of the famous "Pershing" 2-8-0s built by Baldwin between 1916 and 1918 were brought from the United States. This type had evolved from an earlier design for the ROD (see below) and eventually totalled around 1,500, although not all served in France. This fleet was later augmented in 1917 by 250 2-8-0s from American Locomotive Company, a type that proved well suited for French conditions and which was retained in ordinary service after the war. This escalation of the allied presence greatly increased demands on the railway system generally, as evidenced by the two million American troops that were eventually deployed in France.

From 1917, in addition to running the narrow gauge lines, the ROD became increasingly engaged in operating standard gauge trains in France with imported locomotives and rolling stock. By the war's end, the combined number of standard gauge Belgian, British and North American locomotives hired, requisitioned or built specifically for war service exceeded 1600 machines. Thirteen British companies contributed locomotives, most of which had been designed for goods work; many of the 0-6-0s dated from the 19th Century.

Apart from the GWR Class 43xx 2-6-0s, all the engines requisitioned from the British railway companies had seen previous service. Of the locomotives built specially for war service the best known are the ROD 2-8-0s which were closely based on the standard goods engine of the Great Central Railway. A total of 305 were built by private contractors between August 1917 and February 1919; 216 more were completed in 1919 which did not serve overseas.

Although the main focus of the war was the Western Front, fighting took place in other theatres and a need developed to supply further locomotives in support of British forces. These demands were more modest and apart from some of the Manning Wardle petrol tractors, older 0-6-0s were used. The regions concerned where GWR engines were deployed were the Greece, possibly Serbia, and later Turkey. Other areas that saw British locomotives were Egypt, Palestine and Mesopotamia but none of these were from the Great Western.

The political situation in the Eastern Mediterranean was complex and records seem incomplete. The earliest reported deployment of GWR engines in this region was the despatch of some Armstrong Goods engines in 1916 to Serbia. However as an ally of Britain and France, that country had successfully resisted invasion by Austria-Hungary in 1914, but was eventually over-run in late 1915 by a combined force of troops from Austria-Hungary, Germany and Bulgaria. The remnants of the Serbian army were evacuated by British and French naval vessels in early 1916 from ports in what is now Albania and eventually re-deployed at Salonika in northern Greece. This sequence of events makes it likely that reports about the deployment of GWR engines in Serbia are incorrect. It is possible that they had been earmarked for Serbia but actually ended up in Greece.

From the onset of war, the politics of Greece had been unstable with pro- and anti-German factions vying for control of that country. To prevent the Germans from gaining a foothold in this uncertain situation, an allied force was established on Greek soil in October 1915. In June 1917, Greece was induced to declare war on Germany and the Central Powers by which time allied forces based in Salonika (today's Thessaloniki) totalled 500,000. This theatre was also one of static warfare, and was quiet compared with the Western Front until September 1918 when the Bulgarian army was defeated. During the next two months there was a slow advance northwards, dogged by supply shortages, to the southern borders of the Austro-

Hungarian Empire. Because of the terrain, proportionately more use was made of 60 cm gauge temporary lines than in France, with an extensive system fanning out from Salonika.

Turkey was an ally of Germany and the country's principal railway routes had been developed and controlled by German interests since the late 1880s. Following the Armistice, allied forces were deployed in Anatolia and took control of the Turkish railway system until 1923. Records are unclear but it would appear that the ROD fleet at the end of the war was divided into two. Some locomotives were retained in northern Greece until about 1921 and then returned to the United Kingdom while others were shipped to Anatolia. It would seem that those engines used in Turkey were ultimately either legally sold to local railway companies, or destroyed in fighting during the Turkish War of Independence.

The ROD Locomotive Fleet

The types and numbers of standard gauge British-built locomotives to UK loading gauge sent to France:

Railway Company	Class	Introduced	Type	Number
Caledonian	294	1883	0-6-0	25
Great Central	8A	1902	0-8-0	16
Great Central	9J	1901	0-6-0	18
Great Eastern	Y14	1883	0-6-0	43
Great Northern	J4	1896	0-6-0	26*
Great Western	2301	1883	0-6-0	62
Great Western	43XX	1911	0-6-0	11
Lancashire & Yorkshire	¶	1889	0-6-0	32
London & North Western	G	1906	0-8-0	26
London & North Western	17" Coal engines	1873	0-6-0	70
London Brighton & South Coast	E4	1898	0-6-2T	14
London Chatham & Dover	T	1889	0-6-0T	9
Midland	Kirtley 1F	1863	0-6-0	81*
North British	C	1888	0-6-0	25
North Eastern	T	1902	0-8-0	50
South Eastern & Chatham	P	1909	0-6-0T	2
Built for ROD service:				
Kerr, Stuart	Victory	1917	0-6-0T	10
Manning Wardle Petrol Tractors		1914	4-wheeled	11*
ROD type (various builders)	Based on GCR Class 8K	1916	2-8-0	305§

¶ Aspinall's round-topped firebox goods engines from number series 27 to 1297; later classified "27"

* Believed to be the maximum number employed; some might have been short term replacements for locomotives returned to the UK for repair. In the case of GNR Class J4, some records state that only 24 were used in France.

¥ There were erroneous reports of transfers to Italy; locomotives seen there during the war had actually been sold by the Midland Railway to Italian State Railways some years previously.

§ A further 216 of this type were built but not sent overseas

WILLIAM DEAN

Some of the locomotives listed above were transferred from France to the Eastern Mediterranean and Middle Eastern theatres of war, while others were despatched direct from the UK:

Railway Company	Class	Type	Number	Destination	Comments
Great Western	388	0-6-0	22	Serbia (?)/ Greece¶	Direct from UK
Great Western	2301	0-6-0	16	Greece	Transferred from France
London & North Western	17" Coal engines	0-6-0	15	Egypt/ Palestine	Direct from UK
			27	Egypt/ Palestine	Transferred from France
London & South Western	395	0-6-0	36	Egypt/ Palestine	Direct from UK
			5	Greece	Direct from UK
			7	Mesopotamia	Transferred from Palestine
			9	Mesopotamia	Direct from UK
Manning Wardle Petrol Tractors		4 wheeled	3	Egypt/ Palestine	Direct from UK

¶ Eight were lost at sea

The ROD locomotive fleet in France was augmented by locomotives (1) hired from the Belgian government (2) built for foreign railways but requisitioned, and (3) specially ordered from North American builders:

Country	Type	Number	
Australia	2-8-0	10	Built by North British for Australian trans-continental railway; requisitioned
Belgium	0-6-0PT	§	Class 51; 471 were built 1866 to 1905 - a small number were hired by the ROD
	0-6-0	§	Classes 25/ 25bis; outside-framed; built 1884 to 1898
	0-6-0	§	Classes 30/ 32/ 32s; based on McIntosh design for Caledonian Railway; built from 1900
Canada	2-8-0	40	Constructed by Canadian Locomotive Co; delivered mid 1917
Netherlands	4-6-4T	14	Constructed by Beyer Peacock but requisitioned before delivery to Holland
U.S.A.			All built by Baldwin for the UK Government:
	2-8-0	150	Delivered Jul-17 to Feb-19; formed basis for the later Pershing type 2-8-0
	4-6-0	120	70 to France and 50 direct to Egypt
	2-6-2T	75	Delivered Jul-17 to Oct-17
	0-6-0PT	50	Delivered Nov-17 to Feb-18
	0-4-0ST	70	Delivered from Jun-16 onwards

§ Substantial numbers of Belgian locomotives escaped the German invasion and an estimated 225 were hired by the ROD. The actual number for each class is not known.

This list might be incomplete as other locomotives may have been requisitioned or borrowed and their precise status never properly recorded. For example, the ROD ordered ten 2-8-0s in 1918 from Swiss Locomotive and Machinery Works at Winterthur to a standard SLM design but with British-type modifications. These machines were sold to the Czechoslovak state in 1919 and it is uncertain whether they did any work for the ROD.

The Australian engines never saw Australia but were sold after the war to the Nord-Belge company which used them in the Meuse valley. The Belgian-designed engines were ruggedly constructed and considered good steamers; their Achilles' heel was barking power, some having four-wheeled tender brakes only. The engines intended for Holland were handsome as typical of that country's motive power; they were subsequently purchased for use on Parisian suburban services. The Baldwin locomotives were typical of that company's designs, except where modified for European conditions.

With only moderate numbers of British tank locomotives working in France, it must be assumed that the Baldwin construction programme met needs that British companies could not cover, being so hard-pressed on the home front. (The contribution of 0-6-2Ts by the London Brighton & South Coast

Railway resulted from that company convincing the authorities that as a predominantly passenger carrying railway, there were simply no spare 0-6-0s available).

After the war, most of the locomotives on loan were returned to work with their owners but disposal of the fleet built specifically to ROD orders was more complex, and influenced by elements of prejudice and xenophobia. The North American locomotives were considered to be poorly constructed by British standards – perhaps this view was influenced by the experience of English railways with imported US moguls around the turn of the century – although many gave good service in continental Europe for several years. In any event, the ROD was happy to dispose of these locomotives to various European operators. Conversely, the Europeans wished to retain numbers of the GCR-derived ROD 2-8-0 but the British authorities insisted that all should be repatriated, a decision that led to a protracted and costly sales programme as war surplus equipment. The British-built locomotives that had been built specifically for foreign operators could not be used in the UK as they were to Australian and Dutch loading gauges.

In the closing stages of the war and after the Armistice, one other group of locomotives came under the ambit of ROD control. Several German locomotives were seized during advances made by the

British Expeditionary Force in the later months of 1918, and then there was the matter of war reparations. A claim for 5,000 engines (mainly of the "larger type") was lodged by the military authorities as early as 14th November 1918, to be distributed 50% to the British forces and 25% each to the French and Belgians. The logic was that the ROD would operate train services across Belgium into Germany but in the event, this did not occur to any significant degree. Before long, allied demands for German locomotives were substantially scaled back and comparatively few were apparently used by the ROD. A report by a soldier who worked with these engines said that they were generally in better condition than their ROD counterparts.

Unlike World War II, there were few casualties among British locomotives deployed in France. Damage sustained was largely superficial and only one British steam locomotive fell into enemy hands. Midland Railway 0-6-0 No 2717 had to be abandoned in no-man's land at Cambrai in 1917. It was used by the Germans as a machine gun emplacement for a period before being put to railway work by them; it was recovered by the ROD after the war. Records for other theatres of war are less clear and it seems likely that locomotives were lost to enemy action; in particular there appears to be no information on the ultimate fate of four Standard Goods and five Dean Goods transferred to Greece.

Differences in the quality of locomotives contributed by the British companies were noted. For example, the 0-8-0s provided by the Great Central and North Eastern railways were frontline types and were ideal for moving heavy loads. The 0-6-0s lent by the North British were sturdy machines and on their return home they received names (painted on the centre splashers) associated with the conflict. The service of the NER 0-8-0s was recognised in more subtle fashion by the mounting of brass grenades (the badge of the Royal Engineers) above three inverted chevrons (denoting three years' service in France) on the cab sides, later removed to the front sandboxes. The Midland Railway recognised the war service of the Kirtley 0-6-0s by affixing small oval plaques to their cab sides.

The contributions of the South Eastern & Chatham and London Brighton and South Coast railways might

seem modest but these companies were busy on the home front, moving men and materials to the English Channel ports. The most significant omission was the Highland Railway, a company that was heavily committed to meeting the needs of the Royal Navy at Invergordon and the Grand Fleet at Scarpa Flow in the Orkney Islands. The line capacity and motive power fleet of the HR was stretched to and beyond normal limits so that a variety of locomotives had to be borrowed from other railways, including even the far away London & South Western.

The preponderance of requisitioned 0-6-0s in the ROD fleet in the early days caused problems, particularly on main line services as these small locomotives were generally underpowered. Continental freight wagons were larger and of greater individual capacity than the British variety, and trains were universally screw-link coupled. Small engines designed to handle loose-coupled trains were soon found to lack the necessary haulage capacity. Shunting with engines of the small British loading gauge was also difficult because the line of sight from the narrow cabs was restricted by the wider continental wagons.

Generally speaking, older types were inducted into military service and some proved unimpressive. The SECR Class P 0-6-0Ts were returned in 1916 as too small for shunting duties; they were replaced by nine ex-London Chatham & Dover Class T 0-6-0s. The LNWR Coal Engines were used mainly as shunters for which they seemed to lack the requisite power while their small tenders meant frequent calls for water. These engines were in generally poor condition on delivery to the ROD and many did little or no post-war work. A reviewer offered a comment in mitigation that these LNWR engines dated from the 1880's (although there was no need to extend such forbearance to Dean Goods No 2303 built in 1883 and the oldest of the class sent overseas). There was also adverse comment about the Midland Railway not sparing its more modern engines but only providing ageing examples of double framed 0-6-0 goods engines. On the other hand, the LNWR and MR 0-6-0s had a modest axle loading (as did also the Dean Goods) resulting in a "go anywhere" capability that was an advantage when working over hastily and poorly laid trackwork.

Dean Goods Shed allocations as at 31st December 1922

Shed	Nos					Shed	Nos				
Aberdare (3)	2358	2388	2390			**Neath (6)**	2434	2447	2475	2539	2544
Aberystwyth (3)	2322	2457	2528				2557				
Banbury (4)	2402	2404	2444	2461		**Newport (4)**	2309	2314	2414	2530	
Barnstaple (3)	2327	2522	2461			**Neyland (3)**	2319	2323	2350		
Basingstoke (1)	2489					**Oxford (5)**	2343	2427	2429	2470	2559
Birkenhead (2)	2359	2466				**Paddington (7)**	2349	2409	2417	2455	2484
Bristol (28)	2302	2318	2335	2382	2384		2514	2515			
	2389	2391	2394	2395	2398	**Pembroke Dock (1)**	2407				
	2403	2410	2415	2422	2438	**Pontypool Road (8)**	2439	2446	2451	2453	2536
	2440	2443	2458	2473	2480		2567	2568	2577		
	2485	2518	2520	2527	2535	**Reading (14)**	2304	2312	2340	2430	2463
	2547	2564	2570				2471	2479	2488	2512	2540
Cardiff (9)	2303	2396	2399	2424	2441		2546	2561	2572	2580	
	2490	2549	2562	2573		**Salisbury (2)**	2519	2541			
Carmarthen (11)	2311	2315	2336	2345	2351	**Shrewsbury (5)**	2513	2538	2553	2555	2569
	2400	2413	2465	2516	2529	**Slough (1)**	2551				
	2533					**Southall (7)**	2397	2454	2472	2474	2531
Chester (3)	2419	2423	2477				2537	2556			
Chippenham (2)	2525	2526				**Stourbridge (6)**	2356	2408	2426	2462	2575
Corwen (1)	2431						2576				
Croes Newydd (1)	2452					**Swindon (5)**	2329	2338	2357	2545	2571
Didcot (2)	2523	2578				**Taunton (8)**	2316	2320	2381	2405	2435
Evesham (1)	2416						2460	2467	2543		
Exeter (4)	2305	2313	2456	2483		**Trowbridge (1)**	2449				
Gloucester (4)	2348	2383	2428	2574		**Tyseley (10)**	2307	2325	2342	2392	2406
Hereford (6)	2317	2331	2333	2341	2355		2436	2437	2442	2464	2476
	2478					**Wells (2)**	2339	2411			
Honeybourne (1)	2482					**Westbury (6)**	2337	2450	2468	2517	2565
Kidderminster (1)	2321						2566				
Kingham (1)	2412					**Weymouth (2)**	2330	2353			
Lambourn (1)	2481					**Whitland (1)**	2418				
Landore (2)	2360	2486				**Wolverhampton (13)**	2385	2386	2401	2421	2425
Leamington (2)	2459	2469					2511	2521	2532	2548	2550
Llandovery (1)	2354						2552	2554	2560		
Llanelly (5)	2393	2432	2433	2487	2524	**Worcester (13)**	2301	2306	2310	2324	2326
Machynlleth (1)	2346						2328	2332	2344	2347	2352
							2445	2534	2558		

Appendix F

Dean Goods Shed allocations as at 31st December 1933 and installation dates of Automatic Train Control

Sheds	Number of locomotives	Running Numbers						
Aberdare	2	2454 ¥	2484 *					
Aberystwyth	7	2321	2421 *	2424	2438	2445 ¥	2466 *	2559 *
Banbury	3	2385 *	2531 *	2539 *				
Brecon	6	2327	2336 *	2342	2412 *	2459 *	2516	
Bristol Bath Road	4	2381 *	2441 *	2526 *	2543 *			
Builth Wells	1	2405 *						
Cardiff Canton	5	2433 *	2470 *	2478 *	2524 *	2548 *		
Carmarthen	10	2396 *	2407 *	2418 *	2422 *	2440 *	2465 *	2474 *
		2487 *	2572 *	2580 *				
Chester	5	2436 *	2464 *	2511 *	2554 *	2579 *		
Chippenham	1	2415 *						
Croes Newydd	2	2427¥	2555 *					
Didcot	7	2395 *	2397 *	2430 *	2450 *	2463 *	2532 *	2549 *
Ebbw Junction	3	2540 *	2546 *	2571 *				
Ebbw Junction Shops	1	2399 *						
Evesham	1	2536 *						
Gloucester	4	2384	2392 *	2398	2402 *			
Hereford	2	2479 *	2519 *					
Landore	1	2446 *						
Leamington	1	2356 *						
Llandovery	1	2558 *						
Llanelly	2	2360 *	2382 *					
Llanidloes	4	2417 *	2483 *	2514	2522			
Lydney	2	2349 *	2428 *					
Machynlleth	9	2313 *	2341 *	2343	2345 *	2352	2353 *	2449
		2455 *	2490					
Moat Lane	3	2316 *	2401 *	2447 *				
Neath	3	2390 *	2411 *	2530 *				
Newbury	1	2533 *						
Old Oak Common	2	2303 *	2443 *					

ATC fitting dates: ¶ August 1927
* Between June 1930 and August 1931
¥ Between 1936 and 1938

WILLIAM DEAN

Sheds	Number of locomotives	Running Numbers						
Oswestry	7	2337	2339	2354 *	2457¥	2545*	2556 *	2574 *
Oswestry Factory	1	2523 *						
Oxford	2	2332 *	2429 *					
Oxley	6	2389 *	2406 *	2408 *	2451 *	2452 *	2513 *	
Pontypool Road	2	2434 *	2573 *					
Portmadoc	4	2323	2468 *	2520	2576			
Pwllhei	3	2315	2553 *	2560 *				
Reading	6	2305 *	2346 *	2358 *	2404 *	2561 *	2570 *	
Salisbury	1	2357						
Severn Tunnel Junction	3	2480 *	2521 *	2562 *				
Shrewsbury	9	2322 *	2348 *	2419 *	2425 *	2442 *	2460 *	2462 *
		2475 *	2477 *					
Southall	1	2489 *						
Stafford Road	6	2383*	2386 *	2413 *	2414 *	2423 *	2488 *	
Stafford Road Factory	4	2388	2444¥	2525	2550*			
St Philip's Marsh	14	2311 *	2317 *	2340 *	2347 *	2351 *	2426 *	2437 *
		2461 *	2467*	2472 *	2473 *	2535 *	2552 *	2567 *
Stourbridge	5	2320*	2359 *	2469 *	2538 *	2569*		
Swindon	4	2456 *	2528 *	2534 *	2564 *			
Swindon Factory Pool	3	2393 *	2486 *	2541 *				
Swindon Works	5	2301 *	2403 *	2471 *	2512 *	2578 *		
Taunton	5	2410 *	2416 *	2482 *	2517 *	2527 *		
Tyseley	2	2439 *	2575 *					
Wells	1	2400 *						
Westbury	5	2394 *	2435 *	2518 *	2529 *	2566 *		
Weston-Super-Mare	1	2537 *						
Whitchurch	1	2565						
Whitland	4	2409 ¥	2432 *	2476 *	2544 ¶			
Winchester	1	2547 *						
Worcester	13	2310	2325 *	2328 ¥	2350 *	2431 *	2458 *	2481 *
		2485 *	2515 *	2551 *	2557 *	2568 *	2577 *	
Total	212							

ATC fitting dates: ¶ August 1927
* Between June 1930 and August 1931
¥ Between 1936 and 1938

Appendix G
Dean Goods Annual Totals and Withdrawal Dates

The annual totals as at 31st December:

Year	Additions	Withdrawals	Total	Year	Additions	Withdrawals	Total	Year	Additions	Withdrawals	Total
1883	20		20	1921		7	232	1945		11	59
1884	40		60	1929		3	229	1946		3	56
1890	20		80	1930		1	228	1947		2	54
1891	21		101	1931		10	218	1948		2	52
1892	9		110	1932		3	215	1949		3	49
1893	20		130	1933		3	212	1950		2	47
1895	13		143	1934		9	203	1951		3	44
1896	47		190	1935		7	196	1952		8	36
1897	50		240	1936		2	194	1953		24	12
1898	16		256	1937		1	193	1954		8	4
1899	4		260	1938		12	181	1955		2	2
1907		9*	251	1939	8¶	10¶	179	1956		1±	1
1908		10§	241	1940	1¥	108	72	1957		1	0
1910		2§	239	1944		2	70				

One (No 2448) withdrawn following accident; eight withdrawn for conversion to 2-6-2T § For conversion to 2-6-2T
¶ Ten withdrawn on grounds of age; eight re-instated same year ¥ One withdrawn previous year re-instated ± Withdrawn for preservation

Withdrawals by year:

1907	2448/ 2491/ 2492/ 2497-2499/ 2501/ 2504/ 2508
1908	2493-2495/ 2500/ 2503/ 2505-2507/ 2509/ 2510
1910	2496/ 2502
1921	2308/ 2334/ 2387/ 2420/ 2453/ 2542/ 2563
1929	2304/ 2306/ 2318
1930	2355
1931	2302/ 2309/ 2312/ 2319/ 2324/ 2330/ 2331/ 2333/ 2338/ 2344
1932	2307/ 2314/ 2326
1933	2329/ 2335/ 2391
1934	2301/ 2310/ 2311/ 2316/ 2317/ 2336/ 2341/ 2358/ 2396
1935	2303/ 2305/ 2337/ 2352/ 2357/ 2359/ 2397
1936	2346/ 2353
1937	2390
1938	2313/ 2321/ 2328/ 2332/ 2342/ 2347/ 2384/ 2388/ 2394/ 2398/ 2421/ 2450
1939	2417
1940	2392/ 2393/ 2399/ 2400/ 2402-2405/ 2410/ 2412/ 2413/ 2415/ 2416/ 2418/ 2419/ 2422/ 2423/ 2425/ 2427-2430/ 2432-2443/ 2446 2447/ 2451/ 2454-2457/ 2459/ 2461/ 2463/ 2465-2467/ 2469-2473/ 2475-2481/ 2485-2490/ 2511/ 2512/ 2514/ 2517-2522/ 2524 2526-2529/ 2531/ 2533/ 2536/ 2539/ 2540/ 2544-2550/ 2552/ 2553/ 2555/ 2557-2562/ 2565-2567/ 2571/ 2574/ 2576/ 2577/ 2580
1944	2320/ 2389
1945	2315/ 2325/ 2348/ 2360/ 2381/ 2395/ 2406/ 2525/ 2530/ 2554/ 2564
1946	2383/ 2424/ 2535
1947	2345/ 2575
1948	2356/ 2569
1949	2464/ 2523/ 2570
1950	2382/ 2386
1951	2322/ 2385/ 2431
1952	2339/ 2349/ 2407/ 2444/ 2452/ 2482/ 2483/ 2572
1953	2323/ 2327/ 2343/ 2350/ 2351/ 2354/ 2401/ 2408/ 2409/ 2414/ 2426/ 2445/ 2449/ 2462/ 2468/ 2515/ 2534/ 2537/ 2543 2551/ 2556/ 2568/ 2573/ 2578
1954	2340/ 2411/ 2458/ 2460/ 2484/ 2532/ 2541/ 2579
1955	2474/ 2513
1956	2516
1957	2538

Appendix H
The tank v. tender locomotive debate

Tradition was strong in GWR design practice and creation of the vast fleet of 0-6-0Ts under William Dean set a pattern that outlasted the company. Apart from the Class 2021 small saddle tanks, construction of which continued until 1905, and the specialised Class 1361, there was a 30 year interval before creation of a second generation commenced under Collett. The saddle tank layout permitted good access to the valve motion but to retain this advantage when Belpaire fireboxes were introduced, costly modification to the inner profile of the tank was needed. The adoption of pannier tanks was a brilliant compromise that neatly avoided this expense and continuation of this arrangement from 1929 onwards was eminently logical in construction terms. It remains questionable though whether so many locomotives of this type built between then and 1956 were really needed.

A tank engine has certain inherent advantages on short distance and shunting duties but lacks operational flexibility for longer journeys. There is usually also a penalty in greater axle loadings. Strict comparison between tank locomotives and their tender counterparts is only possible where leading dimensions are the same; the table below cites comparative examples from the Dean, Churchward and British Railway eras:

	Class 1813*	Dean Goods*	Class 3150	Class 43xx	Class 82xxx	Class 77xxx
Introduced	1882	1883	1906	1911	1952	1954
Wheel arrangement	0-6-0T	0-6-0	2-6-2T	2-6-0	2-6-2T	2-6-0
Weight - engine - tender	39 tons 12 cwt	c. 33 tons c. 29 tons 5 cwt	78 tons 16 cwt	62 tons 0 cwt 40 tons 0 cwt	74 tons 1 cwt	57 tons 10 cwt 42 tons 3 cwt
Combined weight	39 tons 12 cwt	c. 59 tons 5 cwt	78 tons 16 cwt	102 tons 0 cwt	74 tons 1 cwt	99 tons 13 cwt
Max axle loading	13 tons 10 cwt	11 tons 12 cwt	18 tons 16 cwt	18 tons 4 cwt	16 tons 6 cwt	16 tons 5 cwt
Coal capacity	2 -3 tons	5 tons	3 tons	7 tons	3 tons	6 tons
Water capacity	1250 gallons	c. 2350 gallons	2000 gallons	3500 gallons	1500 gallons	3500 gallons
Tractive Effort lbs	15,285	13,313	25,670	25,670	21,490	21,490
Route colour	Yellow	Uncoloured	Red	Blue	Yellow	Yellow

* As first introduced sharing the same boiler type; Class 1813 as 0-6-0 side tank; Dean Goods with typical Armstrong-vintage tender.

WILLIAM DEAN

With the four GWR designs, the tender versions had roughly double the operational range and a broader route availability. On the other hand, the heavier axle loadings of tank locomotives could bestow certain advantages, as exemplified with Class 3150. The adhesive weight at 56 tons 4 cwt was 3 tons 12 cwt more than the tender version, making the extra "grunt" ideal for banking duties through the Severn Tunnel. The BR designs showed progress in suspension and weight distribution as the axle loading penalty on the tank version had been eliminated

When construction of Class 57xx started, replacement of time-expired machines provided a case for volume production but possibly not in the numbers that actually appeared. The new class replaced basically similar saddle/ pannier tanks many of which were contemporaries of the Dean Goods. It is indicative of the company's tank engine orientation that no thought was apparently given to a replacement 0-6-0 – which could have been based on the modern 0-6-0PT (Classes 64xx/74xx).

In the late 1940s/ early 1950s, the bias towards tank locomotives became even more pronounced when outside contractors added 200 of 0-6-0PT Class 94xx to the original ten built by the GWR. These engines were accompanied by others built after 1st January 1948 – further examples of Classes 57xx and 74xx plus the new classes 15xx and 16xx. Justification for so many of Class 94xx was indeed slim, especially as their duties could have been covered by Class 57xx while their Red route availability matched that of the Castles. On the weight criterion, they could not even be considered replacements for earlier classes:

Class	Built	Number	Route colour
1854	1890-1895	120	Blue
2721	1897-1901	80	Yellow as saddle tanks; blue as pannier tanks
57XX	1929-1950	863	Blue; yellow from 1950 (except Nos 9700-9710)
94XX	1947-1956	210	Red

Lapworth, looking south from the station footbridge on 5 March 1932. *E E Wallis*

Bibliography

Author	Title	Publisher	Date
Allen, Cecil J	The Locomotive Exchanges	Ian Allan Ltd	Undated
Aves, William AT	R-O-D The Railway Operating Division on the Western Front	Shaun Tyas - Donington	2009
Aves, William AT	W D Supporting the British Expeditionary Force 1939-1940	Shaun Tyas - Donington	2012
Behrend, George	Gone With Regret	Lambarde Press	1964
Booker, Frank	The Great Western Railway - A New History	David & Charles	1977
Chacksfield, JE	Sir William Stanier - A New Biography	The Oakwood Press	2001
Chacksfield, JE	CB Collett A Competent Successor	The Oakwood Press	2002
Clements, Jeremy & McMahon, Michael	Locomotives of the GSR	Colourpoint Books	2008
Cook, AF	LMS Locomotive Design and Construction	RCTS	1990
Green, CC	Cambrian Railways Album-2	Ian Allan Ltd	1981
Griffiths, Denis	Locomotive Engineers of the GWR	Guild Publishing	1988
Hamilton, JAB	Britain's Railways in World War 1	George Allen and Unwin Ltd	1967
Haresnape, Brian	Ivatt & Riddles Locomotives	Ian Allan Ltd	1977
Holcroft, H	An Outline of Great Western Locomotive Practice 1837-1947	Locomotive Publishing Co Ltd	1957
Holcroft, H	The Armstrongs of the Great Western	Railway World Ltd	1953
Jackson, David	J.G. Robinson - A Lifetime's Work	The Oakwood Press	1996
Kalla-Bishop, PM	Locomotives at War	Bradford Barton	Undated
Lewis, John & HMRS	Great Western Way	Historical Model Railway Society	2009
Lyons, E	An Historical Survey of Great Western Engine Sheds 1947	Oxford Publishing Co	1972
MacDermot, ET	History of the Great Western Railway Volumes I & II	Ian Allan Ltd	1927 (rev 1964)
Nock, OS	The GWR Mixed Traffic 4-6-0 Classes	Ian Allan Ltd	1978
Platt, Alan	The Life and Times of Daniel Gooch	Alan Sutton Publishing	1987
Pocock, Nigel & Harrison, Ian	Great Western Railway Locomotives Allocations for 1934	Wild Swan Publications Ltd	
Railway Correspondence & Travel Society	The Locomotives of the Great Western Railway	Railway Correspondence & Travel Society	1951 et seq.
Rolt, LTC	Red for Danger	The Bodley Head Ltd	1960
Rowledge, JWP	GWR Locomotive Allocations - First and Last Sheds 1922-1967	David & Charles	1986
Snell, JB	Railways: Mechanical Engineering	Arrow Books	1973
Talbot, Edward	LNWR Eight-Coupled Goods Engines	Talbot, Edward	2002
Tourret, R	Allied Military Locomotives of the Second World War	Tourret Publishing	1976
Westwood, John	Railways at War	Osprey	1980
Whitehouse, PB	Branch Line Album	Ian Allan Ltd	1962
Wolmar, Christian	Engines of War	Atlantic Books	2010
Periodicals	British Railway Journal		
	Journal of the Stephenson Locomotive Society		
	Railway Observer		
	The Railway Magazine		